Knights Templar Encyclopedia

The Essential Guide to the People, Places,
Events, and Symbols
of the Order of the Temple

✦

By

Karen Ralls, Ph.D.

New Page Books
A division of Red Wheel Weiser

This edition first published in 2007 by New Page Books, an imprint of Red Wheel/Weiser, LLC
With offices at:
65 Parker Street, Suite 7
Newburyport, MA 01950
www.redwheelweiser.com
www.newpagebooks.com

ISBN: 9781564149268

Library of Congress Cataloging-in-Publication Data

Ralls, Karen.
    Knights templar encyclopedia : the essential guide to the people, places, events, and symbols of the Order of the Temple / by Karen Ralls.
        p. cm.
    Includes bibliographical references and index.
    ISBN-13: 978-156414-926-8
    ISBN-10: 1-56414-926-9

        1. Templars—history—Encyclopedias. 2. Military religious orders—History—To 1500—Encyclopedias. I. Title.

CR4743.R34 2007
271′ 7913003—dc22

                                                                2007007199

Cover design by Lu Rossman/Digi Dog Design
Interior photos/images on pages 22, 97, 98, 158-160, 162, 163, 184, 190, 193, 195, 197, 199-201, and 203-206 by Simon Brighton; pages 35, 38, and 189 by Alan Glassman; 191, 192, and 196 by Eran Bauer.
Interior by Eileen Dow Munson
Typeset in USA

Dulles, VA
Integrated Books International
10 9 8 7 6 5 4 3 2 1

✦ ✦ ✦

This book is dedicated to

the knights and members

of the Order of the Temple (1119–1312).

Long may your memory continue.

✦ ✦ ✦

✦ ✦ ✦

Acknowledgments and Photo Credits

✦ ✦ ✦

I would sincerely like to thank those photographers who have provided the special photos for this work. As the old saying goes, "a picture is worth 1,000 words." Without clear, lovely images to help us see what the text is describing, no book would be complete.

There are three such special people for this work: Eran N. Bauer of Lincolnshire, U.K., and his wonderful wife, Linda, both of whom have been tireless in their sincere dedication to history, and who have been instrumental in garnering further enthusiasm for not only the history of the medieval Knights Templar in general, but also for the fascinating Temple Bruer site in particular, the ruins of which can still be seen today. Eran's photos are a great addition to any book, and I was most honored with his personal tour(s) of some of the Templar sites in England. Simon Brighton, a gifted English photographer of Templar sites, has done a wonderful job through the years with not only specific photos of medieval Templar sites all over the British Isles, but with a number of others as well. His 30 or so photos of various sites that grace this particular book are greatly appreciated. In the United States, Alan Glassman of Pennsylvania has been tireless in his quest for history and its images for many years. His enthusiasm about Templar history is evident, and he kindly provided photos for this book of some of the Templar-related sites and subjects from his many previous European journeys, and for that I am grateful.

It is a privilege indeed to have the photos of all of these talented visual artists in this encyclopedia, where both word and image are important to get the message across about the Knights Templar and their place in history.

Contents

Preface

The Knights Templar—the famed "warrior-monks" of the late Middle Ages—still resonate in our memory today, some 700 years after their sudden arrests on Friday, October 13th, 1307. Arguably the largest and most influential organization the medieval Western world had ever known, the Order of the Temple (1119–1312) was the first military-religious Order of the Western Church, a "new knighthood." Its members were not only powerful monastic warriors, but also international banking experts, agricultural land owners and developers, seasoned diplomats, businessmen, advisors to popes and kings, guardians of assets, ship owners, and much more.

Yet, even today, many ask: "What are the facts? Who were the Knights Templar and what is the overall picture of the Order of the Temple from the actual, historical record?" In recent years, there have been a number of books written about the Templars for the general reader, stimulating much needed debate and enthusiasm. However, as there is so much conflicting information available today, it also seems that a fair amount of confusion has resulted amidst the fascination with the feats and deeds of these enigmatic knights. Unfortunately, the central Templar archive was largely destroyed in 1571 when the Turks attacked Cyprus, but thankfully not all the records have been lost to posterity. This devastating loss to scholars has left a gap in history, which has often led to much speculation. Contrary to what is often assumed, there *are* records available about the medieval Order; however, not all of them are necessarily found in only one location or library. Historical archives on the Knights Templar exist in several primary categories, in many different countries, under a variety of possible library classifications, and a number of them still await translation, so historians and scholars must work only from what extant records are currently available.

For example, we have access to one of the best sources about the daily life of the Templars: the Rule. It is rather ironic that with all of the books available today about the Knights Templar, very few (outside of academic circles), seriously examine what the 12th-century Rule actually states about the daily life and activities of a medieval Knight Templar. In fact, for various reasons, it gets a mere passing mention at best. But given an opportunity, the Rule yields some interesting fruits, even a few unexpected surprises, as well as details about the medieval Templars' existence. Needless to say, the Rule not only clearly outlines what ideals, principles, and values the Order actually lived by, but also what penalties and penances were allotted to those who broke them—which is valuable information about the practical reality of the Order itself. How, for example, did the knights elect their Grand Master? Who was the patroness of the Order? What precious relic did the Templars guard, day and night? Which saints did the Templars venerate? Why were horse racing and jousting not allowed? Who had the keys to the treasury at the headquarters at the Holy Land? What was the beauseant? Why did the Templar Grand Masters have Saracen scribes on their staff?

The Templar Rule addresses these topics, and it is one key source I have consulted, as well as a host of other medieval period sources, as presented in the extensive bibliography. Other important sources about the Order exist in various forms, such as charters, rolls, various government records, church archives, annals, chronicles, trial proceedings, histories, religious indexes, parish records, and so on. Over the years there have been many academic books and articles written about the Templars, with more being released annually. I have included the major scholarly sources to date on the historical Templar order (1119–1312) in the bibliography.

It must be emphasized, however, that this book only covers information and sources from the time of *the actual existence of the medieval Order itself* (1119–1312) up to the 14th century. It does not include the myriad of later, modern, oral myths and writings about the Templars, which are not considered to be historical evidence for professional historians and religious scholars specializing in the medieval period. Much of the oral tradition did not fully come about until around the 18th century or later, long after the suppression of the historical Order in 1312, so it is not relevant here.

Many questions center on not only the medieval Knights Templar themselves, but related subjects as well, such as the Knights Hospitaller, the Order of Christ, the Cathars, heresy, the Inquisition, Saladin, St. Bernard of Clairvaux, the Grail manuscripts, Templar seals and symbolism, the

Black Madonna, and more. The Templars were also a part of the era in which they lived—the late Middle Ages—so some entries reflect important issues of that time to provide the reader with a broader scope of the Order than merely seeing them as only warriors in the Crusades. It is important to see them within the context of their time.

Other entries clarify matters and answer questions such as: What American president was married in a London church once associated with the Knights Templar? What does the unusual abraxas symbol, that was found on a 12th-century Templar Grand Master's seal signify? And where was the famed Templar fortress—Castle Pilgrim—and what precious relic did the Order possess there? There are a great variety of entries, covering many aspects of the history of the Knights Templar in medieval times.

As many readers today are familiar with, or have already read, a number of the available books on the Templars, an increasing number now want to take their own quest further, and are asking where they might find additional academic sources and facts. Unfortunately, they often seem to feel that such information is largely out of the reach of the non-specialist, or that the material is rather daunting; however, I aim to show that this is not the case! I am pleased to say that far greater library and research resources are available to the general reader than ever before. Thankfully, a lot of academic sources are more readable than one would think; one only needs to know where to look and what specific sources to ask for when consulting a library or digital archive. In fact, many professional librarians are truly among the unsung heroes of our time, because they are knowledgeable and willing to assist the reader, as are many teachers.

As there are a number of well-researched academic books and periodical articles that have been written specifically about the Templars (in order to meet the growing demand for information about which sources are best to consult), I have added a special Recommended Reading section in this work. This focuses on 10 specific Templar research subject areas. I have presented the major academic sources from not only the usual fields of Medieval History or the Crusades, but have also included some of the key works from relevant scholarly disciplines such as religious studies, archaeology, architecture, theology, economics, political science, pilgrimage, and others, as relevant. The Knights Templar did not exist in a vacuum. In order to thoroughly research them properly, one must be aware of the range of expert works that are available in several key disciplines. For example, economic historians' work on the use of money in the Middle Ages, or religious experts' details about medieval pilgrimage, can also provide solid, well-researched facts about the Knights Templar. Please note that these recommendations apply only to the specific period of the historic medieval Knights Templar Order (1119–1312) and not to any time beyond the early 14th century. For each of the 12 subject areas, there are both lists of recommended books and also specific journal articles written by experts that pertain only to a particular subject area regarding the history of the Templars. If it appears in an edited volume, I am only recommending the specific article in question that relates to that subject area of the history of the medieval Knights Templar. So, please look up the name of the article itself, as that is what is being recommended, and not the entire volume.

A first of its kind, this work includes many entries about the various people, places, events, symbols, and more that relate to the historical Order of the Temple (1119–1312). Understandably, in an attempt to answer many of these numerous inquiries in an accessible format, most readers prefer that such material be organized in a simple, easy-to-read, A-to-Z format organized by subject. That has been provided here, along with many related cross references under each encyclopedic entry, and, if appropriate to that particular entry, further suggestions for Recommended Reading sources that relate to that particular entry as well. Some entries will have more of these signposts that others, but I have tried to be as comprehensive as possible for a general reference work of this type. Signposts at the end of each entry are by order of relevance to the topic.

There are also five appendices: Appendix A: chronology of events of the Order of the Temple (1119–1312); Appendix B: a list of Templar Grand Masters; Appendix C: a list of the Popes contemporary with the Order; Appendix D: charges against the Templars; and Appendix E: a list of 54 western European sites related to the medieval Knights Templar order that a modern-day visitor can see today. Following the appendices, there is the full Recommended Reading bibliographic section, listing the 12 key Templar research areas and the details of which particular books and specific journal articles one might best consult for further research on each area. And finally, there follows an extensive bibliography of the major academic works on the medieval Knights Templar order (1119–1312) to date.

Some 700 years later—from 1307 to 2007—we, too, want to learn more about the Knights Templar. We wonder about their power, wealth, beliefs, and legacy. As this is a factual reference work, I have had to clarify what the Order was not, as much as what it was, in order to clearly present each entry. Some new surprises have come forth as well. Although it may seem unlikely that records relating to seemingly mundane subjects such as medieval sheep farming, accounting, or parish supply records, could ever be important sources on the Knights Templar, they often are. But that being said, interesting facts have emerged from the genuine historical record about these extraordinary knights. Many surviving records still await translation, so more information will be released in the coming years. But until then (with some subject areas in particular), no automatic assumptions or conclusions can be drawn at this time for certain.

As serious research is often a rather intensive pursuit including many libraries and archives over a period of years, this particular work is dedicated to all professional librarians, academic medieval historians, and religious studies scholars across the world. And, I might add, to the patience and kind understanding of our friends and loved ones! As a religious studies scholar specializing in the medieval period, it is my hope that this work will provide a helpful resource on the Knights Templar for everyone—the general reader and the specialist alike. I also hope that an increasing number of readers will discover more of the little-known or appreciated sources in the Bibliography. Importantly, this encyclopedia is also dedicated to *all* readers worldwide. May your quest long continue.

It is possible that in the future, new documents or discoveries will be made about the Templars, as periodically occurs with historical records and archives in any field. Archaeology and various religious archives may possibly yield some interesting information in the future. Until then, let us honor the courage and memory of the medieval Knights Templar, 700 years after that fateful October day of their sudden dawn arrest in 1307, to the shock and horror of nearly everyone in Europe.

Perhaps one of their mottoes—"Carpe Diem!" ("Seize the day!")—is relevant not only to our own lives in some way, but also to our own time, as well, as we march into the 21st century, our new frontier.

Dr. Karen Ralls

Oxford, England

Abbasid

The Abbasids were a powerful Arab dynasty in Iraq and Baghdad (A.D. 750–1258), and later, in Cairo (A.D. 1261–1517); they were descended from Abbas, paternal uncle of the prophet Mohammed, and were a prominent Sunni dynasty of caliphs during part of the era of the Knights Templar (1119–1312). They are occasionally confused with the Ayyubids, the dynasty founded by Saladin, one of the most prominent opponents of the Templars during the Crusades. (see **Ayyubids**; **Saladin**; for further sources, see "Crusades and the Military Orders" in the Recommended Reading section)

Abelard, Peter

The Knights Templar, as with many military religious orders in the late Middle Ages, did not merely exist in a vacuum, as they, too, were part of the society around them. Although many Templar knights were illiterate and not at all concerned with intellectual pursuits (as their focus was primarily on the Crusades), their key early advocate, the learned Cistercian abbot Bernard of Clairvaux, was highly influential in intellectual and religious circles and was known to be an especially effective debater. His major dispute with the famed Scholastic philosopher Peter Abelard in the 1140s is but one example of Bernard's tenacity and uncompromising attitudes about certain theological issues, a passionate zeal that had previously been evident with his strong advocacy in assisting the Templar order with obtaining papal recognition in 1129 and regarding his key role in writing the Templar Rule. Certainly, by the 12th and 13th centuries, a period comprising a key part of the era of the Order of the Temple (1119–1312), the Scholastic movement was already prominent in Paris, with input by the leading theologians and philosophers of the time, such as Albertus Magnus, Thomas Aquinas, and others. The brilliant French philosopher and theologian Peter Abelard (1079–1142) also taught in Paris and became master of the school of the cathedral of Notre Dame.

A key influence in the Scholastic movement, and contemporary with Bernard, Abelard attracted many devoted students and, as was characteristic of the time, was known to particularly relish the opportunity to fervently argue and debate.

Throughout his academic life, brilliance—and various disputes—were known to follow. Due to an especially bitter theological dispute with his former master, William of Champeaux, Abelard found it necessary to set up his own school at Mont-Ste-Genevieve in 1112. Later he returned to his old school at Notre Dame, and by all accounts, his thought and writings were brilliant and provocative. Abelard continued his work as a philosopher and theologian, but later, his views on Church doctrine (and the Trinity in particular) would land him in trouble with a church council in Soissons in 1121.

Found guilty of heresy and briefly imprisoned, his works were burned. Later, Abelard established an oratory and convent in Le Paraclet near Paris. His philosophy, which tended to stress the importance of the individual as a personality with both virtues and flaws, was strongly challenged by the powerful Cistercian abbot and early Knights Templar advocate, Bernard of Clairvaux. Bernard had more conservative monastic views and consistently attacked Abelard and his work, even leading the team that investigated the accusations of heresy again Abelard. This trial ultimately resulted in Abelard's condemnation for heresy yet again in 1141, where he was forced to recant his beliefs and more of his works were burned. Bernard's conflict with Abelard later became so bitter that the abbot of Cluny, Peter the Venerable, had to intervene and broker a truce between the two. By then, Abelard was quite ill and retired to Cluny, where he died in 1142; 22 years later, his long-term companion, Heloise, died in 1164. Although both had been buried together at the convent and oratory at Le Paraclet, in 1817 they were reinterred at the Pere Lachaise Cemetery in Paris. The theological conflict between Peter Abelard and Bernard of Clairvaux is an important one not only in medieval history and theology as a whole, but also, to better understand how fervent and formidable a personality was the austere abbot, Bernard of Clairvaux, the same abbot who assisted the fledging Knights Templar in obtaining official papal recognition at the Council of Troyes in 1129, and who had a significant impact on the early Templar order's strict monastic mode of living, as he wrote much of the Templar Rule. (see **Rule; Bernard of Clairvaux; Seven Liberal Arts;** for further sources, see "Bernard of Clairvaux" in the Recommended Reading section)

Abbey

A community of monks governed by an abbot, or of nuns under leadership of an abbess. Abbey was also a term used to refer to the monastic buildings the community lived in, as in the Clairvaux Abbey. Throughout the Middle Ages, abbeys played an important role in church and society and were major landowners. Abbots and abbesses were highly influential figures in the life of the medieval Church. Most notably in relation to the Knights Templar, the major role of the powerful and persuasive Cistercian abbot Bernard of Clairvaux regarding the origins of the Order and at the Council of Troyes in 1129 has long been noted by historians. (see **Origins of the Order**; **Bernard of Clairvaux**; **Clairvaux Abbey**; **Citeaux**; **Rule, Templar**)

Abraxas

(see **Symbols**)

Acre

Form of the Abraxas seen on a 13th century Templar Master's seal

The eastern Mediterranean port of Acre, on the Bay of Haifa, was one of the most strategically located ports in the Holy Land for the Knights Templar during the Crusades. The Templars had several establishments in this area, mainly on the coast. Acre was seized by the armies of the First Crusade and became a major port for the entire kingdom of Jerusalem, the principal crusader state they established. Seized by the Saracens under Saladin in 1187, it was attacked again by the crusader armies in 1189, and then, in the Third Crusade in 1191, Acre was recaptured by Richard I ("the Lionheart") of England and King Philip II of France. Acre remained in Christian possession until about 100 years later, when this city featured in one of the most difficult and devastating battles of all—the fall of Acre (1291). The Templar castle at Acre, the last remaining Christian fortress in the Holy Land, finally fell on August 14, 1291—a devastating event for not only the Templar order, but for all of Christendom. After the fall of the Holy Land, the morale of all Christians suffered, including the Knights Templar. Yet, in spite of an increasingly difficult situation, they fought very courageously (by all accounts). After assisting with the evacuation of as many Christians from Acre on their ships as they could, the Templars fled to Cyprus, taking their treasury, records, relics, and what supplies they could, to establish their new headquarters. This was also a devasting time for all of the other Christian Orders, and the Hospitallers as well as the Order of St. Thomas of Acre—which claimed Richard I ("the Lionheart") as its founder—also moved their headquarters to Cyprus. The Templar order had many properties on Cyprus, second only to the Lusignans, the ruling family. But Cyprus was already a politically complex climate, especially for the Knights Templar. Back in the 1270s, the Templars had previously backed the Angevins rather than the Lusignans for the important title of the King of Jerusalem, that is, the rivals to the current ruling family. In spite of this, the Templars decided to remain on Cyprus, and some scholars believe that this decision on their part certainly contributed to their ultimate downfall as much, if not more, as the trial in France did. Acre had long been important to the Templars as one of its key ports in the East, and it was an important strategic location at the time of the Crusades for not only the Templars, but other Orders as well. The Templar Rule refers to Acre a number of times, a testimony of its overall importance to the knights fighting in the East. The fall of the Holy Land to the Saracens in 1291, following the fall of Acre, was a devastating blow for Christendom in general, but especially so for the Templars. In a real sense, in the years following 1291, historians have commented that the Templars lost much of their *raison d'etre*. An irony of history is that while they bravely fought and won many of the key battles for Christendom in the Crusades—even refusing to convert and willingly facing beheading by Saladin's forces—as time went on and morale lowered throughout western Europe, the Templars ended up being largely blamed for the loss of the Holy Land after the battle of Acre by many in the West. Scapegoats were needed, and as historians have noted, given the beliefs at the time, a growing number felt that the Templars must have somehow fallen out of favor with God to deserve such a fate. But, nonetheless, the fall of Acre is, even today, forever etched in the legacy of the history of the Crusades, as is that of the Knights Templar. (see **Trial; Admiral, Templar; Maritime trade and ports; Thomas of Acre, Order of St.**; for further sources, see "Crusades and the Military Orders" and "Trial of the Templars" in the Recommended Reading section)

Adams, John Quincy
(see **All Hallows by the Tower Church**)

Admiral, Templar

The role of naval warfare certainly had a place in Templar battle strategies, although not as prominent a role as it did for the Hospitallers, who were renowned for their naval fleet during the Crusades. Yet a number of important battles took place by sea; so perhaps inevitably, naval operations also grew in importance for the Knights Templar. The first documented reference to an admiral for the Templar order appears in documents dated 1301, and, for their rivals, the Hospitallers, two years earlier, in 1299. The high seas in the late Middle Ages were a dangerous and challenging environment, a situation that also had an important effect on economics, trade, pilgrimage routes, and piracy. Encountering Saracen or other pirates, however unscrupulous or daring, was simply a rather unavoidable event in the course of doing maritime business on an everyday basis. The last admiral of the Templar fleet, as the Rule informs us in section 143, was the Commander of the Shipyard at Acre. (see **Maritime trade and ports; Acre**)

Admission to the Order
(see **Organization of the Templar order; Rule**)

Advisors, Templar

Members of the various military orders were often key advisors to popes, kings, and other rulers, and the Templars were no exception. In 1177, for example, King Henry II chose Brother Roger the Templar as his almoner. Aymeric St. Mawr, the Master of the Knights Templar in England, was an advisor to King John and was at his side as he signed the Magna Carta in 1215. From the time of Pope Alexander III on, a Templar and a Hospitaller routinely appeared as papal chamberlains, attending to the pope in his private chambers. This meant they often had special private access to the pope, certainly a most powerful position to be in. At the papal court, the Templars served as treasurers, papal messengers, judge-delegates, marshals, and porters—all positions of great trust, requiring the utmost tact and confidentiality. Secular rulers, too, made frequent use of the Templars' reliable services, as even kings such as Henry II consulted with the Templar order regarding his famous dispute with Thomas Becket, the archbishop of Canterbury. In time, the Order of the Temple became an extension of the royal government in both England and France, due to the many key services the Templars provided in a discreet and most effective manner. The Order had various legal privileges; for instance, not having to pay taxes on much of their trade within England, privileges that King Richard I of England had conferred upon the Order in October of 1189, to help the Templars save desperately needed funds for the Crusades. The Templars also served as astute judges and diplomatic mediators in local and regional disputes. (see **Organization of the Order**; **Diplomacy**)

Agnus Dei

The Agnus Dei, or Lamb of God, symbol is found on a number of Knights Templar seals, as well as on those of other medieval orders, such as the Knights Hospitaller. It also appears in many stone carvings in medieval chapels all over Europe. Featuring a lamb bearing a cross or a flag (and sometimes both), the Agnus Dei is symbolic of the martyred Christ and of the concept of sacrifice, and its origin comes from John 1:29: "...Behold the Lamb of God, which taketh away the sin of the world." Certainly the Knights Templar saw themselves as willing to die in battle as martyrs for Christ, so perhaps it is not all that surprising that the Templars would select the Lamb of God as one of the major symbols on the seals of the Order. The image was used by some of the Masters of the Templar order in Europe, especially in England and southern France. The earliest depiction of its use that has survived today is that of the English Templar Grand Master William de la More, who used the Agnus Dei on his seal in 1241. Even today, the name Agnus Dei in Roman Catholic tradition generally refers to discs of wax impressed with the figure of a lamb, blessed at various intervals by the pope, carrying on an old tradition. The lamb usually bears a cross or flag, while figures of saints or the name and arms of the pope are often shown on the reverse. Scholars believe that the Agnus Dei symbol originated in Rome, most likely as a protective amulet or charm, but most maintain that it did not become more prominent in western Christian Europe until the ninth century. In approximately A.D. 820, records indicate that Agnus Dei wax seals were made of the previous year's paschal candle; often, such fragments of the paschal candles would be saved as a protection against tempests and blight and against evil or danger. Such seals were often sent as gifts by popes to kings or nobles. In earlier centuries, the great consecration of Agnus Deis took place only in the first year of each pontificate and every seventh year afterwards, a rule that is still followed at the Vatican today. The Catholic Encyclopedia states that the Agnus Dei discs are now prepared beforehand by monks, and on the Wednesday of Easter week, these discs are brought to the pope, who dips them into a special vessel of water mixed with chrism and balsam, adding various prayers. The distribution of the Agnus Deis takes places with solemnity on the Saturday following, when the pope, after the Agnus Dei of the Mass—"Lamb of God, who taketh away the sins of the world, have mercy on us"—puts a packet of Agnus Dei into the inverted mitre of each cardinal and bishop who comes to receive them. As in the paschal candle, the wax of an Agnus Dei disc typifies the virgin flesh of Christ; the cross associated with the lamb suggests the idea of martyr offered in sacrifice; and as the blood of the paschal lamb of old was believed to strongly protect each household from evil, the purpose of these consecrated discs today is to protect those who wear or possess them from evil or dangerous influences. The manufacture of counterfeits, and even the painting and ornamentation of genuine Agnus Deis, has been strictly prohibited by various papal bulls. There are also some Agnus Deis that are of a grey color, made from wax mingled with the dust which is believed to be that of the bones of martyrs; these are held to need no special consecration from the pope and are treated as relics. Again, we still see—even today—the themes of martyrdom and sacrifice with regard to the Agnus Dei symbol, concepts that the medieval Knights Templar would have greatly resonated with, given their strict monastic Rule and life on the battlefield, especially in the Holy Land. (see **Seals**; **Martyrdom**; **Rosslyn Chapel**)

All Hallows by the Tower Church
This important church is located on Tower Hill in London and was one of the sites in medieval England relating to the period of the arrests of the Knights Templar, as it is located next to the Tower of London. Although it has tangential connections to the Templar order, it is important to note that it was not built by the Knights Templar. Centuries before the arrival of the Romans in early Britain, historians note that Tower Hill was already a central meeting place for the druid priesthood and an important power point in the city. This location has a long and varied history. For more than 1,300 years, a Christian church has stood on this site. In the early 14th century, after the arrests of the Templars, the London knights were imprisoned in the Tower and interrogated there, and also in the church and its immediate environs. Founded 400 years before the Tower of London, the earliest All Hallows church was originally built in A.D. 675 by the monks of Barking Abbey, making it one of the oldest churches in London. But its early Saxon roots are also in evidence, as sometime before 675, the historical record shows that Erkenwald, the bishop of London, founded a Saxon Christian community at Berkynge (Barking), seven miles downriver, and made his sister Ethelburga the

first abbess. Barking Abbey had a large estate near All Hallows, and the church there was most likely used by its representatives. The 1940 German bombing of London revealed a large Saxon arch with Roman bricks, and later, in 1951, half of a circular wheel-head of a Christian cross with Anglo-Saxon inscriptions on it was found under the floor. The Norman church which was built after this early Saxon building was built 10 years after the Tower of London. This Norman place of worship, the only remains of which are now one isolated pillar embedded in the wall of the vestry and a few fragments in the undercroft, had aisles. In the crypt, beneath the present nave of the church, there are three chapels, one of which has a special altar with a Knights Templar connection. Once called the Vicars Vault, this 14th century undercroft chapel High Altar has below it altar stones brought back to England from the Templars' famous

All Hallow Church, London. Its undercroft chapel altar stones were brought back from Atlit in the Holy Land

Photo courtesy of Simon Brighton

Castle Pilgrim at Atlit in the Holy Land. During the Fifth Crusade, the Templars built this extraordinary fortress; it was named in honor of the many pilgrims who helped the Templars build this stronghold. There is also a museum in the crypt that is of interest to many today. In the middle of the 13th century, a chapel dedicated to the Blessed Virgin Mary was built on the other side of the road to the north; this chapel also had a connection with the Templars. Attached to this chapel of St. Mary was a guild, which was later raised to the status of a Royal Chantry by Edward IV in 1465. This chapel's foundation unfortunately disappeared in the 16th century, at the time of the Reformation. The present All Hallows church has a number of early associations with other major guilds, such as the

Worshipful Company of Bakers, Gardeners, and the Watermen and Lightermen. In the All Hallows churchyard, headless bodies were often given Christian sanctuary after their gruesome dismemberment on Tower Hill.

As a point of United States interest, All Hallows church very narrowly escaped the tragic Great Fire of London in 1666 and was only saved by the courage of Admiral Penn, the father of William Penn, the Englishman who went to America to found what would later become the state of Pennsylvania. William Penn was baptized in All Hallows church on October 23, 1644, and was educated in its schoolroom. Also, the sixth president of the United States, John Quincy Adams, was married at All Hallows Church in 1797. However, for clarity, William Penn and John Quincy Adams were not Knights Templar, although they both do have an association with this famous London church. The All Hallows site has many other fascinating associations as well (but the history of the Knights Templar, the connections with the arrests and the Tower of London, the earlier chapel of St. Mary, and the altar stones in the undercroft chapel High Altar from the Templars' Castle Pilgrim at Atlit in the Holy Land, are the major highlights). (see **Atlit**; **Trial of the Templars**; for further sources about the downfall, arrests, and trial, see "Trial of the Templars" in the Recommended Reading section)

Almshouse

Almshouses were originally part of a monastery where alms and hospitality would be bestowed by the monks or nuns upon exhausted pilgrims, as well as the ill or hungry. In the Middle Ages, *alms* was a term meaning money given to the poor for charitable purposes. The Knights Templar collected alms for the poor many times, and in certain areas they played a major role in assisting not only travelling pilgrims, but all Christians in need, in both the Holy Land as well as in their western European territories. Later, almshouses developed into hospitals for the elderly, the poor, or the infirm. (see **Pilgrims**; **Pilgrimage**; **Hospitallers**)

Antioch

Located on the eastern Mediterranean coast across the sea from Cyprus, the city and principality of Antioch was an important strategic location during the time of the Crusades, and was one of the four crusader states organized after the First Crusade. Antioch is especially known for several battles, such as the siege of Antioch (October 1097–June 1098), an important battle that occurred prior to the beginning of the Templar order. But Antioch and its environs also became a key province of the Templar order, with its master having an important political role regionally as well as within the Order itself. The Templar Rule makes it clear that the wide-ranging office of the commander of the lands of Tripoli and Antioch, for example, was an important post in the Templar hierarchy with much responsibility. Antioch was a key area for a number of Crusade-related issues and battles, and it encompasses certain Christian relics. (for further sources about Antioch in relation to the Crusades, see "Crusades and the Military Orders" in the Recommended Reading section)

Aragon
Aragon was a kingdom in northeastern Spain, bordering on southern France and the Pyrenees. In medieval times, the name *Aragon* also indicated the lands held by the house of Aragon, which included the kingdom of Aragon, Catalonia, Valencia, Majorca, and some French fiefs, especially in Provence, Rousillon, and Montpellier. Aragon was an important province in western Europe of the Knights Templar, and was also the origin of several key Grand Masters of the Order. (see **Trial of the Templars**; **Order of Christ**; **Calatrava, Order of**; **Montesa, Order of**; for further sources about what happened in the kingdom of Aragon after the suppression, see "Trial of the Templars" in the Recommended Reading section)

Archives, Templar
The central Templar archives were originally held at the Order's base in Jerusalem, then at the port city of Acre, and after the devastating fall of Acre in 1291, on the island of Cyprus. After the suppression of the Order in 1312 by papal bull, Templar archives, records, and remaining relics were eventually turned over to their rival Order, the Knights Hospitaller.

As the key Templar archive is believed by scholars and historians to have been destroyed by the Turks on Cyprus in 1571, no medieval record of an inner Order within the Templar organization has ever been found. Contrary to much speculation (based on no historical documentation from the time of the Templars) there simply is no evidence of an inner Order, at least not at present. Some key Hospitaller records were also destroyed by the Turks at that time as well, and a number of Templar records were unfortunately destroyed and lost to history. This 16th century destruction of the central Templar archive on Cyprus has been an especially devastating loss for Templar historians, and, as we know, since then, one result is that it has left a rather large gap, through which a number of rather sensational claims have emerged. Scholars maintain that the central archive would have had the land deeds of the Order in the East, detailing the extent of Templar properties and holdings, and also would have yielded far more information about the Order's finances, including specific minutes of chapter meetings, records of Templar business dealings, diplomacy efforts, and so on.

But not all Templar records have been lost to posterity. There do exist a number of Templar archives in various European libraries, archives, and private collections today, but many of these pertain to the Templar commandaries in specific European countries and often deal with important yet far more mundane subjects such as accounting records or sheep farming, as opposed to specific records of extraordinary treasures. It may well be that, similar to the situation with the Dead Sea scrolls and other biblical period manuscripts, additional medieval period Templar records will surface in the future to be translated and analyzed by scholars. A number of documents have been found but have not yet been translated. No doubt in the coming years, a more complete picture will emerge about the medieval Order in not only parts of the East, but regarding further details about the western territories of the Order as well. Until then, no one can make any claims for certain, and inordinate (if not wild), speculations are quite counterproductive, as they take needed focus away from the actual facts about the Order that have emerged from historical documentation. Although it may seem initially less exciting to read about medieval sheep farming and accounting than fabulous treasures, perhaps that ultimately says more about our modern-day culture than anything to do with the Middle Ages. Admittedly, important questions do remain, but so do a number of medieval Templar documents that have yet to be translated or found, as the case may be.

After the Order was suppressed in 1312, the archive was passed on to the Hospitallers. The tragic loss of this central archive makes it difficult to determine, among other things, exactly what property and privileges the Templars held in the crusader states and on Cyprus. Moreover, it is a key reason why there has been so much speculation about the Templars through the centuries, but, as always, we await further discoveries and documentation. (see **Assets, Templar order**; **Relics**; for further sources, see "Assets" and "Relics" in the Recommended Reading section)

Arming jacket
This was a padded jerkin worn under a medieval knight's armor. It is referred to in the Rule of the Templars in several sections, for example, in 138.6 of the Hierarchial Statues, where it is listed along with the other major items that a full knight-brother and a sergeant were allowed in battle, including a hauberk, iron hose, helmet, sword, shield, lance, Turkish mace, surcoat, arming jacket, mail shoes, dagger, bread-knife, and pocketknife, three knives, three horses, one riding animal such as a mule or palfrey, one squire, surcoat, and so on. The Rule also states in section 325 that each brother should wear arming gauntlets when he puts on his arming jacket in order to arm himself, but otherwise he should not wear them without permission. Section 557 regarding further penances gives the stern warning that all brothers of the Temple who leave the house could never take two of anything, including an arming jacket—but if he should ever do that, he would be expelled from the house. (see **Draper**)

Arthurian knights
Often confused with the historical Knights Templar, the knights of the Round Table of Arthurian legend are not the same as the Knights Templar. The Templars were actual historical figures of the medieval Order of the Temple (1119–1312), while the tales and adventures of Arthurian knights such as Percival or Galahad occur primarily in the fictional corpus of medieval Arthurian romances and other literature. Yet both became quite popular subjects in the public imagination in the late 12th and 13th centuries, as they are today. But they do embody different concepts of knighthood. Historically, the Knights Templar were a strict, rather austere Christian military religious Order (the pope's militia), while the Arthurian knights of myth and legend are largely portrayed as either entirely secular, or as having a dedicated Christian religious focus, but, even so, it is still nothing like the strict, Catholic regimen of the Templars during the time of the Crusades. In modern terms, the Templars had far more similarity to what we would think of as a military special forces unit such as the Navy Seals, Marines, Army Delta Force, or the British SAS—an organizational structure that required very austere living conditions and a strict, daily regimen. In medieval times, the Templars were never allowed to play chess, joust, stage plays, see women, drink alcohol, or engage in secular activities such as falconry, for example, as other historical secular knights of their time were occasionally known to do, as the strict military regimen and Christian Rule of the Templars strictly forbade such activities. However, as with many of the Arthurian knights of legend,

they did value proper behavior and high ideals. There were also many other knightly confraternities in the late Middle Ages (in various countries) who also fought for Christendom in the Crusades, but while they were called knights, they are still not the same as the Knights Templar, nor are they identical with the Arthurian knights of legend and romance. Although the Grail romances were written in roughly the same era as the Templars (the late 12th and 13th centuries) and some Grail romances have Templar, Cistercian, or Benedictine themes, there is no evidence that a Templar ever actually wrote a Grail romance. Nonetheless, the memory of the knights of the Crusades, the Knights Templar, and the Arthurian knights of legend continue to inspire many people, centuries later. (see **Chivalry; Grail romances; Relics; Troubadours**)

Arville
In the Loir-et-Cher area of France, between Le Mans and Chartres, Arville is still one of the best-preserved Templar sites. The site includes a chapel, barn, fortified gate, bakery, and dovecote. There is also an excellent Templar museum, housed in the Centre d'histoirie des Ordres de Chevalerie, where the modern-day visitor is led through the history of the medieval Templar order from its beginning to the trial of the Templars. In approximately 1129, the Templars settled in the area, on a wooded estate of some 2,500 acres, donated by a local lord.

Growing in influence, especially in the agricultural sector, Arville became a base for military recruiting and training of knights who were awaiting their opportunity to depart for the Holy Land. It was also an important house of prayer. After the suppression of the Order in 1312, the Templar commandary at this site was eventually transferred over to the Hospitallers, the Order of St. John, who held this site until the time of the French Revolution in 1789. (see Appendix E)

Assassins
(see **Nizari Ismailis**)

Assets, Templar order
The Templars became one of the wealthiest and most powerful organizations the Western world has ever known, with a great variety of assets. During the 12th and 13th centuries, the Order acquired extensive property not only in the West, especially France, but also in the crusader states of Palestine and Syria. It developed an extensive network of thousands of preceptories and commanderies throughout Europe and the Latin East.

Aristocratic families, kings, and fallen soldiers gave the Order thousands of properties, including ports, mills, churches, farms, villages, monasteries, and so on, to assist the Templars in their Crusades. Particularly within the first decade of growth following the Council of Troyes (1129), the new Order was granted lands in nearly every part of western Europe and beyond, a meteoric rise to power that has hardly been seen before or since. The more popular they became, the greater their wealth and the number of new recruits. The ultimate extent of the Templar empire at its height was probably unknown, even to certain kings. Templar wealth was spread widely across numerous commercial activities and subsidiaries, and was supported by diverse elements, so it would have been hard to specify the precise location and form of all their assets at any one given time. With such a huge international empire, the Templar order was similar in concept to our idea of a major, modern, multinational corporation. However, unlike in a large corporation, much of the Templars' wealth that was donated by individuals had to remain in the Templar treasuries and could not be moved without the owner's permission, an early prototype of a bank safe deposit box. While the Templars did not invent banking in the Middle Ages, they were certainly among the earliest in providing arrangements for the safe conveyance of funds, and their castles and key commandaries were some of the few places of safe deposit. In the 13th century, for example, the Templar treasury in Paris virtually served as the French royal treasury. Nobles and many kings were lent large sums by the Order, as were certain popes. The Templars also collected monies and taxes for their clients; later, in some areas (perhaps inevitably) this affected their popularity. Although other religious orders at the time also had financial dealings, by all accounts, none of them had nearly as large or extensive an empire as the Order of the Temple. (see also **Farms**; **Mills**; **Maritime trade and ports**; **Wool**; **Treasuries, Templar**; **Letter of credit**; **Loans, Templar**; **Archives, Templar**; **Relics**; for further sources about the various assets held by the Order, see "Assets" in the Recommended Reading section)

Atlit (Castle Pilgrim)

Long known as Castle Pilgrim, this Templar castle was built during the Fifth Crusade by the Templars, with assistance from locals as well as many pilgrims, hence its name. Atlit and its environs were a strategic location in many battles of the Crusades, and the castle was also the place where the Knights Templar kept a special relic that they particularily prized, that of the heart and body of the virgin saint, St. Euphemia of Chalcedon, a fourth-century martyr. (see **All Hallows by the Tower Church**; **Pilgrims**; **Pilgrimage**; **Relics**; **Saints, Templar veneration of**; for further information about Atlit and the Crusades, see "Architecture," "Crusades and the Military Orders," and "Pilgrimage and Pilgrims" in the Recommended Reading section)

Aventail
This was a chain mail flap that protected a warrior's chin and throat.

Aymeric de St. Maur
Aymeric de St. Maur was a 13th-century master of the Order of the Temple in England. King John, who had heavily borrowed from the Templars for some time, highly regarded the diplomatic advice of de St. Maur and other members of the Order of the Temple in England at the time. Aymeric de St. Maur encouraged King John to sign the Magna Carta in 1215 and was present at the signing of this monumental document. (see **Diplomacy and espionage, Templar**)

Ayyubids
Founded by Saladin (one of the most formidable opponents of the Knights Templar at the time of the Crusades), the Ayyubids were an Islamic Dynasty that ruled Egypt and Syria during the late 12th and early 13th centuries. They originated from Kurdish tribes in Armenia. (see **Saladin**; for further sources, see "Crusades and the Military Orders" in the Recommended Reading section)

B

Baculus
A large ceremonial staff that only the Grand Master of the Order of the Temple was allowed to carry, as in procession or when meeting with dignitaries. The top of the staff featured a large Templar cross within a circle. (see **Symbols**; **Grand Master**)

Bailli
A bailli was a local, provincial Templar commander, who could be either a full knight-brother or a sergeant-brother. He presided over the baillie, an administrative and economic area in that Templar province.

Baillie
The name of the Templar territory under the command of the bailli, the local Templar commander; this was his specific sphere of influence and responsibility. The baillie of the Templars is distinct from the medieval term *benefice*, which meant land tenure associated with an ecclesiastical or secular office. Within each Templar baillie were their preceptories. (see **Preceptory**)

Baphomet
(see **Relics**)

Barres, Everard des
The third Grand Master of the Order, Everard des Barres was from Champagne and served from 1149 to 1152; he offered his resignation from the Order to join the Cistercians at the abbey of Clairvaux for a period of approximately 25 years. (see **Cistercians**; **Clairvaux Abbey**; Appendix B)

Battaile
A medieval French word for the largest organizational unit in a medieval western European army.

Beaujeu, Guillaume de
The 20th Grand Master of the Order of the Temple, Guillaume de Beaujeu was from the castle of Beaujeu, near Gary, Haute-Saône, France. He served from 1273 to May of 1291. By all accounts, he fought most courageously at Acre (1291), where he died in battle. (see **Grand Master**; **Acre**; Appendix B)

Beauseant
The *beauseant* was the famed black-and-white piebald standard or banner of the Templar army. It was most often carried by the marshal, the Order's chief military officer, or by one of his subordinates, such as the gonfanier (the banner-bearer). The beauseant was especially valued within the Order itself, and was a sight known to strike fear into the knights' enemies in battle, and even (on occasion), other Christian military religious orders. In battle, the Templars placed a special guard of 10 knights around their raised standard, and they also carried a second, folded banner to raise again, should anything happen to the first. Early portrayals show that the beauseant was divided vertically in some cases and horizontally in others, but it was always black and white. Symbolically, the black represented the darkness of sin that the Templars had left behind, and the white reflected the pure life of the Order. In addition to the beauseant, a holy relic would also often accompany this retinue, such as the piece of the True Cross that the Rule informs us the Templars possessed. It was believed that such relics—in addition to the beauseant— would give the knights additional help from Heaven. The Saracens were amazed at the tenacity of the Templar Knights, as no Templar could ever leave the battlefield while the beauseant was still raised, no matter how critical the military situation at the time. The policy was that even if their banner was brought down in battle, before they could consider leaving the battlefield, they had to first seek help from their fellow Christians (such as the Hospitallers or any others on site). If no other Christian assistance was available, they would still have to wait for the final decision of the Grand Master or chief officer; if he decided that the banner should finally go down, then—and only then—could a Templar Knight leave the battlefield. To do otherwise was to risk losing one's habit, or, possibly, to be expelled from the Order. The Templars were inordinately courageous in any case, but this policy regarding their standard no doubt contributed to their fearless reputation in battle. In addition, a final policy was that even if the situation on the battlefield was especially dire, the

beauseant itself could never be used as a weapon on its own; should any Templar Knight do so, the Rule states that he should be put in irons and imprisoned, a strict punishment. Some have speculated that the piebald beauseant may be connected to the black-and-white checkered squares of the chess board, though Freemasons point out that the floor of the Masonic Lodge is of similar design. A number of experts believe that the crusaders brought the Persian game of chess back to Europe. The chess player's cry of "Checkmate!" may be a corruption of the original Persian words "Shakh Mat!" which, when translated, mean "the King is dead!" More specifically, in the Arabic-Spanish game of chess, this means "the king is dishonored, defeated, or deposed." While there is no evidence that the Templar beauseant was directly related to chess in any way, such motifs involving a black-and-white checked pattern are nevertheless interesting to note. (see **Organization of the Templar order**; **Marshal**; **Shields**; **Symbols**)

Beraut, Thomas

The 19th Grand Master of the Order of the Temple, Thomas Beraut was from Limousin, France, and served from 1256 to 1273. His surname is sometimes also spelled as Beraud in medieval records. (see **Grand Master**; Appendix B)

Bernard of Clairvaux

Born as Bernard de Fontaine in 1090 near Dijon, France, Bernard was one of the greatest theologians of the Western Church and of the Middle Ages. A renowned Cistercian abbot, Bernard was also instrumental in assisting the fledging Templar order and wrote much of its early Rule. He was also personally responsible for rallying the papacy in getting official recognition for the Templar order at the Council of Troyes in 1129. Historians know that, especially in northern France, the Templar order and the Cistercians were closely associated, and both had connections with Troyes, as did much of Bernard's family. The third son of Tescelin Sorrel, a Burgundian crusader, he was educated at Chatillon-sur-Seine by secular canons. As many historians have noted, even then he illustrated intelligence, wit, and considerable ability in learning difficult subjects. He was also known to inspire others and spoke quite persuasively and eloquently, even at this young age. It was at Citeaux that Bernard, later canonized as St. Bernard, began his religious life, before moving to the monastery at Clairvaux. In 1112, when he was only 22, he arrived at the monastery of Citeaux with 30 nobles from the houses of Tonnerre,

Montbard, and Burgundy. Many were his brothers or other relatives, and all of them were willing to give up everything to join the austere, poverty-stricken Cistercians, which (for some) meant leaving wives and children. As Citeaux was small, Bernard and his entourage were especially welcomed by Abbot Stephen Harding. A few years later, in 1115, Bernard was made abbot of Clairvaux, a new Cistercian monastery. As with many in monastic life, Bernard led an especially strict ascetic life and was especially devout and dedicated; by all accounts (even compared to other monastics), Bernard's regimen was definitely one of the most austere. Even so, his energy levels were widely acknowledged by his contemporaries as extraordinary, and although a rather severe abbot, he was an inspiring one, and was highly regarded across Europe. Early on, as abbot of Clairvaux, Bernard became more involved in Church politics. His natural ability to persuade, charm, cajole, or coerce, when necessary, proved to be quite effective. He soon emerged as one of the most charismatic Church leaders and advocated a number of important reforms. At the Council of Troyes, in 1129, he persuaded the pope that the tiny, fledging Templar order should be given official papal recognition, something that was not ordinarily granted to an order of only nine men. He was especially dedicated to the idea of an entirely new type of knight—monks who were also warriors. In his famous letter, "In Praise of the New Knighthood," written to his colleague and first Templar Grand Master Hugh de Payns, Bernard elevated the knights of the new Templar order above all other orders of the day, including that of its main rival, the Knights Hospitaller. This letter established the image of the Templars as a fierce militia for Christ. Bernard regarded the Templars as an entirely new species of knighthood, previously unknown in the secular world, pursuing an agenda against both flesh and blood and the invisible forces of evil. In 1130, Abbot Bernard took sides in a major papal dispute, preferring Innocent II over his rival, Anacletus. Largely due to Bernard's influence in rallying the Church to recognize Innocent II, he was then made pope. As time went on, the Cistercians continued to gain recruits and power. Their constitution was approved by the papacy in 1119, the same year the first Templars publicly presented themselves to King Baldwin II and the Patriarch of Jerusalem. Bernard was also known to be an especially outspoken abbot, particularly critical of what he perceived to be lax monastic standards. He strongly attacked two famous scholars of his day, Peter Abelard and Gilbert de la Porree. He also had major conflicts with the Cluny order; it is not all that surprising that he had enemies as well as many friends. He was also a major force in rallying huge numbers for the Second Crusade, yet this crusade was a disaster, and some blamed Bernard for it. But by all accounts, Bernard was respected and his writings were widely read and studied. He especially venerated the Blessed Virgin Mary and wrote some 120 sermons on the Song of Songs alone, and his treatise *On Loving God* became a spiritual classic. He was primarily a monastic writer; his rather witty *Steps of Humility and Pride* warned monks that one small slip can then lead one down a further sliding slope to spiritual ruin, is still a classic in monasteries today. Yet Bernard's focus was often on a highly personal mysticism, and he was able to effectively combine both a key role in Church politics as well as that of a gifted mystic. Many historians agree that if it was not for the extraordinary energy, dedication, and enthusiasm of Bernard, the Order's dedicated abbot for some 40 years, the Cistercians may well never have become such a huge organization of international renown. Under his tutelage, they eventually had some 400 houses. He was formally canonized in 1174 and was made a doctor of the Church in 1830. His feast day is August 20th. In the treasury of the Cathedral of St. Peter and St. Paul at Troyes, in Champagne, the bones of St. Bernard of Clairvaux (along with other relics including an important portrait), are still venerated today. Bernard was clearly one of the most extraordinary leaders of the Western Church, and wrote many important works; he was also a significant 12th-

St. Bernard, statue outside Spanish church

Photo courtesy of Alan Glassman

century influence for many in secular life in the late Middle Ages as a whole. His leadership, vision, and courage regarding the initial establishment of the early Templar order will long be remembered in history. (see **Clairvaux Abbey; Cistercians; Rule, Templar; "In Praise of the New Knighthood"**; and for further sources regarding the life of Bernard of Clairvaux, see "Bernard of Clairvaux" and "In Praise of the New Knighthood" in the Recommended Reading section)

Bethany
(see **Mary Magdalene, St.**)

Birds
Falconry was forbidden in the Templar order, as was hunting a bird with another bird. A brother could not go into the woods with a longbow or crossbow to hunt animals, nor should he ever spur on a horse to hunt a wild beast, as section 55 in the Rule outlines. Falconry was expressly forbidden to Templar Knights as it was an especially popular activity of secular knights at the time. (see **Knighthood, secular; Rule**)

Black Madonnas
Although the majority of images of Our Lady are primarily white or light in color, there has always been a tradition of Black Madonnas in western Europe. It may not be fully appreciated or widely known today that during the late Middle Ages, the shrines to the Black Virgin were the most venerated in Europe. Black Madonna shrines are found worldwide, but regarding the medieval period, most are located in western Europe. In addition to many ordinary peasants, a number of royal pilgrims visited these important shrines in the 12th and early 13th centuries, such as Henry II and Eleanor of Aquitaine, Louis XI, and Richard I. Specific Black Madonna shrines also had notable devotees in their day, such as Anatole France and Joan of Arc. Nobles, wealthy merchants, and gifted mystics such as Ramon Lull or Abbot Bernard of Clairvaux made their journeys, too. One poetic verse from 1629 lists some of the key national shrines of Europe (such as Loreto, Italy), all of which, at the heart, seem to represent an ancient tradition of major devotion to a statue of a Black Madonna. Early textual references to descriptions of the images of Virgins as black are few, although the 12th century biblical scholar of Troyes, Peter Comestor, his contemporary, the Cistercian abbot St. Bernard of Clairvaux, and Byzantine historian Nicephorus Callixtus (1256–1335) all wrote on the subject of the Black Madonna at various times. Major important early studies of Black Madonnas in France were presented by Marie Durand-Lefebvre (1937); Emile Saillens (1945), and Jacques Huynen (1972). The first notable study of the origin and meaning of the Black Madonnas in English was presented by American scholar Leonard Moss at a major meeting of the American Association for the Advancement of Science (AAAS) on December 28, 1952. When Moss began his paper, a key study of more than 100 Black Madonnas, every priest and

nun present walked out, it is said. Clearly, the subject of Black Madonnas at that time were seen as quite controversial, as they sometimes still are today. Yet, even so, these rather enigmatic Black Madonna statues have long remained popular with some devoted priests as well as the public, with many effective healings and miracles attributed to them through the centuries. Some modern orthodox Catholic priests simply attribute the darkness of all of these figures to exposure through the centuries to much candle smoke, an explanation no longer satisfactory to an increasing number of experts. The specialists point out that not all Black Madonnas were created from wood; a number of them were carved from stone. Many art historians today believe the concept of a Black Madonna as another form of Our Lady may well be based on the materials often used to make some of her earliest images, such as jet or ebony. Historians show that the Romans brought early images of the goddess Cybele from Phrygia in B.C. 204 to what is now Vatican Hill in Rome and also to other areas in Europe. Some of these early stone images of a black goddess, whom the Romans called Magna Mater, were later Christianized to become the Black Madonna.

The statue of Diana at Ephesus is widely believed to have originally been black. Scholars in some academic fields have noticed the connection between the earliest images of a goddess and the color black, which was considered symbolic of wisdom in ancient times. Several Marys were often venerated at the same site, and many legends have grown around these traditions. One of the most famous Black Madonna pilgrimage sites in France today is Les Saintes-Maries-de-la-Mer, in Provence, where there is a special cult of St. Sara, the patron saint of the gypsies in southern France. This site also has long-standing medieval traditions to St. Mary Magdalene. Clearly more research is needed beyond what possible links historians have already discovered concerning the Black Madonna, the Old Testament Sophia wisdom tradition, the Queen of Sheba legends, and possible connections of the European Black Madonnas with Isis and Egypt. Especially in the Languedoc, sites of devotion to the Black Madonna are often located in the same geographical regions where there were previously Cathar or Templar communities in medieval France, and are still visited by many today. An especially strong Black Madonna tradition existed in the Pyrenees and in parts of Occitania, centered on Montserrat. Many of these sites, especially in southern France, were visited by illustrious medieval pilgrims, including kings, saints, and nobles, so veneration of the Black Madonna is an old phenomenon.

As with many devout Christians at the time, the Templars highly revered Our Lady, the Blessed Virgin Mary, the patroness of their Order, as did the Cistercians and other monastic and religious orders of the time.

The Black Madonna of Montserrat, replica in Barcelona Chapel

Photo courtesy of Alan Glassman

The powerful Abbot Bernard of Clairvaux was certainly one of the most avid Marianists the church has seen, before or since, and was especially instrumental in assisting with official recognition of the fledging Templar order at the Council of Troyes in January of 1129. Historians know that Bernard's reverence for Our Lady was extraordinary. But such devotion also extended to sites of the Black Madonnas as well; again, not something particularly heretical, as that would have been the case for nearly all devout medieval Catholics in the late Middle Ages. Places of pilgrimage relating to the Black Madonna were important to many in the High Middle Ages, including Bernard. For example, on Easter Sunday of 1146, he preached the Second Crusade from Vezelay, a well-known French center of devotion to traditions of the Black Madonna. Bernard was born at Fontaine, which had its own Black Madonna tradition on the outskirts of Dijon where the ancient Lady of Good Hope reigned, so he grew up in an area steeped in legends about the Blessed Virgin Mary and the Black Madonna. Accounts say that the young Bernard, when praying at the nearby shrine of the Black Virgin of Chatillon, received three drops of milk from her breast, perhaps symbolic of not only his love of God, but also his fervent devotion to Our Lady. In the traditions of many ancient cultures, a young initiate would often receive three drops of a special liquid, generally symbolic of wisdom and initiation, and often from a female figure. Descriptions of symbolic acts such as this often find their way into medieval saint's hagiographies, such as this anecdote about Bernard of Clairvaux. Perhaps this was one way for the hagiographers to make the point that, early on, Bernard had been quite dedicated to Our Lady: 14th century French Templars who were arrested, imprisoned, and awaiting their deaths in the dungeons of the tower of Chinon composed a special prayer dedicated to Our Lady, acknowledging St. Bernard as the founder of the religion of the Blessed Virgin Mary. Perhaps they were honoring the initial oath that they took at their reception ceremony. In more recent times, some have suggested that the "Our Lady" patroness of the Knights Templar could only have been Mary Magdalene. However, the Templar services show no evidence for this idea, nor do their Rule, and most of the land donations to the Order were specifically donated in honor of the Blessed Virgin Mary, the mother of Christ, so scholars understandably refute this argument. However, it is known that the Templars on the island of Mallorca venerated a Black Maria and that some medieval French Templar commandaries were near places that had a Black Madonna shrine, particularly in the Languedoc. Even today, the Black Madonna is the patroness of Mallorca. Historians have noted that the Templars' great devotion to Our Lady—including some Black Madonna shrines—would not have been at all that unusual or heretical, especially for a medieval Catholic order. It should also be noted that the Black Madonna is not identical with St. Mary Magdalene. Although it cannot be ignored that a number of Black Madonna shrines often cluster in the same places that were in some way important to the medieval Templars, Cathars, and others, that does not automatically make all of them identical to Mary Magdalene. Nor does it include the historical fact that there was already a long-existing indigenous Pagan black goddess tradition in existence in that area, centuries long before either the start of Christianity or the Templar order. Equally important, when the Templars were persecuted in the early 14th century, their inquisitors never once accused them of revering the Black Madonna, as the medieval Catholic Church did not consider veneration of Our Lady a heresy or view her image as an idol, and this policy included the Black Madonnas. Prominent medieval churchmen, including St. Bernard, often visited sites where Black Madonnas were venerated.

Of the many sites in medieval Europe with key Black Madonna shrines, several are in southern France, in or near Provence, or in the Languedoc, a major heartland of the European Templars and home to the powerful Counts of Toulouse and the Cathar nobles. A number of these nobles were also patrons of the Templar order, but not all of them were. In certain areas of the Languedoc, the Templars are known to have courageously allowed the dispossessed Cathars to bury their dead, who were condemned heretics at the time, on their consecrated land. Yet as much as they may have sympathized with their plight, the Templars did not, as an order, have a policy to defend the Cathars, as they could not defend heretics. In fact, in some areas, historical evidence shows that the Templars let some of the northern crusaders occasionally stay in their homes. With the fall of Montsegur in 1244, the Cathars were almost completely exterminated; but oddly, the one accusation the Inquisition did *not* later charge the Templars with was their affiliation (however loose) with the Cathars; nor did they ever accuse the Templars of Manichaean Gnosticism, a charge that, if they had fervently believed the Templars to be Gnostics, they would have most certainly added to the long list of charges. Historians know the inquisitors were fully aware of Templar connections with the Cathars regarding the burial of Cathar bodies in certain areas, as they were known to have specifically sought out and dug up Cathar bodies that had been given a respectful burial on Templar lands in order to burn them as deterrents to other would-be heretics.

Although in no way can Mary Magdalene and Black Madonnas simply be automatically grouped together and equated—all Black Madonnas are certainly not the same, each having her own unique traditions—neither can they continue to be ignored by scholars, theologians, or art historians. Neither can the Black Madonnas' mysterious blackness continue to simply be dismissed as nothing more than centuries of candle smoke by some priests, which, again, is an explanation that increasing numbers today find distinctly inadequate. What is particularly interesting to historians is that in certain locales, especially in southern France, there has long been a persistent Black Madonna tradition as well as certain connections to Mary Magdalene, in addition to a long-standing ancient black goddess tradition. But, even so, this still does not indicate that all Black Madonnas are symbolic of Mary Magdalene, or that the Knights Templar created the Black Madonnas, or exclusively worshipped only Mary Magdalene, which has sometimes been assumed; the historical record to date does not support this concept. Importantly, in areas such as the Languedoc, there were also a variety of groups that were accused of heresy and pursued by the Inquisition in medieval times. Often small and little-acknowledged today, such groups were nevertheless also a part of the social, political, and historical fabric of the time and cannot be ignored. It is important to examine the entire historical picture at the time, in order to see the Templars within the full context of the late medieval period.

The Templars venerated a number of saints, as exemplified by sections 74 and 75 of their Rule, and although highly regarded, St. Mary Magdalene is not given any particular prominence over the other saints. Currently, further research is being done on the Black Madonnas by many parties—researchers, art historians, scholars, folklorists, museum curators, church archivists, priests, musicologists, and religious orders—and it is only through such an in-depth, interdisciplinary approach that greater clarification is likely to emerge. In the 21st century, the power and influence of the Black Madonnas can no longer be denied. After all, even modern-day popes have fervently prayed at certain Black Madonna shrines, as our news media reports—clear evidence that her deeply important legacy continues to inspire many today. (see **The Blessed Virgin Mary**; **Mary Magdalene, St.**; **Mary Magdalene, medieval celebrations of**; **Pilgrimage**; **Pilgrims**; **Relics**; **Shrines**; **Saints, Templar veneration of**; **Saints in medieval society**; **Women**)

Blanquefort, Bertrand de

The sixth Grand Master of the Order of the Temple, Bertrand de Blanquefort was from Guyenne, France. He served as Grand Master from 1156 to 1168. One side of his seal of 1158 features the symbol of two knights riding on one horse, believed to be the earliest portrayal of this image in the Templar order. (see **Grand Master**; **Seals**; Appendix B)

The Blessed Virgin Mary

The Templar order was dedicated to Our Lady, the Blessed Virgin Mary, who was the patroness of the Order, perhaps seen today as a rather unusual choice for an organization consisting of primarily male military religious warriors. But this practice would not have been all that unusual at the time, as it reflected the great popularity of the medieval cult of the Virgin Mary, with many churches, chapels, and religious orders dedicated to the Blessed Virgin Mary. Such a practice was similar to another medieval fashion at the time—that of the key chivalric concept of being in service to a higher ideal or truth. In many medieval manuscripts, this concept was epitomized as a lady—and in the case of the Templar Order's patroness, it is Our Lady the Blessed Virgin Mary. As with other devout Christians, the Templars saw Our Lady as not only the Mother of God, but also as the Queen of Heaven. The late Middle Ages was a time of peak influence for the cult of the Blessed Virgin Mary, and acknowledgement of the divine feminine in general, as around this same time, many Gothic cathedrals and religious orders were dedicated to Our Lady. The Black Madonna shrines—also shrines in honor of Our Lady—were among the most popular of all in the late medieval period. The Templar order also venerated other female saints, such as St. Mary Magdalene, or martyrs, such as St. Catherine of Alexandria, as we learn from their Rule, but the Order itself was dedicated to Our Lady. It is interesting to note that during the trial of the Templars, some of the brothers were proud to state to their inquisitors under great duress that the cords which they wore around their waists as a symbol of chastity had touched an object, especially the pillar, at the church of the Blessed Mary at Nazareth where Mary received the Annunciation. In addition, an avid devotee of Our Lady and major advocate of the early Knights Templar, Abbot Bernard of Clairvaux, greatly influenced general devotion to the Virgin Mary within the Cistercian order, which was also dedicated to Our Lady.

Our Lady, the Blessed Virgin Mary, also shows up on documents regarding donations of land to the Templars. In several sections throughout their austere Rule, we know that a Templar's day was very demanding, starting at around 4 a.m., when he would rise for the first religious service of the day, Matins. Regarding Our Lady, it is interesting that section 306 specifically states that "the hours of Our Lady should always be said first in this house...because Our Lady was the beginning of our Order, and in her and in her honor, if it please God, will be the end of our lives and the end of our Order, whenever God wishes it to be."

Mary was also linked with the Knights Templar in other ways, even in reference to specific locales or relics. For instance, one tradition states that the Annunciation had taken place in the Temple of the Lord (the Dome of the Rock area on the Temple Mount) and that a stone on which Mary rested her head was located outside the famous Templar castle at Atlit in the Holy Land, known as Castle Pilgrim. By hours, section 306 in the Rule is referring to the religious canonical hours, special prayers to be said at certain times, such as the Lord's Prayer. In Templar houses and commandaries, according to the Rule, prayers to Our Lady should be said first in the day, to be followed by others at specific intervals throughout the day. Templar novices at their reception into the Order were required to make their solemn pledges to Our Lady, the Blessed Mary as well as to God, as she was their patroness.

The great dedication that Templar knights showed for their patroness may also be illustrated, by all accounts, in what has been described as a final and extraordinary display of courage of the last Grand Master of the Templars, Jacques de Molay. After recanting the confessions he had earlier made under great stress and torture in prison, he said at his final hearing, to those assembled, in part: "...Before heaven and earth and with all of you here as my witnesses...I declare, and I must declare, that the Order is innocent. Its purity and saintliness is beyond question...." De Molay had claimed the Order was innocent, and had shocked everyone present, as he had recanted his earlier confessions—a crime under Inquisition rules. Later that day, along with Geoffrey de Charney, the Templar preceptor of Normandy (who had also recanted his earlier confessions), the last Templar Grand Master was led to the stake on the orders of the French King Philippe IV. De Molay surprised his captors again, however, as he asked that his hands remain free—as he wanted to pray, and he then made some remarks before the crowd that had assembled on an island in the Seine in Paris, thus: "...In this faith I wish to die. Witness my faith, and I pray you that towards the Virgin Mary, in whom Our Lord Christ was born, you turn my face...." It would appear, according to this medieval account written by eyewitness Geoffroi de Paris, that de Molay in his final, most difficult hours, had sought solace in not only God and Christ, but especially from the Mother of God and patroness of the Templar order, the Blessed Virgin Mary. (see **Women**; **Mary Magdalene, St.**; **Mary Magdalene, medieval celebrations of**; **Black Madonnas**; **Saints, Templar veneration of**; **Relics**; **Shrines**; **Pilgrimage**; **Saints in medieval society**)

Bouillon, Godfroi de

Godfroi de Bouillon has become a figure of legend whose life has left an indelible mark on popular consciousness from medieval times until today. The leader of the First Crusade (1096–1099), he became the first Christian ruler of Jerusalem since it had fallen to the Muslims in A.D. 637. Although he had been granted the title Duke of Lower Lotharingia by the German emperor Henry IV in 1087, he was not as rich or influential as other aristocrats of his time. When he left France in 1096 for Jerusalem with other members of his family, he mortgaged all of his lands and sold all of his possessions to fund the expedition. History records that he fought courageously, and, in July 1099, after a long and particularly bloody battle, his armies took Jerusalem, regaining the Holy Land for Christendom. The Latin Kingdom of Jerusalem was founded. With great humility, Godfroi famously refused to accept the crown of Jerusalem, preferring instead the title Defender of the Holy Sepulchre. He died soon after, probably of typhoid, on July 18, 1100, and was succeeded by his brother Baldwin I, who did accept the crown of king of Jerusalem.

Godfroi's only official act as Defender of Jerusalem was to reapprove the charter of an abbey located on Mount Sion, an imposing hill outside the city walls of Jerusalem, which was rebuilt on the site of an earlier, fourth-century Byzantine church. Scholars maintain that monks present on the site in 1099 may have been Augustinian, yet the community there was known as the Order of Notre Dame de Sion; its church was called the Mother of All Churches. There is a charter signed by a Prior Arnaldus dated July 19, 1116, and Arnaldus's name shows up again on another charter dated May 2, 1125, this time in conjunction with Hugh de Payns, the first Grand Master of the Knights Templar. But Godfroi himself was not a Knight Templar, as has sometimes been assumed, as the Order did not publicly emerge until later, in 1119, 11 years after his death. Godfroi de Bouillon is also known to have paid special reverence to Stenay and to Orval Abbey, where the relics of Dagobert II were kept. In the Middle Ages, Godfroi was remembered in poetry as a descendent of the mythical Swan Knight and was featured in a number of extraordinary French tapestries, as well as having the status of one of the Nine Worthies, the greatest warriors of all time. (see **Payns, Hugh de**; **Origins of the Order**; **Canons of the Holy Sepulchre**; **Nine Worthies**; for further sources, see "Origins of the Order" and "Crusades and the Military Orders" in the Recommended Reading section)

Brunete

Mentioned in the Templar Rule, a brunete was a fine woolen cloth that was worn only by men of rank. In the Templar Order, a member's appearance and supplies were organized by the officer known as the draper. (see **Draper**; **Organization of the Templar order**)

Burell

This was a coarse woolen cloth, referred to in the Rule, to be given to sergeants and squires to wear in lieu of the availability of a black robe, which they were entitled to wear. Only full knight-brothers, however, were allowed to wear white mantles. (see **Mantle**; **Draper**)

Cahors
The remains of what was once a medieval Templar castle, chapel, and church can still be seen in this city. Cahors is in the Lot district of France, and a recommended place to visit, among many, when in the area. (see Appendix E)

Calatrava, Order of
A Spanish order founded in 1158 by Abbot Raymund Serrat of the Cistercian abbey of Fitero. The main purpose of the Order of Calatrava was to defend the castle of Calatrava, as it controlled access to Toledo from the south. The General Chapter of Citeaux accepted it as part of the Cistercian order in the year 1187, after which the Order of Calatrava was put under the jurisdiction of the abbey of Morimond; both knights and chaplains of the Order were monks. The rule of the Order of Calatrava was adopted by the Portuguese Order of Christ, one of the orders that, after the suppression of the Templars in 1312 by papal bull, a number of Templar Knights joined. The Order of Calatrava was annexed to the Spanish crown in 1482, which was finally approved by the pope in 1523. It was unique in that it did not require its knights to be of noble birth. The Order was suppressed by the Spanish government in 1835, but was reestablished in the diocese of Ciudad Real in 1851, although this, too, was suppressed by the government in 1931. (see **Christ, Order of**; **Citeaux, monastery of**; **Montesa, Order of**; **Trial of the Templars**; **Aragon**)

Caliphate
A caliph was a supreme leader of the Islamic world, and the territory he ruled was called a caliphate. In the 12th century, during part of the era of the Templar order, there were several rival caliphates. (see **Saladin**; **Ayyubids**)

Canon Law

The law of the Church, as opposed to the law of the state or other secular authorities.

Canons of the Holy Sepulchre

Officially called the Regular Canons of the Holy Sepulchre of St. Augustine, these canons had been previously established on the Temple Mount in Jerusalem before the early beginnings of the Templar order (1119). After the success of the First Crusade, Baldwin I, king of Jerusalem, drew up the first constitution of the Equestrian order of the Holy Sepulchre of Jerusalem in 1103; the Regular Canons of the Holy Sepulchre were later established by Gibelin of Sabran, archbishop of Arles, and Arnulf de Roher, the patriarch, in 1114. The Regular Canons followed the customs of the abbey of St. Victor in Paris, whose rule and habit had been given by Godfroi de Bouillon when he founded the community for the purpose of guarding Christ's tomb, the Holy Sepulchre. In 1119, the early Templars, under the direction of Hugh de Payns and Godfrey de St. Omer, were given accommodation by King Baldwin II in his palace, the Lord's Temple (the Dome of the Rock area today) on the southeastern side of the Temple Mount platform, which the crusaders had earlier dubbed Solomon's Temple. The Regular Canons of the Holy Sepulchre also gave the first nine Templars an area around the Lord's Temple. The early Templars took the three monastic vows (chastity, poverty, and obedience) and, according to Archbishop William of Tyre's chronicle, had eventually intended to become regular canons. The first nine Templars made their vows to the patriarch of Jerusalem, Warmund of Picquigny. Not all chroniclers' accounts agree exactly on the details involving the earliest years of the Templars in Jerusalem, and although information about this period in Templar history is sketchy, nearly all accounts say that the Order was definitely operational by 1120 at the latest. Due to the lack of concrete information about these earliest years, a number of questions remain today. But the earliest Templars lived by the Augustinian rule. It was not until the changes instituted later by Bernard of Clairvaux and others at the Council of Troyes in January of 1129 that Benedictine and Cistercian influences became far more predominant in the Rule. (see **Origins of the Order**; **Rule, Templar**; **Godfroi de Bouillon**; for further sources, see "Origins of the Order" in the Recommended Reading section)

Casalier
An officer commissioned to guard one of the Templar order's farms or casals; mentioned in the Templar Rule.

Castellan
An officer comissioned to guard one of the Templars' castles, such as Atlit (**Castle Pilgrim**).

Castle Pilgrim
(see **Atlit**)

Cathars
The Cathars of the Languedoc were dualist heretics who probably presented the greatest doctrinal challenge faced by the Catholic Church in the 12th and 13th centuries. The word *cathar* comes from the Greek word *katharos*, meaning "pure." The Cathars professed a neo-Manichaean dualism, a belief that there are two main principles, one good and one evil, and that this world, the material world, is evil. Similar views were held in the Balkans and the Middle East by the medieval religious sects of the Paulicians and the Bogomils, with whom the Cathars were closely connected. However, the Cathars are not the same as the Knights Templar, as they have often been confused, perhaps because both Christian groups had been accused of various heresies and specifically targeted by the Inquisition. They did, however, have some of the same patrons, especially in the Languedoc area of southern France. The Cathars were dissident, pacific Christians who would not accept the orthodox position that an omnipotent and eternal God could have been responsible for the material world of matter, as to them, this world was the product of an evil creator, not a beneficient one. The Cathars believed that matter was evil, and that Man (Humanity) was an alien sojourner in an essentially evil world. Therefore, the main aim of Man was to free his spirit, and restore it with God. They lived a devout lifestyle; they had austere rules for fasting and were strict vegetarians. The Cathars also allowed women to be perfecti, or priests. They did not believe in a Last Judgement, believing instead that this material world would end only when the last of the angelic souls had been released from it. They believed in reincarnation, and that souls could take many lifetimes to reach perfection before their final release. In many ways, Catharism represented total opposition to the Catholic church, which they basically viewed as a large, pompous, and fraudulent organization that had lost its integrity and "sold out" for power

and money. The Cathars could also not accept the orthodox beliefs regarding the Eucharist and other sacraments of the church, as this implied that Christ would have actually lived on this earth in the flesh, been crucified, and resurrected from this evil, material world—a concept that they felt a divine, good Being such as Christ would never do in the first place, as God (that is, Christ, in the orthodox Christian view) would never exist in this material world, only in Heaven. So they rejected a fundamental tenet of the orthodox church: the Incarnation. In many ways, the Cathars differed significantly from the Templars, who, on the whole, maintained far more orthodox positions, judging from the Rule they lived by. Unlike the Templars, who were a military religious Order, the Cathar church was organized into dioceses whose bishops presided over an order of succession consisting of elder and younger sons, deacons, and perfecti (their priesthood). Many supporters were among the nobility of the Languedoc, which was one of the most sophisticated, wealthy, and cosmopolitan civilizations in all of Europe at the time. Many laypeople supported the Cathar perfecti (priests) by becoming credentes, and most took the consolamentum oath when near death, as the hard, ascetic rigors of the perfecti daily life were too demanding for the average person. By becoming credentes, one could then marry and have a family, while the perfecti lived a monastic life. It is also known that the Cathar perfecti frequently traveled in pairs while doing their ministry. They were great healers, renowned doctors, and herbalists. Overall, the Cathars had many followers, with the largest numbers residing in southern France and northern Italy. Inevitably, with such radical beliefs, large numbers, and loyal patrons, they became a definite threat to the Catholic church, and the Inquisition was finally launched on them, culminating in one of the bloodiest, most ruthless crusades the world has ever seen. Various crusades were first preached to the Cathars, but to no avail, as they utterly refused to repent.

Bernard of Clairvaux was known to have said that he thought they basically lived very good lives, yet, technically, acknowledged that they were heretical Christians. Others, however, took a far more severe line, especially the Dominican order, which was expressly organized to pursue the Cathars and eliminate the Albigensian heresy. Eventually, as all else failed, a policy of ruthless violence was instigated by a desperate church, resulting in many deaths and atrocities, fueled by the greed of northern French barons who supported the crusades against the wealthy Languedoc in the south. The Inquisition persisted in earnest, and, in some areas, whole villages or cities were annihilated, including women, children, and even Catholics—with the justification that this serious heresy must be eliminated no matter what the consequences. Arnold Aimery, the papal legate at the siege of Beziers, famously ordered his men: "Show mercy neither to order, nor to age, nor to sex...Cathar or Catholic, Kill them all...God will know his own...." Finally, by the end of the 14th century, Catharism largely vanished from history. But because of the final, fateful siege of Montsegur in 1244, when many were burned alive, the Cathars and their memory, live on today. The Templar order could not officially defend heretics; however, as the Cathars were denied a proper Christian burial (as they were officially heretics), in some areas in the Languedoc, the Templars were known to have allowed them to bury their dead on their lands—after all, they were fellow Christians. Later, unfortunately, the Inquisition often sought out these specific graves to exhume them and burn them again. In spite of such a tragic past, now, some seven centuries later, the memory and legacy of the Cathars continues today. (see **Heresy**)

Champagne fairs
(see **Fairs, Champagne**)

Chapter meetings, Templar
Major meetings called general chapters took place at the Order's head-quarters in the Holy Land, or at one of its leading houses in the East. They were similar to what we might think of today as an important annual meeting at a business conference. Chapter meetings of the Templar order, similar to most major modern-day company board meetings, were held in secret so as to keep all internal business within the Order. Templar chapter meetings were also held in their preceptories in the West. These were chapter meetings of the Master and central convent, and involved input from the leading Templar officials of the Order from all of Europe, as the Order had an extensive empire over a vast area. Chapter meetings were similar to the courts held by secular rulers, at which business was discussed and legal cases heard. Unfortunately, no concrete information is known about how often Templar general chapters were held, due to the scarcity of records. In addition to the major general chapter meetings, ordinary chapter meetings were also held weekly at each major Templar house as well, as the Rule informs us. These began and ended with prayers led by the chaplain and were presided over by the Master of the house. Unfortunately, there are no specific records of these meetings, as the Order's central archive has been lost to posterity, most likely

destroyed by the Turks in 1571 upon their invasion of Cyprus. (see **Archives, Templar**; **Organization of the Templar order**; for further sources, see "Organization, Structure, and Rule of the Order" in the Recommended Reading section)

Charges

At least 104 articles were brought against the Templars in France; these were based primarily on testimony from French king Philippe's informers and from confessions made under torture. The intent in medieval heresy trials was to convict the already guilty—that is, to prove the charges—rather than to discover the truth. Legal concepts, such as "due process" or a "trial by jury," as we know them today, simply did not exist at the time of the trial of the Templars. Historians have grouped the charges against the Knights Templar into six major categories: (1) reception into the Order, (2) idolatry, (3) heresy, (4) sodomy, (5) charity and the acquisition of property, and (6) secrecy of proceedings.

One of the most infamous charges against the Templars was that of denying Christ and/or spitting on the cross. Yet their behavior had been just the opposite; when 80 Templars were captured after the loss of the castle at Safed, the sultan offered to spare them if they would deny Christ. Every single one of them refused and was either flayed alive or beheaded, hardly illustrative of men familiar with denying Christ. Historians have since determined that many of the charges were in fact carefully crafted, and stemmed from popular myths and superstitions about so-called heretics and magicians that were common at the time. Interestingly, before 1307, the Templars had hardly ever been accused of heresy, unlike the Hospitallers, for example, whom Pope Gregory IX had accused in 1238. Many of the same categories of charges against the Templars had also been leveled at the Cathars or had been used during the European Witchcraft trials of the 13th century. Aside from the Templars in the Middle Ages, a number of others, too, were often accused of various crimes, including Jews, gypsies, lepers, and a host of other religious groups. It seems that the powerful Templar order, especially after the fall of Acre in 1291, fell prey to such accusations for largely political reasons between the French king and the pope. Accountable only to the papacy, the Order had become very wealthy and powerful, so, in time, it also became feared as well, a rather easy target for envy in particular. Finally, they were the primary focus of the Inquisition, prompted by King Philippe IV and Pope Clement V. The medieval definition of exactly what constituted "heresy" was rarely very specific; it was molded and shaped according to how the prosecutors wanted to create their case and who was in power at the time. (see **Trial of the Templars, summary of**; **Heresy**; **Clement V**; **Philippe IV le Bel**; Appendix D; and for further sources about the trial, interrogations and downfall of the Templars, see "Trial of the Templars" in the Recommend Reading section)

Chartres, Guillaume de
The 14th Grand Master of the Order of the Temple, Guillaume de Chartres was the son of Milon IV, count of Bar-sur-Seine in Champagne, France; he served from 1210 to 1219. (see **Grand Master**; Appendix B)

Chas-chastiaus
This was a type of medieval wooden siege-tower that was closely associated with mining or trenches in battle.

Chausses
Armor for the upper legs and thighs, either padded or made of chain mail.

Chevauchee
Medieval French term for a raid into enemy territory.

Children
Many medieval religious orders did allow the reception of children into their orders; a child would then take a vow to that particular Order. However, the policy of the Order of the Temple, as with section 14 of the Rule, was that this was not advisable. The Rule says that children who would be considered as a possible future Templar knight should not take a vow until they were older and were able to bear arms, that is, until they had proper training and could make the decision on their own, so as to not regret it later. This was partly because the Templar order did not have a training program per se, as brothers were expected to already be largely skilled in matters of warfare. If the young person had training and was older (no longer a child), then the parents could bring the child to the Master and brothers of the house for further questioning and so on. (see **Rule**)

Chivalry
Chivalry was a rigid moral system and a strict code of proper conduct for a feudal knight in the Middle Ages. Its main values were those of courage, loyalty, charity, courtesy, respect for women, honesty, and

benevolence. Enshrined in a number of important writings of medieval literature, including many of the Arthurian Grail romances and the *chansons de geste* of the troubadours, chivalry was especially required of all men in the knightly class. Although the Knights Templar maintained similar chivalric values in addition to those of their military religious order, they were not the same as the secular knights of their time (the legendary Arthurian knights of the Round Table), with whom they are sometimes confused. The ideals of chivalry in the Middle Ages were extolled in the literature of courtly love and widely promulgated by the troubadours in a number of countries, especially southern France. In many a medieval tale and song, the ideals of courtly love were expressed as the unattainable love between a knight and a married woman of the aristocracy, yet, it was also often secretive and supposedly always unrealized. At a time when most marriages were arranged purely for feudal, political, and economic purposes, the idea of individual love between the two parties was not generally a normal reality; hence, the phenomenon of courtly love and its popularity at the time. Two of the major sponsors of courtly love literature were Eleanor of Aquitaine and her daughter, Marie de Champagne—in Eleanor's reign alone, Chrétien de Troyes's, *Lancelot* and Andreas Capellanus's famous *On the Art of Love* was written, as well as Guilluame de Lorri's *Roman de la Rose*. The modern-day romantic myth of a "knight in shining armor" meeting a "lovely damsel" also has its origins in the literature of the Middle Ages, although it is not identical with the courtly love literature's concept of the ideal knight and has nothing to do with the daily life of a medieval Knight Templar. The precise meaning of courtly love is still being debated by scholars today, but the power and beauty of these medieval stories and songs still resonates with us today. The great popularity of the Arthurian romances, the troubadours and chivalry in general eventually led to the idea of creating chivalric orders. The Templars were a military religious Order with strong chivalric overtones that highly emphasized service to others and God—perhaps best exemplified by their famous *Non nobis Domine* motto: "Not unto us, O Lord, not unto us, but to your name give the glory." (see **Arthurian knights**; **Grail romances**; **Knighthood, secular**; **Chretien de Troyes**; **Troubadours**)

Chrétien de Troyes

A 12th century poet and troubador, Chrétien de Troyes was unquestionably one of the very best medieval French writers and poets of his time. Yet although he lived during part of the Templar era, he was not a Knight

Templar, as has sometimes been alleged. Chrétien was born in 1135 and wrote four complete works and fragments of others, but his most famous poem is *Le Conte du Graal*, about the adventures of the young Percevel. This masterpiece, written in 1190, was the first Grail romance and remains one of the most important writings of medieval French literature. He was a university graduate who later joined the court of the influential Countess Marie de Champagne, the daughter of Eleanor of Aquitaine. A number of historians believe that he may have served in a high ecclesiastical office later in life, although this has not been proven. (see **Grail romances**; **Chivalry**; **Arthurian knights**; **Knighthood, secular**; **Troubadours**)

Christ, Order of

Founded in Portugal and approved by papal bull in 1319, after the suppression of their Order in 1312, a number of Templars joined the newly established Order of Christ. The knights of this Order became known as the Knights of Christ. They wore a white mantle with a red cross that had a white twist in the middle, which also has been translated as a double cross of red and silver in some medieval documents. Initially, the Order of Christ was located at Castro Marim; later, its headquarters was relocated to Tomar, the location of the castle of the Knights Templar. It grew quite rapidly, as by 1321 it already had 69 knights, nine chaplains, and six sergeants. It adopted the Order of Calatrava's rule, but placed itself under the spiritual direction of the Cistercian abbey of Alcobaca. The lands of the Templars in Portugal after the suppression were given to the Order of Christ. After the 15th century in particular, the Order of Christ became heavily involved in the exploration activities of the Portuguese princes and explorers. The famous explorer Prince Henry the Navigator became the administrator of the Order in 1420 and used the best geographers of the time; another famous explorer, Vasco de Gama, was also a member. In the earlier part of the 16th century, the Order had declined in numbers, and, by 1551, the Order of Christ was brought under the Portuguese crown and then became purely honorific of the senior Portuguese royal honor, though the chaplains continued to live a monastic life at Tomar. In 1834, the Order was secularized. An Italian branch of the Order of Christ became the supreme honorific Order of Knighthood of the Holy See. (see **Calatrava, Order of**; **Trial of the Templars**; **Tomar**; **Aragon**)

Churches donated to Order
(see **Assets, Templar order**)

Church of the Holy Sepulchre
(see **Canons of the Holy Sepulchre**)

Cistercians
The Cistercians were one of the most influential religious orders in medieval times, but unlike the Templars they were not a specifically *military* religious Order. Their very earliest history has Benedictine roots going back to 1098, involving Robert of Molesmes and his successors. (see Molesmes, Robert) Founded in its major phase in approximately 1120 by Stephen Harding at Citeaux abbey in France, the Cistercian order spread rapidly throughout Europe and reached a peak in the twelfth century under the able leadership of their abbot, St. Bernard of Clairvaux. They became known as the "white monks," as they wore white habits to distinguish themselves from the Benedictines, who wore black habits. The name "Cistercian" and that of their first monastery, Citeaux, both come from the word *cistus,* of the *Cistaceae* rockrose family, which we know today as the simple five-petalled "wild rose." This rose was very popular in medieval symbolism involving depictions of the Blessed Virgin Mary, of whom the Cistercians, Templars, Hospitallers, and the Teutonic knights all honored as the patroness of their respective Orders. The Cistercians were among the key Orders that spearheaded the building of the Gothic cathedrals, among other things, and their gifted Abbot Bernard of Clairvaux was certainly one of their most influential leaders. He was also extremely influential in assisting the fledgling Templar order with obtaining official papal recognition at the Council of Troyes in January of 1129. The Cisterican order also helped spearhead the chivalric Order of Calatrava, which adopted some elements of the Cistercian constitution in their Rule. (see also **Bernard of Clairvaux; Citeaux, monastery; Clairvaux Abbey; Molesmes, Robert of; Origins of the Order;** for further sources, see "Origins of the Order" and "Bernard of Clairvaux" in the Recommended Reading section)

Citeaux, monastery of
The location of the "mother" monastery of the Cistercian order, the "White Monks" of the Middle Ages. It was at Citeaux that Bernard de Fontaine, later canonized as St. Bernard, originally started his religious life, before he moved to Clairvaux, where he later became abbot. He arrived

at Citeaux in 1112, with 30 nobles from the houses of Tonnerre, Montbard, and Burgundy, many of whom were his relatives and all of whom were willing to give up everything, which for some even meant leaving wives and children, to join the austere Cistercian order. Bernard was only 22 years old at this time and his relatives were considerably older; so naturally, this has often been referred to as a prime example of his extraordinary talents, piety, and ability to persuade others. In 1115, Bernard moved to a new monastery at Clairvaux, where he would spend many decades. Unquestionably, Bernard had great influence on the 12th-century Church, and he was also instrumental in getting official papal recognition for the Templar Order at the Council of Troyes in 1129. Historians know that, especially in northern France, the early Templars and the Cistercian order were closely associated, and both had connections with Troyes. (see **Bernard of Clairvaux**; **Cistercians**; **Robert of Molesmes**; **Origins of the Order**; **Hughes I, Count of Champagne**; **Clairvaux Abbey**)

Clairvaux Abbey
Clairvaux Abbey was founded in 1115 in a wooded part of the southern Champagne region, and, largely due to what many historians agree was the extraordinary enthusiasm and influence of the Cistercian abbot Bernard of Clairvaux, the Abbey became the head of some 300 other Cistercian houses, an amazing accomplishment by all accounts. It was here that Bernard lived for many years, often referring to this Cistercian monastery at Clairvaux as an entrance to "the heavenly Jerusalem." Some scholars suggest this specific mention of Jerusalem may have been not only because he lived during the time of the Crusades, when Jerusalem was on every medieval person's mind, but also because of his close association with the early circle of what later became the Knights Templar order, who are best known to us today as those who defended and won "fortress Jerusalem" for Christendom in 1099 and in a number of battles afterward. The Knights Templar, in Bernard's view, were to combine the best of both the practical and the spiritual—"lions in war, lambs in the house." (see also **Bernard of Clairvaux**; **Robert of Molesmes**; **Origins of the Order**, **Cistercians**; **In Praise of the New Knighthood**; for further sources, see "Bernard of Clairvaux" and "Origins of the Order" in the Recommended Reading section)

Clement V

Regarding the history of the Knights Templar, Pope Clement V (1264–1314) is known as the pope who was contemporary with the arrests, downfall, and trial of the Order in the 14th century. His name was Bertrand de Got and he was born at Villandraut in Gascony, France in 1264. He studied civil and canon law at Orleans and Bologna, and was bishop of Comminges in 1295. He became the archbishop of Bordeaux in 1299 and was aided to power, as a number of historians believe, by the French king, Philippe IV. Having been crowned as pope in Lyons on November 14, 1305, he served as pope from 1305 to 1314 at Avignon. Under persistent pressure from King Philippe IV, Clement V decided to remain in Avignon, rather than risk going back to Italy for political reasons, in what was already a challenging period in general for the papacy. So in the year 1309, Avignon, rather than Rome, became the papal seat. Historians believe that such conditions and papal conflicts at the time, plus the continous pressure from Philippe IV throughout his career, may have also led Clement V to later exonerate Philippe IV and his officials in the death of Pope Boniface and to then accuse Boniface—posthumously—of various heretical charges. Of course, history has shown that Clement V would later play a key role in the downfall of the Knights Templar as well; again, accusing them of various charges that, upon further examination, are similar to those levelled earlier at Pope Boniface and, to an extent, also to those issued against the Cathars as well. A significantly weakened figure, certainly having endured heavy pressures from King Philippe IV for years, unfortunately, by the time of the Templar arrests in October of 1307, Pope Clement V seems to have found it most difficult to put forth a stronger defense of the Knights Templar. In fact, on a number of occasions, he was not properly or fully informed about Philippe IV's moves against the Templars, including, incredibly, the initial arrests of October 13, 1307. Clement V presided at the important Council of Vienne in 1311, at which he declared that as the charges against the Templars were "not proven," the Order itself was not guilty. He also pointed out that by then, due to some seven years of lurid Inquisitional hearings and a number of trials, the Templars had become so defamed in the eyes of the public that they could simply no longer be operable or hope to gain new recruits. In 1312, he issued the final papal bull that suppressed the Order of the Temple, and, shortly thereafter, he also issued another important bull in Templar history, which, to the great chargrin of King Philippe IV, decreed that all Templar properties, assets, and archives were to be transferred to another military religious Order—the Hospitallers—rather than to any secular body. All Templars were to be freed; many joined other monasteries or orders, or were pensioned off if they were elderly. Pope Clement V died on April 20, 1314, at Roquemaure. (see **Trial of the Templars**; **Charges**; **Philippe IV le Bel**; **de Molay, Jacques**; **Heresy**; Appendix D; and for further sources about the downfall and trial of the Order and Clement V's role in it, see "Trial of the Templars" in the Recommending Reading section).

Coif

Part of a knight's armor, the coif was originally a part of the hauberk; in the thirteenth century, however, it became a separate hood of chain mail to help protect the head. The coif is specifically referred to in the Templar Rule; for example, in section 162, the Rule tells of how a brother could protect his head with an iron coif , without permission, while trying out his horse when in a squadron, but he could not take it off. He did, however, need permission to take his shield or lance in those circumstances, however. No brother could charge or leave the ranks of a squadron without permission. (see **Arming jacket**; **Draper**; **Hauberk**)

Commander, Templar office of

The Commander of the Kingdom of Jerusalem was the treasurer of the entire Order and was in charge of the strong room at their headquarters. He shared power with the Grand Master in a way that prevented either from having too much control over funds. For example, a Templar Grand Master could keep a lockable strongbox of his own in the treasury but was not allowed to hold the key to the room itself. Another policy was that anything the Commander received was first seen by the Grand Master and then recorded in writing, so that the list could later be available for inspection if necessary. The Commander of the Kingdom of Jerusalem also oversaw all nonmilitary assets of the Order, such as pack animals, houses, villages, and the ships and storage vaults at Acre. Needless to say, it was a most important position within the Order of the Temple. (**Organization of the Templar order**; **Assets**; **Treasuries, Templar**; **Letter of credit**; **Loans, Templar**; for further sources and information about the officers of the Order, see "Organization, Structure, and Rule of the Order" in the Recommended Reading section)

Confrere

A confrere was an associate brother who served with the Templar order for a shorter length of time and who did not take the strict monastic vows like full knight-brothers. Married brothers, for example, could be confrere; but as the Rule states, they could not live in the same house as the brothers who had pledged chastity, as they were married and had wives. Confrere were to leave part of their estate to the Order upon their death, and the rest to their lady, to support her during her lifetime. In addition, although highly valued, like the sergeants and squires, confrere could not wear white mantles, which were only to be worn by full knight-brothers. (see **Rule**)

Consoeur
This was an associate sister who was with the Templar order for a shorter length of time; a female equivalent of a confrere. (see **Women**)

Constantinople
Constantinople was the capital of the Byzantine Empire, now known as Istanbul. (see **Hagia Sophia**)

Convent
The Templar brothers who made up the actual fighting force of the Order—the full knight-brothers, or, the Sergeants.

Cope
Referred to in the Rule, a cope was a large hooded cloak which covered the Templar's whole body; it was fastened at the top by a string or by a special hook, somewhat similar to a cape.

Council of Troyes
This was an important church council held in January of 1129 at which the fledging Templar order was given official papal recognition, primarily due to the efforts of Abbot Bernard of Clairvaux. It is a key event regarding the earlier years of the Order, after which the Order rapidly grew in prestige, power, and wealth. But the early period that finally lead up to this famous council is also rather interesting to note. In 1104, Hughes I, the powerful count of Champagne, attended a synod in Troyes, at which many eminent people were present, to hear an abbot from Jerusalem whose name was not recorded, but historians maintain that matters in the Holy Land at the time were most likely discussed. A series of other meetings followed this intial meeting, all instigated primarily by Count Hughes. In 1104, Hughes left for the Holy Land and returned some four years later to Champagne. In 1114, he again traveled to the Holy Land, along with Hugh de Payns, the first Templar Grand Master. In a letter

written by Ivo, the bishop of Chartres, Hughes was criticized for leaving his wife as he made this second trip and referred to the count having taken his vows "to the 'knighthood of Christ" (*militi Christi*) in order to take up "that gospel knighthood" (*evangelicam militiam*). Interestingly, St. Bernard would use the very same imagery years later in support of the Order of the Temple, even though Ivo did not mention the Templars in his letter to Hughes I. Historians have attempted to determine precisely what Ivo meant by Hughes's vows to this unspecified "knighthood of Christ," largely concluding that Hughes may have taken simply crusader's vows to go to Jerusalem, which many did at the time, or, he may have vowed to join a confraternity of knights formed to protect the Christian holy places in the Holy Land, again, something that many did at the time. Before the First Crusade in particular, such knightly confraternities were more common. Some historians maintain that as such groups of wealthy warriors agreed to work together towards a common aim (that is, defending churches against bandits), it is plausible that Hughes joined a confraternity. Yet others point out that someone as wealthy and influential as the Count of Champagne certainly would have been much more likely to have joined an Order rather than a confraternity. At this quite early date, we know it was not the Templars, as Ivo did not mention them by name, either, but it is known from the historical record that Hughes I later—in 1125—did officially join the Order of the Temple. (see **Hughes I, Count of Champagne**; **Bernard of Clairvaux**; **Origins of the Order**; **Rule**; **Canons of Holy Sepulchre**; for further sources, see "Origins of the Order" and "Organization, Structure, and Rule" in the Recommended Reading section)

Craon, Robert de

Robert de Craon, son of Renaud, lord of Craon and Egmagen, Anjou, France, was the second Grand Master of the Order of the Temple; he served from 1136 to 1149. Under Robert de Craon's leadership, the Templar order received its now-famous papal bull *Omne datum optimum* of 1139, which made them answerable only to the pope and gave them the right to have their own chaplains, among other important privileges. Many Templar historians also believe that at some point during Robert de Craon's reign as Grand Master, the Latin Templar Rule was most likely translated into French, as the translation had been completed after the time of the Council of Pisa on May 30, 1135.(see *Omne datum optimum*, **Grand Masters**; **Rule**; Appendix B)

Cressing Temple

The preceptory of Cressing Temple was probably one of the earliest in England. The manor with its church was first granted to the Order by Queen Matilda by a charter dated at Evreux in 1136 and later confirmed by King Stephen. Cressing and its environs were a very rich agricultural area, with wheat, corn, barley, and oats grown there. Today, one can still see two of the original large wooden Templar barns, which were carefully restored in 1987 by the Essex County Council: the Barley Barn, built around 1200–1220, and an even larger barn, the Wheat Barn, which was built in approximately 1260. In addition to these two barns and other features on the property, the preceptory at Cressing Temple also had five corn mills. Money that was raised from large, prosperous Templar farms like this massive complex at Cressing made it possible for the Knights Templar to channel much-needed funds to their brothers in the east, to fight in the Crusades. At Cressing Temple, the Templars had three chaplains for their services and to pray for departed benefactors. There was a chapel dedicated to St. Mary on the site, and, later, in 1153–54, a market at nearby Witham was added to the lands belonging to Cressing. Cressing Temple is unique, especially as nowhere else in England can be found such complete farm buildings, such as the granaries, that date from medieval times. In its heydey, it was a huge agricultural complex comprising some 2,000 acres. These two great Templar barley and wheat barns are also important structures in their own right regarding the general medieval history of England as well. (see Appendix E)

Crusader states

There were four major principalities that were established by Christian crusaders—the Latin kingdom of Jerusalem, which was the primary crusader state, set up after the First Crusade in 1099; Antioch, set up in 1098; Edessa, also set up in the year 1098; and Tripoli, in 1109. Acre, a major port in the kingdom of Jerusalem, was the last Christian fortress that remained in the Holy Land, due to noble efforts by the Templars, Hospitallers, and other crusaders, until it finally fell in 1291. (see **Acre**; for further sources about the Crusades and the role of the crusader states in them, see "Crusades and the Military Orders" in the Recommended Reading section)

Decoration

Templar knights were strictly forbidden from having any undue decorations, finery, or "pomp" on their mantles, clothing, or anything that belonged to them. This was partly in reaction to the many secular knights of the day who were often rather ostentatious, something that Bernard of Clairvaux commented on in his famous letter, "In Praise of the New Knighthood." The sin of pride opposed the genuine values of a Templar knight, as when one first joined the Order, the Order itself and its policies would always take precedence over one's own free will. Section 18 of the Rule states that the mantles should be without any finery or specific show of pride, especially with no piece of fur on his clothes, as no one brother's mantle or clothing should stand out in any way over the others. In section 52, it states that no brother should ever have shiny gold or silver on the bridle of his horse, his stirrups, or his spurs; again, the emphasis is on one's humility and lack of individual pride, as was also the policy in most monastic Orders. Bernard of Clairvaux strongly condemned knights decorating their bridles in his "In Praise of the New Knighthood" letter. (see **Rule**; **Draper**; for further sources, see "Organization, Structure, and Rule," "Bernard of Clairvaux," and "In the New Knighthood" in the Recommended Reading section)

Diocese

In the Middle Ages, as in current times, a diocese indicates the specific area or territory that is presided over by a bishop.

Diplomacy and espionage, Templar

Members of the various military orders were advisors to popes, kings, and other rulers, and the Templars were no exception. In 1177, for example, King Henry II chose Brother Roger, the Templar, as his almoner. Aymeric St. Mawr, the Master of the Knights Templar in England, was a major advisor to King John and was at his side as he signed the Magna

Carta in 1215. From the time of Pope Alexander III on, a Templar and a Hospitaller routinely appeared as papal chamberlains, attending to the pope in his private chambers. This meant they often had coveted private access to the pope himself. At the papal court the Templars served as treasurers, papal messengers, judge-delegates, marshals, and porters, holding positions of great trust. Secular rulers also frequently relied on the Templars' advice and diplomatic skills. The Order became an arm of the royal government in England and France, due to the many reliable, discreet services the Templars provided. It had various legal privileges, such as not having to pay taxes on much of their trade within England, to help the Templars save money for the Crusades. The Templars also served as judges. In some countries, such as England, for example, high-ranking Templars presided in criminal matters, except for cases involving major crimes punishable by hanging or mutilation, which went to the king's courts. Many a medieval common thief was probably tried by the Knights Templar. Because they acted inconspicuously as monk-messengers for kings, nobles, and popes, the Templars were also ideally suited for espionage, as they were much less likely to be stopped or questioned by authorities, as they were religious men.

Domme
Domme was one of the medieval fortresses where the French Templars were imprisoned. A rather fascinating array of various medieval Templar "graffiti" and carvings on the walls can still be seen today at this site; their possible meanings remain unclear to date. (see Appendix E)

Draper
The Draper issued clothes and bed linen, and could also distribute gifts made to the Order. He was not only keeper of the famed white mantles, but also ensured that every brother was dressed "decently," as the Rule states. He was also responsible for ensuring that all brothers kept their hair and general appearance and items clean and properly presented, and so on, in the role of an inspector. The Draper could also remove items from a member when he thought that member had more than what was proper, or, if he thought he was being in any way ostentatious or acting with unnecessary individual pride. In keeping with the New Knighthood concept of living simply, Templars were not allowed many personal belongings, and certainly nothing showy or ostentatious, such as fur on their mantles or gold on their horses' bridles, for example. (see **Organization of the Templar order; Haircut; Decoration**)

Eral, Gilbert
The 12th Grand Master of the Order of the Temple, Gilbert Eral served from 1194 to 1200; he was originally from Provence. (see **Grand Master**; Appendix B)

Espalier
Espaliers were metal shoulder protectors on a Templar knight's armor and were given to them by the Draper of the Order after their investiture.

Eugenius III, Pope
Pope Eugenius III, Cistercian abbot and friend of the highly influential Abbot Bernard of Clairvaux, served as pope from 1145 to 1153. He is important regarding the history of the Knights Templar, as he issued the now famous papal bull *Omne datum optimum*, which meant that from that time onwards, the Order of the Temple was accountable only to the papacy. Its other major privilege to the Templars, among other items, was that they could now have their own chaplains. This bull was issued when Robert de Craon was Grand Master of the Order. (see *Omne datum optimum*; **Red Cross**; **Martyrdom**; **Craon, Robert de**; **Cistercians**; Appendix C)

Fairs, Champagne

The famous medieval Champagne fairs at Troyes began as a result of the increased trade traffic between Europe, the Mediterranean, and the Middle East. These fairs were certainly exciting, colorful events; the quality of the merchandise, especially the exquisitely woven cloth, was very high, attracting expert buyers from all over Europe. The period of their greatest success corresponds to the Plantagenet period as well as the era of the Templar order (1119–1312). However, by the 14th century and after the Black Death, the fairs began to wane significantly. Champagne, especially the area around Troyes, was the location of the beginnings of the Templar order, as the early Templars had strong links with both Champagne and Burgundy. In their heydey, there were six annual Champagne fairs. Each fair was held at a town that sponsored it; for example, two were held at Lagny-sur-Marne and Bar-sur-Aube, and also, at Provins and Troyes, each running for a period of approximately 49 days, or seven weeks. The Templars' house in Provins, in Champagne, was one of the most important preceptories in northern France. Historians acknowledge that Templar influence was a key factor behind these popular fairs, perhaps not all that surprising in that they were largely viewed as very trustworthy, and were also the wealthiest organization in western Europe at the time. In fact, in certain instances, it is known that merchants were rather keen on doing business with the Templars. The French king Philip of Valois granted the special privileges of the Champagne fairs to the Templars, which meant that they could then engage in trade and collect tolls and tithes in certain cases. The Order often received specific rights similar to this connected with trade in many European countries, not only France, and were often also allowed by the relevant authorities to hold weekly markets and annual fairs on their own Templar lands. At the fair in Provins, the Templars were allowed to levy certain tolls on produce and Templar wool that had been turned into beautifully woven cloth at Bruges and other places. Champagne's trade laws in medieval times had a profound influence on later commercial policies—for example, the *troy weight*, originating from the fairs of medieval Troyes, is still used to weigh gems and precious metals such as gold and silver in our modern world of the 21st century. (see **Assets**; **Troy weight**; **Letter of credit**; **Wool**; **Farms**; for further sources about the various assets of the Order, see "Assets, Templar" in the Recommending Reading section)

Farms

Especially following the return of the early Templars from the Holy Land in the autumn of 1127, in an effort to assist the Templars, many kings, nobles, and aristocratic families donated lands or estates to the fledging Order. Such donors often gave the Templars large tracts of undeveloped land or properties that they could not, or did not, necessarily want to work themselves, for various reasons. As the Templars generally had the available manpower, labor, and funds to invest in developing such lands or estates, they were often able to make them fertile and productive; if they did not have the time or labor to do so, they often let out the land to tenants for a tithe, which was often 1/10th of all produce. In certain conditions, renting out the land saved the Order additional expenses of cultivation, but due to especially challenging economic conditions in western Europe in the late 12th and early 13th centuries, renting out land no longer became nearly as profitable, so the Templars, similar to other religious orders at the time, simply worked the land themselves.

In certain areas, they became very efficient indeed and the profits from agricultural produce added to the Order's coffers. For instance, wheat and barley production in the fields around their preceptory at Cressing Temple in Essex, England was especially bountiful, and the original medieval Templar barns at this site have recently been restored. At other locations, largely due to the often phenomenal success of the Templars' efforts at working the land, they would also unfortunately sometimes arouse the envy of their neighbors. For instance, on one occasion in 1274 at the Templar preceptory at Lydley, in Shropshire, England, Templar servants taking oats to market were violently ambushed by jealous locals, led by Sir John Giffard, who stole all of the oats and harrowed the grain into the ground using horses stolen from the Templars' carts. Unfortunately, for some reason, it seems that the Templar servants were traveling without their usual armed guard at that time, but the Order ended up taking legal action against John Giffard. Obviously, grains and produce, similar to their sheep, were very valuable assets of the Templars in Europe, who needed to consistently raise vast amounts of money to assist their brothers fighting in the Crusades in the East. (see **Assets**; **Fairs, Champagne**; **Wool**; **Cressing Temple**; and for further sources, see "Assets" in the Recommending Reading section)

Feast days, Templar

As the Templars were a military religious Order, they strictly avoided conducting business on major Christian feast days of Easter, the Ascension, and Christmas, the three feast days of the Virgin, the Feast of St. John the Baptist, or on saints' days of particular interest. The busiest months for receiving deposits were near All Saint's Day (November 1) and throughout November, and after the Feast of St. John the Baptist (June 24), which took place in the month of July. The Templar Rule also refers to a number of specific saints and their feast days were observed in Templar houses. Templar Rule section 75 specifically lists which feast days were to be venerated in their Templar houses on a regular basis every year: the Nativity of Our Lord; the feast of St. Stephen; St. John the Evangelist; feast day of the Holy Innocents; the eighth day of Christmas, which is New Year's Day; Epiphany; St. Mary Candlemas; St. Mathias the Apostle; the Annunciation of Our Lady in March; Easter and the three days following; St. George; Sts. Philip and James, the two Apostles; the feast day commemorating the finding of the True Cross; the Ascension of Our Lord; Pentecost and the two days following; St. John the Baptist; St. Peter and St. Paul, the two Apostles; St. Mary Magdalene; St. James the Apostle; St. Laurence; the Assumption of Our Lady; the nativity of Our Lady; the Exaltation of the Holy Cross; St. Matthew the Apostle; St. Michael; Sts. Simon and Jude; the feast of All Saints; St. Martin in winter; St. Catherine in winter; St. Andrew; St. Nicolas in winter; and St. Thomas the Apostle.

In section 74, the Rule lists the specific feast days and fasts that all brothers of the Order—whether based at battle in the Holy Land or in a European Templar house—should venerate, no matter where they were based. These feast days and fasts include: St. Peter and St. Paul; St. Andrew; St. James and St. Philip; St. Thomas; St. Bartholomew; Sts. Simon and Jude; St. Matthew; the vigil of St. John the Baptist; the Ascension; the vigil of Pentecost; the ember days; the vigil of St. Laurence; Our Lady in mid-August; All Saints; and Epiphany. The Rule also states very clearly in section 76 that "none of the lesser feasts should be kept by the house of the Temple. And we wish and advise that this be strictly kept and adhered to." (see **St. Mary Magdalene; Saints, Templar veneration of; Saints in medieval society; Relics; Shrines; Pilgrimage;** for further sources about the Templar order and specific relics of saints, see "Relics" and "Pilgrimage and Pilgrims" in the Recommended Reading section)

Food

Similar to their Cistercian and Benedictine counterparts, the Templars were required to eat their meals in absolute silence. The only person allowed to speak was the chaplain, a priest, who would bless their meal, and either he or a clerk would read passages from the Bible during their meals. The Rule states in section 23 that the Templars should eat together, in silence, but if a brother would be in need of something at the table, he should adopt "the signs used by other men of religion," that is, the silent sign language that monastics often used, such as those employed by the Cluniac monks, for example, where bread would be indicated by a circle made with two fingers and the thumb, and so on. If, the Rule says, for some reason, a Templar brother was not accustomed to such signs and found it necessary to speak, he could only then do so very quietly and with all humility at the table, to request what he needed. The Rule bases this policy on several biblical verses, including "Eat your bread in silence" and "I held my tongue." While the Cistercian monks were totally vegetarian, as we learn from section 26 of the Rule, the Templars, however, were required to eat meat—either mutton, veal, beef, goat, or fish—at least three days a week in order to keep their strength up and remain constantly ready for combat. This did not apply, however, to Christmas, All Saints, the Assumption, and the feast of the 12 apostles. The rest of the week the Templars were served vegetables, cheese, and bread, as was the usual custom in other medieval monasteries. They ate at least twice and sometimes three times a day. As there was a shortage of bowls, the Rule also says that the brothers should eat in pairs and, a bit later, that "it seems just to us that each brother should have the same ration of wine in his cup." However, at times the Rule makes clear distinctions as to who may eat what, and when, as illustrated by the phrase at the end of section 26: "And on Sundays all the brothers of the Temple, the chaplains and the clerks shall be given two meat meals in honor of the holy resurrection of Jesus Christ. And the rest of the household, that is to say the squires and sergeants, shall be content with one meal and shall be thankful to God for it." A further reference to food—this time, to the humiliating punishment of eating on the floor instead of the table—occurs in section 95.1, where it states that any brother who received such a penance may never rise from the floor without direct permission of the Master of the house. (see **Rule**; **Prayers**; **Organization of the Templar order**)

Frank

Although the term "the Franks" originally meant a Rhineland Germanic tribe, a "Frank" was a general name used by the Muslims and Byzantines in medieval times to refer to most western Europeans at the time of the Crusades. (see "Crusades and the Military Orders" in the Recommended Reading section)

Freemasonry

Freemasonry remains a fascinating subject of great interest today, for both Freemasons and non-Masons alike. But, for clarity, modern-day Masonic groups are not the same organization as the historical military religious Knights Templar order (1119–1312) of the Catholic Church, with whom they are sometimes confused; modern-day Freemasonry has its own Masonic Knights Templar degrees and groups. But Freemasonry is perhaps one of the most misunderstood organizations today, with many erroneously assuming that there is only one "unified theory" of Freemasonry, for example. In fact, Freemasonry has many branches, each with its own unique history and traditions. Perhaps the teachings and practices of Ancient, Free, and Accepted Masons might be better defined by what it is *not*. There are many different Masonic orders worldwide, and much confusion has arisen in the popular mind as to who Freemasons are, what they believe, and what they do in lodge meetings. Freemasonry is not a religion, nor does it teach a specific theological creed or impose a specific dogma; Masonic sources state that Freemasons are encouraged to explore such issues for themselves. They also state that Freemasonry is not a political organization, and further emphasize that Freemasonry is more properly a system of morality that is taught by oral tradition using allegorical and dramatic pageants that are based on special symbols. This may be in part because the existing historical record shows that in much earlier times, the medieval stonemasons in their guilds taught their new members morality and trade secrets without infringing on religious matters. In the process of educating their members by oral tradition, the medieval stonemasons also often performed ritual plays or pageants based on legends of the origins of the craft of stone masonry.

The precise origin of Freemasonry is a complex topic that has been researched by Masonic scholars for years and, according to the Website of the Grand Lodge of England: "...the honest answers to the questions when, where and why Freemasonry originated are that we simply do not know. Early evidence for Freemasonry is very meager and not enough has yet been discovered—if indeed it even exists—to prove any theory. The general agreement amongst serious Masonic historians and researchers is that Freemasonry has arisen, either directly or indirectly, from the medieval stonemasons (or operative masons) who built great cathedrals and castles."

The early medieval craft guilds are thus worthy of further study in this regard. One of the more well-known legends central to Freemasonry is that of Hiram Abiff, the allegorical story of a murdered apprentice. We also witness the many "mason's marks" in Gothic cathedrals and other ancient and medieval buildings today. The official beginning of the Grand Lodge of England was in 1717; the Grand Lodge of Ireland, around 1725; followed by the Grand Lodge of Scotland in 1736; and many others after that. However, there is certainly evidence of operative Scottish lodges before 1717, as exemplified by the groundbreaking research of Professor David Stevenson of the University of St. Andrews, and others. Another key Masonic work was written in 1723 by a Scottish Presbyterian minister James Anderson, called *The Constitutions of Freemasonry*. This work confirmed that all Freemasons must believe in a supreme being. A number of experts continue to research the complex topic of the origins of Freemasonry. One of the leading worldwide Masonic research lodges is the Quatuor Coronati Lodge No. 2076, founded in London in 1886, for the purpose of further detailed research, study, and discussion of Masonic antiquities, history, and doctrine. Many other Masonic research lodges also exist worldwide. Masonic sources state that the three principles of Freemasonry are Brotherly Love, Relief (Charity), and Truth. In lodges today, supporting charitable organizations in the local community is seen as important. Freemasons claim that Freemasonry is not a secret society, but instead, "a society with secrets." Various debates about Freemasonry and/or its origins will no doubt continue, and further research is being done today by Masonic scholars, academics in related disciplines, and members of the public, to shed more light on the history of Freemasonry, a subject of continuing interest today. There are a variety of Masonic traditions worldwide; therefore, not all Freemasons necessarily agree with each other about the origins of Freemasonry—in fact, some vehemently disagree with each other, as is often the case with many other organizations. While some Masons advocate the concept of a direct succession from the historical Knights Templar military religious order (1119–1312) to the organization that became modern-day Freemasonry, a number of others, in agreement with most academic historians and archivists today, hold that there is no documentable historical evidence to prove such a claim. But as many agree, at the heart of Freemasonry is its symbolism and allegorical teachings. Masonic brochures all over the world state that Freemasonry is "a peculiar system of morality, veiled in allegory and illustrated by symbols." And as is becoming more widely acknowledged today, a number of the founders of America and signers of the Declaration of Independence in the 18th century were Freemasons, such as George Washington, Benjamin Franklin, and others. But for clarity, the medieval military religious Templar order of the Catholic Church with its austere monastic Rule—the Order of the Temple (1119–1312)— is not the same organization as that which eventually became modern-day Freemasonry via the medieval stonemasons' guilds. Nevertheless, researchers await further discoveries and conclusions by Masonic historians and others on the interesting and complex subject of their origins. (see **Guilds, medieval**)

G

Garnache
A sleeveless cloak worn by members of the Order; it is referred to in the Rule.

Gaudini, Thibaud
The 21st Grand Master of the Order of the Temple, Thibaud Gaudini was from the region of Provence in France and served as Grand Master from 1291 to 1292/1293. (see **Grand Masters**; Appendix B)

Geometry
None other than St. Bernard of Clairvaux had defined God as "length, width, height, and depth." As Bernard was one of the key supporters of the early Knights Templar and instrumental in writing their Rule, this definition of God has interested many for some time. Yet, he was living at a time when not only the famed Scholastics were teaching in Paris, but also when geometry itself was prominent among the famed medieval Seven Liberal Arts—geometry, grammar, logic, rhetoric, arithmetic, astronomy, and music—and so it was very highly valued and studied. Clearly, design, number, and proportion were also important to the Templars as they built their castles in the Holy Land and a number of churches and chapels in the West. The Order also had its own mason brothers with section 325 in the Rule stating: "No brother should wear leather gloves, except the chaplain brother…. And the mason brothers may wear them sometimes, and it is permitted them because of the great suffering they endure and so that they do not easily injure their hands; but they should not wear them when they are not working." As the Rule shows, these mason brothers were members of the Templar order who specialized in building skills, though they were not full knight-brothers, however. The mason brothers of the Templar order may also have worked with local stonemasons where construction was taking place and/or may have worked with masons from other orders or guilds. However, few specifics are

known, as few records about medieval stonemasonry survive on the whole, and many of the Templar archives were also destroyed or have disappeared. It is also possible that specific information about Templar order mason brothers may not have ever been recorded at all. More documentation is needed, too, about the meanings of the mason's marks carved on medieval buildings and cathedrals, and scholars from various disciplines are currently conducting research in these areas; it is a rather complex subject and an interdisciplinary approach is required.

But nonetheless, it is known that St. Bernard was translating material relating to sacred geometry after 1128. There were various medieval "rumors" that the Templars had perhaps retrieved something from the Ark of the Covenant, perhaps the Tables of Testimony, that would have had formulas relating to the divine law of number, measure, and weight. Supporters of the theory that Gothic architecture may have had Templar origins point out that, shortly after the Templars returned from the Holy Land in the autumn of 1127, a major change occurred in Europe. Although there is no direct evidence for this, it is interesting to note that, in addition to the Gothic cathedrals beginning to appear in France—which is one issue—the fact is, too, that some of the Templars' own buildings had interesting architectural design changes around this time as well. The Philosophical Cross, the plan of the Third Temple as prophesied by Ezekiel is illustrated in some of the Templars' building schemes, and many have noted that the Temple Church plan in London was based on the Tau Cross. But although these certainly show an awareness of geometry, proportion, and so on, it does not prove that the Templars built the Gothic cathedrals per se. The Cistercian order, under the charismatic Abbot Bernard of Clairvaux, had a primary role in helping to spearhead further growth of the Gothic style. Yet, the Templars were indeed good builders. In 1139, Pope Innocent II granted the Templar order the right to build its own churches, so, after that, understandably, more Templar churches and chapels began to be built in western European areas as well.

Earlier in 12th century Jerusalem, the Templars built (among other things) three of the magnificent central bays of the porch of the al-Aqsa mosque during the time when the Order's headquarters was originally based there (from 1119 until they moved their headquarters to Acre after the Battle of Hattin in 1187). Their famous castle at Atlit, dubbed "Castle Pilgrim," was built in 1218, specifically at the direction of William of Chartres, the 14th Templar Grand Master. So the Templars probably had learned more than a little about geometry, mathematics, and certain architectural designs in the East. The Templars have long been known for building some of their churches with circular naves, illustrative of their devotion to the Church of the Holy Sepulchre in Jerusalem. Eventually, in some areas, however, round churches were gradually considered rather suspect in certain areas in the Christian West, and were thus discouraged. The Knights Templar were especially interested in the design of the Temple of Solomon; the order had many members, but only a minority were full knight-brothers. Others could affiliate with the Order as what we might now call specialist outside consultants, perhaps as an expert in translation or a skilled builder from a guild, for instance. But in the Latin East, some of these outside experts were Arabs; for example, Grand Master Jacques de Molay was known to have had a Saracen scribe who accompanied him on important business in the Holy Land. Knowledge of subjects such as astronomy, mathematics, the telescope, herbal medicine, and even mouth-to-mouth resuscitation came to western Europe via crusader contacts in the East. No doubt the Templars played a role in the new cultural flowering that brought Europe out of the so-called Dark Ages. Geometric symbols have been found on the walls of the prison tower of Chinon Castle, where 60 Templars, including its highest officers, were imprisoned in 1308, so it is known that at least some Templars were familiar with geometry. While not easily accessible to view today, these symbols include stars, various geometrical grid patterns, hands with a heart carved on them, and so on. Other Templar "graffiti" symbols are also to be found at Domme, in France, where the Templars were also imprisoned, and at various other sites. These carvings remain largely undeciphered today and it is possible that more may be found at other Templar-related sites in the future. Further archaeological and professional iconographical research needs to be done by experts before anything definitive can be said about them at present.

Geometry was also one of the Seven Liberal Arts and sciences during the late Middle Ages, perhaps yet another indicator of why such an influential figure as Bernard of Clairvaux would define God in terms of geometry. The Great Architect concept is also very predominant in Freemasonry as well, although it is important to realize that the historical medieval Templar order (1119–1312) is not the same organization as modern-day Freemasonry, which arose out of the medieval stonemasons' guilds and has many branches all over the world today. (see **Seven Liberal Arts**; **Gothic cathedral architecture**; **Guilds, medieval**; **Hagia Sophia**; and for further sources about Templar architecture, see "Architecture and Archaeology" in the Recommended Reading section)

Gold and silver
(see **Assets, Templar order**)

Gothic cathedral architecture

Built in the period between 1140 and 1300, the early and High Gothic cathedrals are among the most stunning interpretations of the divine Order in stone. From popular images of elusive monks working in darkened cloisters, as in *The Name of the Rose* by Umberto Eco, to cathedral imagery in films or in glossy guidebooks, Gothic cathedrals continue to inspire us today. Regarding the history of the Templars, we know that akin to all Catholics in late medieval times, they, too, regularly venerated saints in their houses, and, on occasion, their officers would visit cathedrals or their shrines; and sadly, of course, we recall from history that, in October of 1307, the charges against the Templar order were read out on the steps of one of the most extraordinary Gothic cathedrals of all—Notre Dame de Paris. So what are Gothic cathedrals and why were they so important in the Middle Ages?

"Gothic" is known to us today as the specific name for a special medieval architectural style that featured high naves, flying buttresses, pointed arches, rib vaulting on the ceilings, stained glass windows, and intricate stone carvings in cathedrals. Yet, a great irony is that the term "Gothic" actually pertains to the Goths, a northern people, who had nothing at all to do with this kind of architecture. But today, of course, the word *gothic* can also mean something intriguing, dark, or mysterious. Examples of this type of architecture today would be the majesty of Westminster or Canterbury or the unique "philosopher's carvings" of Notre Dame de Paris. Just what is it about these buildings that are so unique and captivating? The High Gothic style is especially noted for its focus on "upward" orientation, tall naves, and its emphasis on letting in much light—something very different from the previous Romanesque style, which featured round arches and darker interiors. Gothic cathedrals were seen by their creators as houses of light dedicated to the Glory of God, the epitome of the "Heavenly Jerusalem" on earth. Yet, here and there, they exhibit rather unusual carvings and inexplicable details that would appear to be based on much earlier philosophies from the ancient world that had been assimilated by the medieval Christian church and found their way into the cathedral designs. The whole cathedral gives the visitor or pilgrim the impression of soaring into the heavens, of being lifted up.

Appearing nearly overnight, the new Gothic style caught on quickly, beginning in France in the 1130s and ending in the early Renaissance, when a preference for more classical designs returned. But the extraordinary flowering of this new 12th century style began under Abbot Suger in the Benedictine abbey church of Saint-Denis (1130/1135–1144) in Paris, the burial place of many French monarchs. After the middle of the 12th century, the cathedrals of Noyon, Senlis, Laon, and Notre Dame de Paris also began to express this new Gothic style, and, especially by the beginning of the 13th century, Gothic architecture had reached its mature form in the cathedrals of Chartres, Reims, Amiens, and Bourges. The style reached its climax with the conversion of the abbey church of Saint-Denis from 1231; the royal palace chapel of the Sainte-Chapelle in Paris; the cathedral at Troyes; and the royal castle chapel of Saint-Germain-en-Laye. Other countries in Europe gradually began to adopt the Gothic style, as it emanated from France—the mother lode of Gothic design, one might say. Laon and Chartres were the first to have a wide influence, followed by Reims and parts of Amiens, and from around 1180, it then spread first to England (Canterbury, Wells, Salisbury, Lincoln, Westminster Abbey, and Lichfield), then on to Germany (Marburg, Trier, Cologne, Strasbourg, and Regensburg from 1275), and to Spain (Burgos and Toledo), for example. The Cistercian order in Burgundy, founded in 1098, also contributed to the rapid spread of Gothic architecture in France.

The Romans used only geometry and the repeated use of the semicircular arch to build their vast empire. Many churches, right up to the time of the first Gothic cathedrals, featured these round arches, which were defined as "Romanesque." But new innovations followed in the 12th century with the introduction of *the pointed arch*—a hallmark feature of Gothic design. The flying buttresses in the cathedrals were located on the sides to support the great weight of the tall Gothic buildings, so the cathedral could soar higher as well as help support the weight, and the pointed arch came from the necessity of transferring the extra weight from above. All in all, it was as much a type of science as an art to design and build these extraordinary cathedrals.

It is not often realized today that the term *Gothic* was actually first used in a disparaging way by Renaissance critics. They did not like its lack of conformity to the standards of classical Greece and Rome, which they clearly preferred. Ideologies change, regimes come and go, and this includes architectural styles. A closer look, however, reveals that the medieval architects who built the Gothic cathedrals were firmly rooted in the ancient use of geometry and proportion. This is seen in the overall cruciform shape of a cathedral, and in the rhythmic, intricate patterns found in stained glass windows, and also in the rib vaulting that criss-crosses the ceiling of a Gothic cathedral. But many variations in design occurred within the definition of Gothic, with each country or region having its own special characteristics. Contemporary attitudes to Gothic architecture do not emerge clearly from the written sources, as there was no continuous tradition of writing about the visual arts at that time (the 11th–13th centuries), leaving us very few records today. So, to really understand these exquisite edifices, it is often more a question of the symbolic reading of the building and not merely relying on written sources, as, after all, in the Middle Ages, the biblical and other stories and images portrayed in the carvings of cathedrals were used to educate the public, as literacy was rare.

God's presence was seen as universal, but the cathedral was his home in two special ways; one, he was the architect of the universe, the supreme master-mason; the other was the High Altar, where every day, God's Body and Blood were present in the Mass. These were "automatic assumptions" at the time, and not mere speculations. So, the power of God, Christ, or the saints was not doubted or questioned at the time. Neither was the value and power of Our Lady—to whom most Gothic cathedrals were dedicated. For the peasants, the cathedral was a rather distant vision. But when it was being built, they might find work hauling the enormous amounts of wood and stone needed for building, or find themselves compelled to lend their carts and their labor—that is, "a fair's days work for a fair day's wage." Perhaps they might contribute something, according to their resources, to the cathedral building fund, and when it was finished, they, too, could also join with their parish priests on Whit Sunday for the great processions to the cathedral. Or they might choose to go as pilgrims on the feasts of the saints who were buried there. The enormous naves of medieval cathedrals were also intended to provide shelter for the large throngs of ordinary folk on such special occasions. So, from king to peasant, they would all congregate under the same roof.

The great layman, similar to the peasant, was usually only an occasional visitor to the cathedral. He had often endowed charities to help finance the cathedral and to help save his, and his families', souls from death, so when he came to the cathedral, he might find, as at Autun, a stirring reminder of the Last Judgment to greet him over the west portal; or as in the Pardon Cloister at Old St. Paul's, a dramatic representation of the Dance of Death. In spite of their legendary pomp at times, such great men, too, would gather under the same roof for the same feasts or processions as the peasants. Even though medieval Europe was a strictly hierarchal agrarian society, the role of merchants and artisans was *not* a secondary one. The peasant might live near to subsistence level, but in the mid to late Middle Ages, neither he nor his lord was wholly dependent for survival on a single year's harvest. Ironically, too, compared to today, a medieval peasant in the long run actually had much greater overall job security, as there were no redundancies and many more public holidays—in some areas, the medieval church insisted on 80 a year! So peasants, too, when they could, were also allowed to contribute to the building of a cathedral and attend the major feast days and processions. In the building of Chartres Cathedral, for instance, everyone in the society of the town and the diocese, and of the country around it played their part, including the king himself. The top of the lay hierarchy was the king—or in Germany and (more remotely) in Italy, the Holy Roman Emperor.

The design of a medieval cathedral put God himself at the head of the social hierarchy. Gothic cathedrals were homes for all in society, the masses of ordinary folk as well as the kings and bishops, but especially for their most treasured inhabitants after God and Christ himself—their saints. Even though peasants and artisans could contribute and attend feast days and processions, the higher strata of the clergy—bishops, canons, priests, and so on—were in the cathedral far more often, similar to permanent fixtures on the scene. So, in this overall climate, the cathedrals came to be built. The society that developed the Gothic style was still largely feudal in organization, but no longer anarchic as in the earlier Middle Ages; it was also roughly concurrent with a major part of the Templar order. It was strictly hierarchical, yet everyone in the community in some way had a chance to participate or contribute. Cathedrals were often the town's community center as well as a key place of worship. And a Templar house, preceptory, or property was often not terribly far away.

The Templars and Cathedrals

In the 12th and 13th centuries, the Cistercian monks were connected with the medieval Knights Templar through the powerful Abbot Bernard of Clairvaux—the same influential figure who was instrumental in assisting the fledging Templar order with obtaining the necessary papal approval in 1128 and, intriguingly, who also said that God was "length, width, height and depth." So, the time of the Templar order (1119–1312) was also roughly within the same time period as the building of many Gothic cathedrals. Although there is no evidence that the Templars had a role in building the Gothic cathedrals, a number of medieval guilds certainly did, who, in certain places and times, invariably had interactions with many of the major religious orders of the day, the Templars included. However, although some have suggested that the wealthy Templar order may have possibly assisted with the financing of the Gothic cathedrals in some way, there has been no historical documentation to date to confirm this, due to the relative scarcity of accounting documents that have survived from medieval times. But although Bernard of Clairvaux and the Cistercians, and other orders, especially the Cluniacs, were heavily involved in supporting what can only be described as a rather extraordinary boom in the new Gothic architectural style concurrent with the Templar era, it does not mean that the Templars built the cathedrals. Literally overnight, so to speak, in the 12th and 13th centuries, it seemed that the designs of Gothic cathedrals were spreading like wildfire. The primary guild involved in building the Gothic cathedrals, of course, were the medieval stonemasons, who carried on much of their traditions orally. The Templars had their own mason brothers, as section 325 of their Rule confirms, but they were not full knight-brothers in the Order, rather highly valued associates. They were the only Templar brothers allowed to wear leather gloves, except for the chaplains, as the Templars were quite busy building their own chapels or buildings in the West, and their castles in the East. Nor were the Templar mason brothers identical with the medieval stonemason's guilds. Many talented craftsmen did join the Templar order, as they were needed in the Crusades, such as blacksmiths, cooks, and so on, but as there are few surviving historical records detailing precisely who built the cathedrals and the intricacies of the specific financial details, not much can be said for certain, although some accounting rolls and records do exist, informing us which guilds donated stained glass windows and other materials. But as the cathedrals were major projects of the church, and the Templars were the wealthiest religious order at the time, scholars speculate that they would have most likely tried to donate whatever resources they could toward a major cathedral in their area, providing they had surplus capital that was not needed in the Crusades. But, quite frankly, as the Crusades were incredibly expensive, most of the assets generated from Templar commandaries in the West were desperately needed in the East, and were often channeled there as soon as possible. Unfortunately, as there are not many surviving archives about Templar building expenditures, and the central Templar archive was destroyed by the Turks in 1571 on Cyprus, historians continue to remain hopeful that more documents may be found in the future to clarify Templar financial affairs. Sadly, one of the major Gothic cathedrals that does have a specific historically documented connection to the Knights Templar is Notre Dame de Paris, but not because the Templars built it. Instead, upon the steps in front of this towering Gothic masterpiece, the learned theologians, scholars, and king's prosecutors read out the charges against the Order in October of 1307 to the shock and horror of the French public. (see **Guilds, medieval**; **Geometry**; **Seven Liberal Arts**; **Saints in medieval society**; **Trial**; for further sources about Templar architecture, see "Architecture and Archaeology" in the Recommended Reading section)

✦

Grail romances

Given the complexities of medieval dating, scholars cannot always determine the precise date for a manuscript, however, historians note that many of the Grail romances were written in the period between 1190 and 1240, roughly synonymous with the peak of the Templar order. Many were authored by monks, in particular, the Cistercians and Benedictines. These two Orders of the Church, although totally distinct from the military-religious Templar order, also had associations with the influential Cisterican abbot Bernard of Clairvaux, a key early supporter of the Knights Templar as well. There is no historical evidence that a Templar wrote a Grail romance, although some Grail romances do have Templar-related themes, details, and motifs. Contrary to popular belief, there is in fact no "single Grail story"; this is a rather unfortunate misconception today.

Many of the motifs in the Grail stories come from earlier pagan Celtic themes that were later amalgamated into Christian themes as well. But the medieval Grail romances are of a very great variety and do not always agree with each other. One could say there is a prototypical Grail story, but, even then, it is an amalgamation of various themes, people, and places from different medieval manuscripts.

The actual medieval manuscripts describe the Grail as a cup or chalice, a relic of the Precious Blood of Christ, a cauldron of plenty, a silver platter, a stone from Heaven, a dish, a sword, a spear, a fish, a dove with a communion Host in its beak, a bleeding white lance, a secret Book or Gospel, manna from Heaven, a blinding light, a severed head, a table, and more. Obviously, the Grail can take different forms in these legends, all depending on how it chooses to reveal itself to the seeker. In Chrétien de Troyes's *Le Conte du Graal,* for example, the Grail is a platter bearing a single Eucharist wafer. In Robert de Boron's account, the Grail is the chalice Christ used at the Last Supper. In the *Queste del Saint Graal,* it is the dish from which Christ ate the Passover lamb, which now holds the Eucharist wafers. Wolfram presents it as a luminous pure stone. The anonymously written *Perlesvaus* describes it as five different things. There is no single Grail story, and no single Grail—this point cannot be emphasized enough. The Grail can manifest differently to each seeker. It can be an earthly object, and it may be the goal of a spiritual search, and often, it is both. Yet ultimately, it remains a mystery.

Another popular misconception is that both the Templars and the Arthurian knights are the Grail knights, that is, that the Templars are the same as the Arthurian knights of the Round Table. This is not the case, as, in fact, the Templars were Christians as part of a strict military-religious Order, and although some of the Arthurian knights are portrayed as Christians in the legends, many of them are distinctly secular knights, a lifestyle that the historical Knights Templar would never have been allowed to live. Had they done so, they would have been immediately expelled from the Order. Yet, in principle, both the Templars and the legendary Arthurian knights highly valued the chivalric code. One of the earliest known late medieval instances of the Grail motif is found in *Le Conte du Graal,* written by Chrétien de Troyes in 1190, just a few decades after the Templar order's founding. Chrétien's main character, Perceval, is a guileless knight, the archetypal Fool, whose primary trait is innocence. He sees the Grail during a feast at a mysterious castle presided over by a lame man called the Fisher King, a tale familiar to many today. But, unfortunately, Chrétien died before he could finish his story, so other writers attempted to complete it. These versions, called the *Continuations*, expound on Chrétien's version and added in other Grail themes, such as the Grail floating on a platter in midair, the bleeding lance, or a broken sword, and so on. As more *Continuations* were written, other details were added, such as a chess board or a Precious Blood relic, and Perceval has even more challenging adventures. Burgundian poet Robert de Boron wrote two Grail romances, *Joseph d'Arimathie* and *Merlin*, his most famous works, sometime between 1191 and 1200. De Boron gives the reader a distinctly Christian focus to his Grail story, presenting the knights' quest as a spiritual search rather than the usual courtly adventure undertaken for a lady's love or a king's honor. Early 13th century prose versions of Robert de Boron's works link the Grail story more closely with Arthurian legend. *Diu Krone*, by Heinrich von dem Turlim, presents Sir Gawain as the hero, while the Cistercian *Queste del Saint Graal* features Galahad. In the latter, the quest for the Grail becomes a search for mystical union with God. Only Galahad can look directly into the Grail and behold the divine mysteries. The *Queste* presents Galahad as the son of Lancelot, thus contrasting chivalry inspired by divine love, as with Galahad, against that inspired by human love, as between Lancelot and Guinevere. This is the best-known version of the Grail story in the English-speaking world. It was the basis for Sir Thomas Malory's famous late 15th century prose work *Le Morte d'Arthur*—in turn, the storyline sources for much of the film *Excalibur* and the musical *Camelot*. These are only some examples of the many fascinating themes and legends about the Grail that have come down to us through the centuries.

But what about specific Templar-related elements in the Grail legends? Although there are several romances that may have Templar aspects to them, by all accounts the clearest is that of Wolfram von Eschenbach's *Parzival*. Wolfram, a gifted Bavarian poet, wrote several unfinished works and *Parzival,* which was composed between 1197 and 1210. There is no evidence that Wolfram was a Knight Templar. But in this famous work, the Grail is portrayed as a luminous stone that fell from Heaven, and not as a cup or chalice, as is often the case in other versions. He uses the term *lapsit exillas* for this stone; it can be translated as either a "stone from Heaven" or a "stone from exile," leading some scholars toward the concept of a meteorite. Later in the story, Wolfram says the Grail stone is an emerald that fell from Lucifer's crown during the war in Heaven, and that it was brought to earth by the neutral angels.

He also implies a celestial component to the Grail: it originally came from the stars. But next, in his story, he reveals the elite guardians of this precious stone—Grail knights he names as *Templeisen*.

Technically, the medieval German word for "Templars" is *Tempelherren*, but scholars acknowledge that Wolfram seems to have wanted his *Templeisen* to be seen as Templars in the mind of his audience. *Parzival's* unique focus on the Templars may be partly because both Wolfram and his patron, Hermann I of Thuringia, were known to have had an interest in the Crusades and the East. We also know, for instance, that in his earlier work, *Willeham,* Wolfram shows a sympathetic interest in Arabic lands and Muslim culture. His patron, Hermann I, had gone on the German Crusade of 1197–98. Wolfram was also fascinated by astrology, which was gaining popularity in 12th-century European courts following the influx of Arabic texts in Latin translation from Spain. Some scholars believe that Wolfram's Mount of Salvation, on which the Grail castle sits and where the *Templeisen* live, may be a veiled allusion to Mount Sion in Jerusalem, because the original nine Templars lived on the Temple Mount. However, unlike the historical medieval Templars, the *Templeisen's* shields don the symbol of a turtle dove rather than the red cross of battle. In his tale,Wolfram states that Parzival is related to the Arthurian line through his father and to the Grail family through his mother's side of the family. His Grail family is not the courtly society of Arthurian legend but more a divinely chosen elite, of which the *Templeisen* and others whom the Grail has silently selected are to dutifully carry on its noble tradition. Women are also included in the Grail family in Wolfram's account. Although there is a Grail succession in his version, he also says the Grail lineage derived from it is a secret that, ultimately, only the angels are privy to. Certain people are designated by God, through the mechanism of the Grail, to guard the Grail for posterity. So in Wolfram's version, the Grail knights that guard the luminous stone are portrayed as "proto-Templars"; obviously, his audience would have well understood this, as his tale was written in 1205, during the height of the Order's power and influence. But interestingly, he does not specifically call them Templars, either—he made up his own word, *Templeisen*, and chose the peaceful turtle dove as the symbol on their shields.

There are other chivalric motifs in the early 13th century Old French Arthurian romance *Perlesvaus,* known also as *The High Book of the Grail.* This story was written by a Benedictine monk. Here, the Grail castle sits in both the earthly and the heavenly Jerusalem. The hero, Perlesvaus, is a knight of Christ, although he is not specifically described as a Knight Templar per se. Perlesvaus travels across the seas to an island where he visits the Castle of the Four Horns. Here, he meets 33 men in white robes with red crosses on their habits, very reminiscent of the mantles of the knight-brothers of the historical Templar order. The shield of Perlesvaus has a red cross with a gold border around it, similar to, but not identical with, the shields of the medieval Templars. The *Perlesvaus* tale emphasizes the idea of holy war against the infidel, an obvious reference to the Crusades, of which we know the Templars played a key part. This story also tells of how Arthur and his knights tried to forcefully impose the New Law of Christianity in place of the Old Law. In this version—unusual for a Grail romance—Arthur's knights are portrayed collectively as a kingdom and not merely as individuals on a personal quest. This very much resembles the Templars' warrior-monk code, where the group identity always superceded any one individual's personal quest or egoistic concerns.

And, finally, in the *Queste del Saint Graal* tale, written by a Cistercian monk in 1215 for another crusader patron, Jean de Nesle, there may be other chivalric or Templar metaphors. Here, we met Sir Galahad, portrayed as a descendant of King Solomon, who is described as very devout, chaste, and destined from birth to find the Grail. Galahad is not specifically described as a Knight Templar, however, he is a secular knight. But at a monastery of the white brothers, Galahad receives a special white shield with a red cross on it that is said to have once belonged to Joseph of Arimathea; this may be because he is shown to be a direct descendant of Joseph through his mother. The historical Templars who were full knight-brothers wore white mantles with a red cross on them. It is interesting to note that in *Perlesvaus*, the Grail castle *is* Jerusalem itself; in the *Queste* the Grail knights go to Jerusalem with the Grail, but only *after* they complete their quest. When Galahad, Perceval, and Bors reach the Grail castle, they encounter nine more knights who have achieved the Grail. All 12 knights then celebrate communion together, and Christ himself is the priest, analogous to the Last Supper. Galahad, after eating the consecrated host administered by Christ, has a vision of himself as Christ crucified, and dies in ecstasy before the altar. Bernard of Clairvaux, in mystical states, sometimes experienced himself as Christ crucified, and he was also known to have made reference to "Solomon's Bread," special bread from the time of Solomon's Temple. In the *Queste* tale, Galahad symbolizes the secular ideal of Christian knighthood.

As one can see, there are a number of theories about possible chivalric or Templar-related elements in some of the Grail romances. But even though one could argue that some Templar-related allusions are present in various Grail romances, it must also be stated that none of them specifically name the Knights Templar. Only Wolfram's *Parzival* comes closest, with his Grail knights, the *Templeisen*. (see **Arthurian knights**; **Knighthood, secular**; **Relics**; **Chivalry**; **Chrétien de Troyes**; **Troubadours**; for information about relics and the Templar order, see "Relics" and "Pilgrimage and Pilgrims" in the Recommended Reading section)

Grand Master, office of

A Templar Grand Master was elected for life. A powerful individual not only in the Templar order itself, but as part of the entire medieval political and religious scene, the Grand Master was treated with the utmost respect by many kings, nobles, and popes as well as his own men. His opinion and decisions would affect many a battle. No longer an ordinary knight, upon his election, he was entitled to four horses—a luxury at the time of the Crusades—and a major entourage that included at least one chaplain, two knights, a clerk, a sergeant, a Saracen scribe for diplomatic missions and interpreting, a cook, and a servant to carry his shield and lance. But although he certainly had considerable power, he was not to make unilateral decisions, such as whether to wage war or negotiate a truce, without first consulting the Chapter, a committee of the top officers of the Order. He also had much to say about the distribution of funds and could take out some money from the central Treasury for his own travel needs, but not without first consulting the Commander of Jerusalem, who was the treasurer of the Order and guard of the keys to the treasury stronghold. The Templar Grand Master also served as a spiritual head of his Order, leading his knights into battle when he was present. By the 1160s, the office of Grand Master held much power and prestige, especially among the crusading armies in Outremer (the "Latin East" in the Holy Land) and also among the Saracens and other leaders there. By the end of the 13th century, when de Molay served as Grand Master, there were at least 970 Templar houses, including commanderies and castles in both East and West, serviced by a membership of probably at least 7,000, excluding employees and dependents, who must have been at least seven or eight times that number. Similar to the major officials of other military religious orders, the Templar Grand Master had his own seal, which he used to validate approved documents. Probably the most famous Templar Grand Master was Jacques de Molay, the last Grand Master, who was unjustly burned at the stake by the French king Philippe IV in 1314. (see **Organization of the Templar order**; **Grand Master, election of**; **Baculus**; **de Molay, Jacques**; Appendix B; and for further sources about the role of the Grand Master, see "Organization, Structure, and Rule" and "Jacques de Molay" in the Recommending Reading section)

Grand Master, election of

Many have wondered how the Templars chose their Grand Master. The procedure was that after the funeral of the previous Grand Master, which was attended by many dignitaries and leaders in the Holy Land, all the provincial Templar officers in the East would meet in Jerusalem to appoint a Grand Commander to govern until a new Grand Master was chosen. Demonstrating respect for the international character of the Order, though without specifying national divisions, the officers from various countries would choose an electoral college of 13, who, after a night of prayer, would choose the new Grand Master. These 13, symbolic of Christ and his 12 disciples, were a group of eight knights, four sergeants, and one chaplain, in order to reflect the diverse countries from which the membership was drawn. A majority decision was acceptable, having the usual aim of selecting someone already in the Holy Land, although the history of the Order shows that this did not always happen. When the name was announced, the new Master was acclaimed by the brothers and then, while the chaplains sang, they all carried him to the chapel before the altar, as a means of offering him to God. In theory, these elections were structured according to the now-famous papal bull *Omne datum optimum* of 1139, which said that only a professed brother of the Order could be elected. The hierarchical statutes that set forth the procedures for the election give the impression—quite rightly—that it was more important to elect the right person than to elect someone quickly. But the process wasn't always so straightforward, because at least seven of the 22 Templar Grand Masters were appointed through the direct influence of a secular ruler. According to policy, whatever occurred within the electoral conclave was supposed to be kept secret until the result was announced. This is similar to how the Vatican selects a new pope, which is done by a special conclave of Cardinals that meets privately, until the famous "puff of smoke" comes out of the chimney signaling to the world that they have made their choice. (see **Grand Master, office of**; **de Molay, Jacques**; Appendix B)

Guilds, medieval

Generally speaking, in the Middle Ages, a guild was an association of craftsmen or merchants formed for mutual aid and protection, and to further their own professional interests. The medieval guilds were of two main types: the merchant guilds and the craft guilds. Merchant guilds were associations of nearly all of the merchants in a particular town or city, whether they were local or long-distance traders, wholesale, or retail sellers A modern-day analogy might be a type of local chamber of commerce association, which exists for the benefit of its members in the community. Certainly by the 13th century, the merchant guilds of western Europe were officially recognized by many town governments. They often included the wealthiest and most influential citizens in many towns and cities. In the larger towns, a guildhall would often be provided by the merchants' guilds, where their meetings and other events would take place. The merchant guilds became intimately involved in regulating and protecting their members' interests, both in long-distance trade and local town business. Guilds eventually controlled the distribution and sale of food, cloth, and other staple goods, so they often gained a powerful monopoly.

Today, when the words "medieval guild" are mentioned, one often thinks of tired apprentices toiling away from dawn to dusk in a busy master's workshop, or of a young craftsman learning difficult, intricate skills and secret "tricks of the trade." There may be a small grain of truth in the stereotype, in that yes, apprentices did work very hard in the medieval guild system, but the rewards, when finished, were equally great. In fact, our modern-day usage of the word "masterpiece" comes from the final project presentation of a hard-working apprentice to his guild Master, after many years of dedicated service. To have one's "masterpiece" accepted meant that one was now on the road to being allowed to set up one's own workshop and become a "master" himself, some years later. It varied from guild to guild as to what the specific policies were, but this was certainly a major step, a kind of graduation.

The medieval craft guilds were associations of all the artisans and craftsmen in a particular branch of industry or commerce. For example, there were guilds of weavers, bookbinders, stonemasons, architects, painters, metalworkers (the "Hammermen"), bakers, dyers, embroiderers, leatherworkers, and so on. Although its roots were in earlier times, the medieval craft guilds system became much more widespread in the 11th century in Europe, as towns and cities started to develop. A guild craftsman was a very skilled person in his specialized area of expertise. Most skilled craft artisans in medieval guilds were men, although girls and women were certainly involved in highly skilled crafts, too, such as intricate embroidery, tapestries, and weaving, although opportunities for boys and men were more numerous in the Middle Ages regarding apprenticeships and other opportunities.

The skilled craftsmen in a town usually consisted of a number of family workshops in the same neighborhood. The powerful masters of these workshops related to each other as specialized experts in their chosen areas of expertise and would train young people, often sharing apprentices between them. These crafts masters would agree as a group to regulate competition among themselves, promoting their own as well as the entire town's prosperity. The crafts guild members would agree on some basic policies governing their trade, setting quality standards, and so on. So from very local beginnings, the early craft guilds of the Middle Ages gradually developed into larger, more sophisticated networks and associations of highly skilled craftsmen. In fact, some towns became famed far and wide for producing particularly high-quality work in their crafts workshops, with their skilled masters becoming as widely known as a celebrity might be today.

Members of the craft guilds were divided into three distinct categories, those of *master, journeyman*, and *apprentice*. The master was a very accomplished craftsman who took on apprentices very selectively. Usually these were boys (or girls, in a few cases, depending on the craft) in their teens who were provided food, clothing, shelter, and an education by the master, in exchange for working for them for free as an apprentice, often for a fixed term of service that could last anywhere from about five to nine years. After this, an apprentice could become a journeyman, who was allowed to work for one or more masters and was paid with wages for his labor. Once a journeyman could provide direct proof of his technical and artistic skills, by showing his "masterpiece" as a kind of demanding final exam, he might rise even higher in the guild and become a master on his own some years later. Then—and only then—could he set up his own workshop to hire and train apprentices himself. The path to becoming a master was a long and difficult one.

Masters in any particular craft guild tended to be a highly select inner circle, who possessed not only technical competence, but also proof of their wealth and social position. Masters also had to guard their trade techniques and initiation rites very closely. Apprentices would flock to be trained by certain masters, hoping to be fortunate enough to be chosen for a place on a specific apprenticeship program. But many apprenticeships were hereditary, and other masters might only accept a very few apprentices a year, so it was a highly selective process. It is difficult to overstate the great importance of these guilds in trade and commerce prior to the industrial revolution. As history has shown, in many areas in the Middle Ages, they literally *were* the economy. The specific traditions of the western European craft guilds remain rather mysterious—trade "secrets" of the various crafts guarded by the guild. But as these and other mysteries were passed on orally, historians do not know for certain what the specific nature of these secrets were; also, some secrets and knowledge were passed down symbolically. For example, the masters of the stonemason's guild recorded every member's name and mark where necessary. In many medieval cathedrals, for example, mason's marks were carved on certain walls, pillars, and crypts. But other guilds also had their own unique marks and symbols to identify work done by their workshops in their specific area.

In addition to marks or symbols, some guilds had other ways of communicating their more specialized concepts and religious traditions; in some cases such knowledge was carried on by traveling musicians, troubadours, Meistersingers, and others. It is also important to realize that although there were stonemasons among the guilds, they differed from many of the other guilds in two major ways: (1) as their work necessitated they moved about more and traveled from site to site, which created more of a need for special recognition signs and so on; and (2) the stonemasons especially tended to have a much richer tradition about their past than a number of the other guilds, with some of their legends and allegories going all the way back to Enoch or the Temple of Solomon, for instance. Gradually, these medieval stonemason guilds developed into what many believe may be the beginnings of modern-day Freemasonry. Many Masonic scholars around the world continue to research the history of their origins from a number of different perspectives. It must be noted, however, that not all Masonic scholars today necessarily agree on these matters, so we await their further research and perspectives in the future.

Naturally, the Templar order, akin to other religious orders at the time, had interactions with various guilds. The Templars also had their

own mason brothers who were not full knight-brothers, but as the Rule in section 325 informs us, other than the chaplains, the mason brothers were the only members of the Templar order who had specific permission to wear leather gloves. The Rule states that this was because of the difficult work they did and to help prevent the possibility of injury. The Templars built castles, chapels, and other edifices. Their mason brothers are not the same as a member of a medieval stonemason's guild, however, as the mason brothers of the Templars were specficially members of the Order of the Temple. (see **Geometry**; **Gothic cathedral architecture**; **Seven Liberal Arts**; **Rosslyn Chapel**; for further information and sources about Templar architecture and archaeology, see "Architecture and Archaeology" in the Recommended Reading section)

h

Haircut

The Templars had short haircuts, but could wear beards or moustaches as long as they were always kept tidy, as we learn from their Rule, sections 21 and 22. Here, it specifically states that it was the Draper's responsibility to ensure that each Templar's haircut was so well cut that it could be examined from both the front and from behind. The Rule goes on to advise that all Templar houses should firmly adhere to that policy, as well as applying it equally with respect to beards and moustaches. While Templars could wear beards, they were also advised not to have them (or their habits) too long. Later, in section 532, care of one's hair is also mentioned along with other criteria to carefully tend to after one made amends for any sins or penances in the Order. Overall, tidiness is emphasized in several sections of the Rule about not only haircuts and beards, but regarding a Templar's clothing as well. (see **Draper**; **Decoration**)

Hagia Sophia

A major inspiration for such medieval period luminaries as Abbot Suger and Bernard of Clairvaux, the Hagia Sophia is the famous "Church of the Holy Wisdom," or Sophia, in Constantinople, a city today known as Istanbul. Built by the Emperor Justinian I in the sixth century, it became the apotheosis of Byzantine art and wealth, with highlights including its rare marbles, gold candelabra, and extraordinary mosaics on its ornate ceilings. Through the centuries, this Byzantine church has endured many changes, among them being earthquake damage, being converted into a mosque, being re-converted to a Christian church, and, since 1935, being made into a museum by the Turkish government. The Templars, however, did not build or restore the Hagia Sophia, as has sometimes been erroneously put forth; however, one of their most enthusiastic early supporters and writers of their Rule, Bernard of Clairvaux, did take an interest in this church, as did many of his contemporaries in late western medieval Europe.

The Hagia Sophia was built in honor of the glory of the Temple of Solomon—clearly something that Abbot Suger of St. Denis and Abbot Bernard of Clairvaux would have been quite interested in, especially given the prominence of the study of geometry in 12th century France. They wanted to draw the very best inspiration from Christendom—East or West—to build churches to the utmost glory of God, the very epitome of a "Heavenly Jerusalem" on earth. The whole idea of a Gothic cathedral as a place where the Heavenly Jerusalem touched the earth meant that they would naturally consider the meaning behind the Temple of Solomon as well. But the Hagia Sophia went even further than that, apparently, as its exquisite mosaics and beautifully decorated interior were so incredibly intricate and ornate that the emperor Justinian I was reported to have said "Solomon, I have surpassed you!" Long coveted by leaders of both the Muslim east as well as the Christian west, understandably, the capture of Constantinople in 1204 was considered a major victory by the armies of Christendom. And, at the heart of this extraordinary city was the Hagia Sophia. But some 250 years later, Constantinople was again attacked, this time by the Ottoman Turks in 1453. The young sultan Mehmet II, converted the church into a mosque, a process in which many Christian treasures were pillaged and mosaics defaced or destroyed. Later, in the 19th century, the first efforts were made to restore Justinian's church to its former glory—a monumental task. As significant damage had been done over time, many specialists and restoration experts painstakingly worked over a period of years to again reveal its beauty and glory for all to see and experience today. However, it is not, and never has been, a site of the Templar order. (see **Geometry**; **Bernard of Clairvaux**; for further sources about Templar architecture and buildings, see "Architecture and Archaeology" in the Recommended Reading section)

Harding, Stephen

After the death of the abbot Alberic at the "mother" Cistercian monastery of Citeaux in 1109, the Englishman Stephen Harding then assumed power and became abbot. An especially gifted scholar, Harding consulted with Jewish rabbis and other learned men to better study the Hebrew of the Old Testament. He proved to be a very effective administrator, and also deserves credit for giving shape to the early Cistercian ideal, which combined practical daily work with a life of devout prayer, based on the earliest versions of St. Benedict's Rule. As we know, Bernard of Clairvaux, one of the earliest and most influential advocates of the early Knights

Templar, was also a Cistercian and helped write their Rule. (see **Bernard of Clairvaux**; **Cistercians**; **Citeaux**; **Clairvaux Abbey**; **Molesmes, Robert of**)

Horse racing and jousts

Although full Templar knight-brothers as well as sergeant-brothers had elite horses for battle, and roncins for daily tasks, the Old French Rule makes it clear that horse racing, however, was rarely permitted, and only with the permission of the Master. Riding elsewhere without a specific approved purpose was also not allowed. In addition, practice jousts were only permitted in the Master's presence, not on one's own or with other knights or members of the Order. Such strict policies were part of the overall emphasis in the Order on most of the activities of secular knights being expressly forbidden in the Templar order, as well as saving valuable manpower, supplies, and time toward proper, disciplined training for battle. (see **Knighthood, secular**; **Roncin**)

Hauberk

A key part of a knight's armor; the hauberk was a coat of mail with coif covering the head but leaving only the face uncovered. (see also **Coif**)

Heresy

In the Middle Ages, a heresy was a religious belief or opinion in opposition to the orthodox doctrine of the Church, that is, it was seen as an "error of the faith." A heretic was a person accused of heresy; there were many different kinds of heresies as there were heretics. Obviously, the accused saw themselves not as heretics, but as true believers. At a trial for heresy, the primary objective for the prosecutors of the Inquisition was to prove the charges of the Church, rather than to ascertain the truth, as is often assumed today for a "trial." Third-party witnesses were often not used at all, such as with some of the areas where the Templars were tried. It was legal to torture heretics in certain countries; for example, in medieval France, where it was used against the imprisoned Knights Templar. Such methods would involve being put in tubs of scalding hot water or extremely cold water; being beaten or having one's skull cracked; notorious devices such as the rack, which stretched the limbs to the breaking point; the thumbscrew, which, lined with metal studs, would gradually crush a heretic's thumb in a painful grip; or, the strappado, a device that would raise the victim up into the air while heavy weights were attached with a rope to the victim's hands. Not too surprisingly, in the trial of the French Templars, for example, where torture was most widely used, there were also a correspondingly large number of "confessions"; in areas where torture was not used, or employed very lightly, there were few, if any, confessions. Many medieval heretics were burned at the stake for their beliefs; and, perhaps most notably for Templar history, are the cases of the last Templar Grand Master, Jacques de Molay and the Preceptor of Normandy, Geoffrey de Charney, who were ordered to be burned by the French king Philippe IV in March of 1314. Famous medieval heresies were, for example, the Albigensians (Cathars), the Waldensians, or the Lollards, to name but a few.

Some medieval heretics were famous in their own day as well as now, such as Joan of Arc. The Inquisition was established via the Dominican order in the mid-13th century specifically to exterminate the Albigensian heresy in the Languedoc; it then extended to Italy, Spain, and Germany. In Britain, heresy was relatively rare until the latter part of the 14th century, when the authorities strongly pursued the Lollards. The arrests of the Knights Templar began in France, at dawn on Friday, the 13th of October 1307, followed by the later arrests of Templars in other countries. (see **Trial of the Templars**; **de Molay, Jacques**; **Philippe IV**; **Clement V**; **Cathars**; for further sources about heresy in relation to the Templars, see "Trial of the Templars" in the Recommended Reading section, as well as Appendix D)

Hospitallers
The shortened name of the Order now properly called "The Sovereign Military and Hospitaller Order of St. John of Jerusalem, called of Rhodes, called of Malta." In the time of the Templars, they were known as the Hospitallers. Still an official religious Order in the Roman Catholic Church today, the Hospitallers were originally formed to serve their medieval hospital in Jerusalem. It was a major beacon of hope to many hungry and exhausted Christian pilgrims. As many more increasingly weary or badly ill Christian pilgrims began to arrive in the Holy Land, a much greater need for medical services became apparent. Answering this need, the Hospitallers rose to the challenge. Due to the general lack of surviving records from the medieval period, it is not known for certain how long the Hospitallers' earliest hospital or hospice had been in Jerusalem. But it was one of the earliest and was certainly well established by the early 12th century by the time the Knights Templar arrived. A women's hospice dedicated to St. Mary Magdalene was also founded nearby.

Evidence does exist for other foundations of certain hospitals in Jerusalem before the First Crusade, including one in the ninth century and one in 1039. Yet, none of these were consistently in service, until a Benedictine abbey called St. Mary of the Latins started a hospital just to the south of the Holy Sepulchre around 1080, most likely staffed by monks from the abbey next door. The dedicated and energetic supervisor of this hospital was named Gerard, and he later became the first Grand Master of the Hospitaller order. Today, it is believed that this early hospital was assisted financially by the influential, wealthy merchants of the Italian port city of Amalfi, and that it was established as early as A.D. 1020. Sometime before 1113, this early hospital broke away from its monastic "parent" and became independent.

On February 15, 1113, Pope Paschal II sanctioned the establishment of the Order of the Hospital (the "Hospitallers") by papal bull and the Order was dedicated to St. John the Baptist and placed under the protection and authority of the Holy See. This early hospital in Jerusalem was said to have held up to 2,000 patients. In 1120, the supervisor Gerard died. A skull that is highly revered as the relic of the head of the Blessed Gerard, the founder of the Order of the Hospital, is preserved today in the Convent of St. Ursula in Valletta, the capital of Malta. Around 1126 the Hospitallers started to take on military responsibilities in addition to taking care of the sick. Of course, the Knights Templar were the major military Order around at the time and also assisted pilgrims; but the Hospitallers kept their medical services going in a more major way under these difficult circumstances, as that was their primary purpose.

Unlike the Templars, who were known for their trademark white mantles with red crosses, the Hospitallers initially had black mantles with a simple white Latin cross on them. But by 1126, the eight-pointed Maltese cross design was adopted by the Blessed Raymond du Puy, the second Grand Master of the Order. The Hospitallers first became a religious order under their able leader, Brother Gerard, after the conquest of Jerusalem.

Maltese cross, associated with the Knights Hospitaller
Courtesy of Simon Brighton

Similar to most fellow Christians in early 12th century Jerusalem, they, too, welcomed the presence of the early Knights Templar in the area, as the Templars provided needed protection for pilgrims, among other functions. The Hospitallers were officially approved by the pope in 1113 and followed the rule of St. Augustine; however, they did not become a military religious order until later, around the 1180s, after the Templars had been established as such following the Council of Troyes in 1130. After the fall of Acre in 1291, similar to the Knights Templar, the Hospitallers also transferred their headquarters in the east to Cyprus, and then to Rhodes by 1310. By all accounts, they were especially renowned for their naval fleet during the Crusades.

Famagusta Hospitallier and Templar Chapel, North Cyprus
Photo courtesy of Simon Brighton

The Hospitaller's main devotion, after Christ and the Blessed Virgin Mary, was to St. John the Baptist, their patron saint. Driven out of Rhodes by the armies of Suleiman the Magnificent in 1523, they were relocated to Malta by 1530. Napoleon drove them from Malta in 1798, so the Order then transferred its headquarters to Rome in 1834. In Malta, the Hospitallers had established a sovereign state, and even today, the Order still claims sovereign status, and has its own passports and diplomatic privileges. It is involved in charitable work involving hospitals, ambulances, and other medical concerns.

Although fellow Christians, the Templars and the Hospitallers were often strong rivals in medieval times, and after the trial and suppression of the Templar order in 1312 by papal bull, most Templar lands, properties, buildings, archives, relics, and other goods, as decreed by the pope, were transferred to the Hospitaller order. (see **Knights of St. John's Co-Cathedral**; **Krak des Chevaliers**; **Trial**; **Maritime trade and ports**; for further information and sources about the Hospitallers and other military orders, see "Crusades and the Military Orders" in the Recommended Reading section)

Hughes I, Count of Champagne

Born in 1077, Hughes was the third son of Thibaud I, the count of Blois, Chartres, Sancerre, and Champagne. Hughes was to eventually become Hughes I, the count of Champagne, one of the most powerful men in all of medieval western Christendom. He was also a key figure in the early developments of the Templar order. In March of 1096, when he was only 19, the First Crusade left for the Holy Land; this entourage included his older half-brother, Stephen de Blois, who was married to Adele, the daughter of William the Conqueror. Although he was involved with an assembly of bishops and nobles in Reims who had discussed this important crusade, he was still rather young and did not immediately set out with the others, but went to Jerusalem later.

One of the most important figures in the early foundation of the Knights Templar, Hughes I's court was centered at Troyes. Although historians know that he was very active in the Order's earliest years, he did not officially join the Templars himself until late in 1125, some six years or so after the first public emergence of the Order in 1119. Hughes I donated the land on which the first Cistercian monastery had been built at Citeaux; ironically, when he made his Templar vows, he had to pledge fealty to his own vassal, Hugh de Payns, as he was the first Templar Grand Master. Hughes's willingness to do so shows that he sincerely believed in what he was doing. Even though he joined the Order of the Temple at this rather late date, his involvement regarding the earliest foundations of the Order is clear. Not much is known about his specific activities in 1106 or 1107, or about his (or Hugh de Payns's) activities in the Holy Land during these years, but nearly four years later, around the year 1108, historians know that Hughes returned to Champagne and met with an important group of nobles and clergy, the same ones he had met with earlier at Molesmes in 1104. As his signature is missing from all documents between 1104 and 1108, many historians believe that he and Hugh de Payns were in the Holy Land during these years. Unfortunately, however, medieval chroniclers also make no reference to any of their activities in the Holy Land; perhaps records have simply not survived, or, their activities and whereabouts were not documented. We do have a letter that Ivo, the bishop of Chartres, wrote to Hughes, which rather strongly chastises him for leaving his wife to return to Jerusalem in 1114. Historians acknowledge that after this, Hughes then returned to Champagne partly due to the Bishop's pressure. Nevertheless, by late 1125, Hughes decided to leave his family for good to join the fledging Templar order, which at that time still had only nine knights. We know he stayed in Jerusalem for about two years, returning with the rest of the early Templars in the autumn of 1127. Unfortunately, not much detailed documentation exists from medieval chroniclers about the specifics of the first nine years of the Order in particular, but from what does exist, the key role of Hughes is clear at that time, and later, after he officially joined the Templar order in 1125. Hopefully, in the future, more documents will be found and translated about Hughes and his role regarding the early founding of the Knights Templar. (see **Origins of the Order**; **Hugh de Payns, Hugh de**; **Organization of the Templar order**; for further sources detailing the origins of the order, see "Origins of the Order" as well as "Organization, Structure, and Rule of the Order" in the Recommended Reading section)

Incense and the spice trade

Particularly in the 13th century, when trade vastly increased due to rapidly growing population, an influx of many goods came into western medieval Europe. At this time, the medieval money supply was at a peak, not to be reached again for several centuries; naturally, this increased the demand among the wealthy elite of the time for more luxurious items, such as fine perfumes, ointments, incenses, and spices. So kings were not alone in demanding and obtaining such spices and perfumes, as nobles and churches needed them, too, as did some individuals. Unfortunately, for many today, and for a variety of reasons, the predominant economic view of medieval life has tended to be rather stereotypical—that of pathetic, sweating serfs toiling on their laird's manor, receiving little if anything in return for their efforts, desperately trying to sell their wares at the local market. Of course, life was feudal and difficult for many; however, the entire picture is much more comprehensive than this, with the term "Dark Ages" now largely viewed by experts as outdated. There were, in fact, many facets of medieval trade, money, and exchange of goods, including various products of the spice trade—perfumes, ointments, oils, and incenses. Although historians know that many of these luxury commodities were brought back to western Europe by returning crusaders, there is little evidence that the full Templar knight-brothers were directly involved in doing so, as they were far too busy with fighting in the Crusades. However, similar to many in the late Middle Ages, the Templars needed to work with a number of associates regarding trade and commerce, within their own Order as well as with various secular contacts on land or by sea, as necessary.

Although the Saracens were the major enemies of the Templars, the Templars were on better terms with Arabic contacts due to their great skills in diplomacy than were other religious orders at the time. As history has shown, many precious perfumes and oils came from Arabic or eastern locales, as, in fact, they still do, to a large degree. Regarding their maritime trade activities, historians know that the Templars were involved in shipping not only men, horses, and equipment for battle, but also pilgrims, produce, wine, olive oil, and other commodities, as much money was desperately needed by the Order to finance the expensive Crusades in the East. As the church needed a steady supply of frankincense, myrrh, and other oils for its services from the East, scholars believe that some military religious orders such as the Templars and their associates would have likely arranged for such goods also to be brought back to Europe when they could, in conjunction with other religious orders, guilds, and Christian secular merchants of the day.

It is important to realize that the overall definition of "spices" at that time was far more all-encompassing than it is now, as we currently tend to think of them mainly as culinary spices, such as pepper, and herbs; for example, the generic heading of "spices" as imported by Italians from Alexandria and the Levant to European capitals, and sold there by grocers or *speziali* was far broader than our narrow modern definition of kitchen spices and herbs. Such a wide definition of spices could conceivably include things such as sugar, candied fruits, gems, wines, or even items such as gold leaf or rosewater. Many of these types of ingredients were also used in medicine, where, for example, in Florence, the *speziali* and *medici* formed a single guild. Aromatic incenses such as frankincense and myrrh for burning in church also counted as spices, as did soaps, glue, dried rhubarb, gems such as turquoise, dyes such as indigo, or even elephant tusks—the variety was endless. Ginger was used for mulled wine, still a persistent favorite at Christmas in many European countries, and also for spicing meat and fish. Cloves were used in a similar fashion, and were also in high demand by apothecaries (shops akin to a pharmacy), for pain relief; in fact, oil of clove is still used by many dentists today.

Sources for spices were widely scattered—throughout India, Indonesia and southeast Asia, mainly—and were transported to Europe via ship, through the Persian Gulf or the Red Sea, and by caravan or pack train, with many tolls along the way, and much danger of loss. Pirates often lay in wait especially for a richly laden spice ship—an especially "lucky find" for them. The trade was lucrative for many merchants bringing back incenses and oils, so specific sea routes that would permit a ship to sail from Europe all the way to the East, load up, and sail back safely to the West was kept as secret as possible. Although most spices were from the

East, some were produced by Europeans, such as sugar and cumin seed. Later, by the early 15th century, saffron was by far the most expensive commodity, and was directly imported into Prussia by the Teutonic Knights, another Christian military religious order roughly contemporary with the Templars. But, by far, the primary sources of many medieval spices, dyes, and fine incenses, oils, and perfumes were known to be from the "exotic East," building up a kind of folklore of its own over time, an aura of exclusivity.

Churches, of course, needed their incenses, oils, and wine for religious ceremonies, and these would have been necessary commodities in the spice trade for the West. Thousands of Christian communities needed wine for Mass, oil for consecration and unction, and incense for services and at shrines. In a sense, incense was a kind of interfaith product of sorts, as well as others oils used in religious ceremonies and anointing rituals as not only Christians needed them. But the constant need for incenses and oils meant that unbroken trading contacts had been long maintained for centuries between the Christian and Islamic worlds, often over a distance of more than 4,000 miles, a great distance in those days.

Venice played a key role in medieval trade; as it had become a great sea power and controlled the Adriatic Sea, so it became very wealthy from its trade with the East. There was great trade between Byzantium and Venice—the "gateway to the East"—bringing precious oils, perfumes, and spices into western Europe, from as early as the ninth century. Historians acknowledge that various types of special perfumes, especially musk, were brought to Europe in the late 11th and 12th centuries from Arabia, through trade with the Islamic world and with the returning crusaders—not all of whom were Knights Templar, of course. Even today, many have heard stories from the great medieval travelers about exotic spices and adventures from Europe to the East, such as Rabbi Benjamin (1160–1173) or Marco Polo (1254–1324); authors of literature, such as Chaucer or Shakespeare also mention exotic spices at certain junctures in their work. There are archives from the reign of Edward I to show that spices and other aromatic luxury commodities were traded in medieval England; a fair number in France, Spain, and other European countries exist as well. By the 13th century, too, East India had developed an especially powerful trade network for cloves and nutmeg, and would later also become famous for its tea.

Bruges, Belgium was the major point for not only the export of manufactured medieval European goods, but also for receiving imports for the

Low Countries and much of northern and northwestern Europe. Bruges acted as a key focal point for the wealthy Italian merchants, too, who would often collectively purchase such rare commodities at its port. The Templars also sold wool at Bruges and had dealings with cloth merchants here as well; they would later sell their finely woven cloth at fairs in France. Spice ships were understandably among the most strongly guarded, and from the port at Bruges, spices were brought by the counts of Flanders, the dukes of Brabant, and the counts of Hainault-Holland and others. At the port of Bruges, one could find exotic luxuries from the Levant and Alexandria, and even fresh oranges and lemons from Cordoba in Andalusia, as citrus trees were introduced from India into the Mediterranean by Arab merchants. Fresh citrus produce such as this was a genuine luxury at this time, perhaps something rather hard to believe in our current day. Medieval Spain itself also received many precious perfumes from Arabia from as far away as Baghdad and Syria. Arabian perfumes were exquisitely developed to a very high degree, using ingredients from India, North Africa, China, and Egypt, producing a larger scale of perfumes than other areas.

The range of what was available to buy or sell at ports such as Bruges was quite extensive. Certain medieval fairs, too, provided a rich mercantile environment, such as those at Champagne. This was also due to the fact that from the middle of the 12th century to the beginning of the 13th century, a network of roads was organized in France as a consequence of a rapidly growing economy. Fairs attracted huge numbers, who came to purchase luxurious silks, jewelry, rare cloths, and so on. Many of the merchants there obtained their goods from distant places, including precious oils, fine perfumes, and exotic spices from Arab merchants, making such fairs famed for their commercial opportunities and extraordinary offerings for the purchasers. As the key Champagne city of Troyes was also a central point for the medieval Knights Templar, they, too, were involved in some of the commercial enterprises and issues surrounding tolls at the Champagne fairs, as historical documents show.

But, unfortunately, there was a darker side to the increase in the medieval spice trade as well, affecting churches, families, and towns. Even after the time of the suppression of the Templar order in 1312, the remainder of the 14th century saw not only other groups accused of various heresies, trials, and economic challenges, but also the terrible ravages of plague, the Black Death. (see **Fairs, Champagne**; **Wool**; **Maritime trade and ports**; **Assets**; **Farms**)

"In Praise of the New Knighthood"

This famous letter was written by Abbot Bernard of Clairvaux to his colleague Hugh de Payns, a co-founder of the early Templar order, which elevated the Order of the Temple above all other orders of the day, including its main rival, the Knights Hospitaller. This letter established the image of the Templars as a fierce spiritual militia for Christ. St. Bernard regarded the Templars as an entirely new species of knighthood, previously unknown in the secular world, pursuing a double conflict against both flesh and blood, and the invisible forces of evil.

The Templars were known to be especially fearless, believing that in the sight of the Lord they would be his martyrs. As a holy militia fighting for Christ, the Templars were willing to put aside the usual temptations of ordinary secular life for a dedicated life of service. They accepted many sacrifices, such as living by a strict religious Rule apart from secular society; giving all of their personal property to the Order; not shaving their beards; and having no ornamentation on their clothing, no luxurious foods, no women, little meat at meals, and so forth. They were something similar to a spiritualized version of modern-day elite military Special Forces—such as the famed U.S. Navy Seals, the Marines, or the British SAS—who live by far more rigorous standards than other soldiers. They were elite Special Forces for Christ, the most disciplined fighting force in western Europe.

Contrary to popular belief, the Templar knights were not monks, although they did take the three monastic vows of poverty, chastity, and obedience. They were devout men who followed a religious Rule of life and wore a distinctive mantle, but who, unlike monks in a monastic environment, did not live in an enclosed house. Most monks prayed and fought spiritual battles, but as we know from the history of the Crusades, the Templars also valiantly fought many bloody physical battles in the defense of Christendom as well. Not everyone agreed initially with St. Bernard's idea of combining spiritual devotion with physical fighting. A number of churchmen saw these two functions as largely incompatible, as there was great concern about sins and souls in medieval society. Even St. Bernard himself struggled with some of these issues, and we know the Byzantines were reportedly quite shocked to see so many priests who bore arms in the crusader armies. Even so, in general, the Templars gained much respect as they demonstrated their battle skills and won victories. The power of the New Knighthood concept was so strong that even the Order of the Hospital of St. John of Jerusalem, also known as the

Hospitallers or the Order of St. John, had to adapt by adding to their official Rule a new knightly monastic ideology. This new idea combined knighthood and monasticism into a code for a community of warrior-monks, of which the Templars were a leading example. (see also **Bernard of Clairvaux; Knights Hospitaller; Payns, Huge de**; for further sources about this letter, see "In Praise of the New Knighthood" and "Bernard of Clairvaux" in the Recommended Reading section)

Jolly Roger

The now infamous Roger de Flor has become known as one of the most successful pirates of the late 13th century. Roger de Flor was a key player in the late 13th-century naval scene and commanded a vast army of mounted Catalan knights and mercenaries. Seen as powerful—and feared—by his contemporaries, Roger achieved much success on the high seas and eventually married into the Byzantine royal family. He was also the only man from foreign parts who held the Byzantine title of "Caesar," no mean feat in those times. But as a young man, he began his life on the sea aboard a Templar ship in Marseilles. Hardworking and talented, by age 20, he was a sergeant-brother in the Templar order and assisted them in many battles. Brother Roger and the Templars bravely evacuated the citizens of Acre, a major port city in the Holy Land in 1291, but unfortunately Roger engaged in a bit of piracy himself during the process and helped himself to some of the proceeds. Jacques de Molay, the last Templar Grand Master, was understandably furious about this severe breach of ethics, immediately expelled him from the Order, and denounced him.

After this expulsion from the Templar order, Roger immediately fled. Not long afterward, however, as it often happens in such situations, he set up his own piracy business and ended up becoming one of the most successful, notorious privateers on the high seas in the late Middle Ages. Some surmise that the story of Roger de Flor might be one possible origin for the pirates' skull-and-crossbones insignia and its nickname, the "Jolly Roger," yet no specific evidence exists about the de Flor legend in this regard. A number of other theories exist about the possible origin of the "Jolly Roger" pirate flag symbol, but the story about Roger de Flor is one of the legends that has a specific Knights Templar connection. In any case, it is interesting to note that he was immediately expelled from the Templar order by the Grand Master, an indication of the Order's strict Rule and disciplinary procedures. (see **Maritime trade and ports**; **Admiral**)

Judges, Templar

The Templars advised many kings and popes, but today it is perhaps not so widely realized that they also served as judges. In England, for example, high-ranking Templars presided in criminal matters, except for cases involving major crimes punishable by hanging or mutilation, which went to the king's courts. Many a medieval common thief was probably tried by the Knights Templar. (see **Advisors**; **Organization of the Templar order**; and for further sources about the various functions, organization, and officers of the Templar order, see "Organization of the Templar order" in the Recommended Reading section)

K

King Arthur
(see **Arthurian knights**; **Grail romances**; **Romanticization**)

Knighthood
(see **Knighthood, secular**)

Knighthood, secular
Knighthood in the Middle Ages could take many forms. The medieval Knights Templar was organized as a Christian military religious order, distinct from many other secular knights of the era who were members of various knightly confraternities. They are also not the same as the famous Arthurian knights of legend, the knights of the Round Table, as has sometimes been assumed. The idea of a "new knighthood" regarding the early Templar order was largely instigated by the powerful Cisterican abbot, Bernard of Clairvaux, who wrote his famous letter to his colleague and first Templar Grand Master, Hugh de Payns. This letter, titled "In Praise of the New Knighthood" described his unique vision of a new order of monks who would combine the functions of both warrior and monk in a way the Western world had never seen before. Bernard insisted on a very austere Rule, partly due to his vociferous reaction to what he considered to be the increasingly lax and immoral excesses of the secular knights of the day. For example, he often complained about their idle words; outbursts of laughter; jousting; playing chess and games of dice; hunting; falconry; going to soothsayers, jesters, or storytellers; and staging plays. He especially criticized their pomp and pride and said that these were to be strictly avoided by monastic knights, especially the Knights Templar, who were to be exemplary models of the best ideals of knighthood and chivalry. Bernard's renowned powers of persuasion were legendary. The Templars, in his view, should ideally combine the best of both the practical and the spiritual—that is, they should be "lions in war and lambs in the house." The Templar Rule outlines what behaviors,

attitudes, and precautions need to be taken by all members of the Order, from full knights to associates, and has an additional section titled "penances" for punishments of transgressions of the rules, such as being put in irons, losing one's habit, eating on the floor, or outright expulsion. (see **"In the New Knighthood"**; **Bernard of Clairvaux**; **Origins of the Order**; **Chivalry**; **Arthurian knights**; **Rule**; for further sources, see "In the New Knighthood" and "Bernard of Clairvaux" in the Recommended Reading section)

Knight-brothers

These were the prestigious full knights of the Order. Contrary to popular belief, not all members of the Templar order were in fact full knights, as only a small number of members in the Order were in this category. The knight-brothers were the only members who were allowed to wear their prestigious white mantles with red crosses on them. Although a number of men filling Templar officer positions largely came from the knightly class, especially the full knight-brothers, not all of them did. The initial status of an incoming Templar novice largely depended on their social standing in secular life before entering the Order, but, on the whole, full knights were those from the higher echelons of society, whereas the sergeants and others were not. But by the late 12th century, the Templar knight-brothers had hardened to become more of a knightly caste of their own, as by then it was largely necessary to be originally of knightly class before one could initially join the Order at the level of knight-brother. Those from the noble classes had already obtained the necessary training in jousting and other important knightly skills, and they also had the funds to pay for their expensive equipment, horses, and clothing for their early training as knights. After his investiture as a full knight-brother, the new brother then received weapons, such as a sword, a shield, a lance, a Turkish mace, a dagger, a bread knife, and a pocketknife, and also articles of clothing, including two white mantles and a heavier cloak. Each full knight-brother, according to section 138 of the Hierarchal Statutes of the Rule, was allowed three horses and a squire but could not have any additional horses or equipment without specific permission from the Master of the house. However, the Rule further states that some knight-brothers did have a fourth horse and a second squire, but these, too, would only be allowed by specific permission from the Master of the house.

While the full knight-brothers wore white mantles with red crosses on them, the sergeant-brothers wore black short-sleeved tunics with a red cross on the front and back, and black or brown mantles as opposed to the white ones of the full knight-brothers of the Order. Among the sergeant-brothers there was a further division. The Templar Rule shows that they were intended to be part of the fighting force, which they generally were, but some sergeants became trial notaries, craftsmen, blacksmiths, masons, or cooks, for example, depending on the specific needs of the Order at a particular location or time. The Templar Rule gives a number of instances where the distinction between full knight-brothers and the sergeants and squires is made, in addition to further items about the confrere, or associates of the Order as well. (see **Draper**; **Mantle**; **Organization of the Templar order**; **Confrere**)

Knights of Christ
(see **Order of Christ**)

Knights Hospitaller
(see **Order of the Hospital of St. John**)

Knights of the Round Table
(see **Arthurian knights**)

Knights of St. John's Co-Cathedral (Malta)
Located on the island of Malta, this extraordinary edifice, officially called the "Knights of St. John's Co-Cathedral," remains an important site for many individuals and organizations, especially the Knights of St. John. As art historians and architectural experts have long noted, this cathedral has a number of unique symbols carved in the walls and ceiling, and etched on its marble floors. Housing some of Europe's greatest art works, many today believe that it is a "must see" for visitors to Malta. Jean Parisot de la Vallette, the founder of Valletta, the capital of Malta, and also the 49th Grand Master of the illustrious Knights of St. John, is also buried here. Also in Valletta is the 16th century Knights of St. John Grand Masters Palace with its grand rooms, now Malta's Presidential Office and Parliament House. However, for clarity, this is not a medieval Knights Templar site (although on occasion it has sometimes been confused as such by modern-day visitors); rather, its primary connection is with the Order of St. John rather than any Knight Templar affiliation. (see **Hospitallers**)

Krak des Chevaliers

The Krak des Chevaliers was in fact a major Hospitaller fortress in the Holy Land, located in Syria; it has sometimes been confused with one of the major castles of the Knights Templar, especially that of Atlit, the famed "Castle Pilgrim" of the Templar order in the East. Krak des Chevaliers was built by the medieval Knights Hospitaller from approximately 1131 to 1136. In 1187, its powerful, dramatic lord, Reginald of Chatillon, attacked Saladin's forces, and—perhaps not unpredictably, given it was the time of the Crusades—in the following year, Saladin attacked and reclaimed Krak des Chevaliers. The fortress was later recaptured by the crusaders again, and finally fell to Baybars, a Muslim leader, in the late 13th century. (see **Hospitallers**; **Atlit**; for further sources about Templar architecture and the military orders in the Crusades, see "Crusades and Military Orders" and "Architecture and Archaeology" in the Recommended Reading section)

Lamb of God
(see **Agnus Dei**; **Seals**)

Land
(see **Assets and farms**)

La Rochelle
(see **Maritime trade and ports**)

Le Morte d'Arthur
(see **Grail romances**; **Arthurian knights**)

Leopold V of Austria
(see **Richard I ("the Lionheart")**)

Letter of credit
An early form of the letter of credit was developed in western Europe by the Knights Templar regarding pilgrimage, but another form was also in use at the famed medieval Champagne fairs in France. These fairs were key events for not only nobles, merchants, and the public, as one might expect, but also for the Templars as well. At these large, bustling fairs, drawing visitors from far and wide, the use of letters of credit that promised full payment of a debt at the next fair were known to be in use by merchants, and was one of the earliest forms of a credit transaction in western Europe. The Templars gained a great deal commercially from these fairs, especially from selling finely woven cloth made from wool, for example; the Order was also granted special trading privileges pertaining to the fairs, inciting some envy among other traders. The Templars were also granted the right to hold weekly markets and annual fairs at many of their local commanderies throughout various locations in Europe. (see **Assets**; **Champagne fairs**; **Troy weight**; **Loans**; **Safe deposit**; **Treasuries, Templar**; **Pilgrimage**; **Wool**; for further sources about trade, see "Assets" in the Recommended Reading section)

Loans, Templar

At the time of the Templars (1119–1312), Church law forbade the practice of usury (lending money for interest). So the Templars had to recover their administrative costs in other ways, mainly by adding a service charge, similar to a handling fee, instead of charging interest directly. This same basic procedure is akin to the process of traveler's checks today. So when traveling abroad and using traveler's checks, we can be mindful of their medieval Templar origins. There are very few complaints on record concerning how the Templars handled other people's money, even huge transactions for kings. The nobility, kings, and, occasionally, even popes, would borrow heavily from the Templars, not only because they were generally regarded as extremely trustworthy, but, as warrior-monks, valuables were far safer with them than nearly anyone else at the time, given the dangers of travel. Rare accusations that they were greedy did not usually refer to their loan practices per se. Some Templar loans from southern France did include a clause about a fixed fee due the lender, which may have caused some resentment, but by and large the Templars were regarded favorably. So what had started out as basic financial services provided to pilgrims—a sideline to crusading—had in due course developed into a full-scale financial empire spanning many countries, akin to a modern-day multinational corporation. (see **Assets**; **Treasuries, Templar**; **Letter of credit**; **Champagne fairs**; **Wool**; **Troy weight**)

London
(see **New Temple, London**)

Lord's Temple

The "Lord's Temple" was the term used by the early crusaders to refer to what we now know as the area of the Dome of the Rock on the Temple Mount in Jerusalem. This phrase is distinct from what the crusaders called "Solomon's Stables," which was the area underneath the southeastern section of the Temple Mount platform—dubbed "Solomon's Temple" by the earliest crusaders—where the Templars were initially given accommodation by King Baldwin II in 1119. As the "Solomon's Stables" area was large enough for some 2,000 horses in late medieval times, the Templars were known to have stored their horses here, as well as conducted architectural building work on the Triple Gate and other areas. (see **Canons of the Holy Sepulchre**; **Origins of the Order**)

M

Magna Carta
(see **Aymeric de St. Maur**)

Mainz
(see under "Germany" in **Trial, aftermath of**)

Mantle
The mantle was a religious habit worn by a Knight Templar, either white or black, depending on one's rank in the Order. During the first nine years of the order, the Templars wore simple, ordinary clothes with no mantle. When they were initially based at the Temple Mount area in Jerusalem during their earliest years, they would not have been wearing their trademark white mantles, as permission to do so was received only after the Church Council of Troyes in 1129. Here, they were given a specific religious Rule, and the mandate to wear a white mantle as a full knight-brother, and a black or dark brown one as a sergeant-brother and squire. The key symbol of the trademark four-armed, equidistant red cross of the Knights Templar was not added to their mantles until 1147, when Pope Eugenius III issued his papal bull allowing them to wear it as a symbol of Christian martyrdom.

The Templar Rule makes specific reference to the mantles of the brothers in many places, outlining how it may or may not be worn; for example, in section 280, it states that no brother should ever be without his mantle when the canonical hours are sung, and that if any brother is eating or drinking, he should also not be without his habit; and later, in section 324, it says that no brother should ever hang his mantle around his bed on hooks, as he was always to honor his mantle. As a primary symbol of the Order of the Temple on the battlefield as well, taking proper care of one's mantle, equipment, horses, and weapons was essential. Each Christian military religious order had its own mantle colors and insignia, and the Knights Templar were no exception. (see also **Red cross**; **Draper**; **Decoration**; **Rule**; **Eugenius III, Pope**; **Symbols**; **Organization of the Templar order**)

Marco Polo
(see **Nizari Ismailis**)

Maritime trade and ports
The huge empire of the Knights Templar not only involved land and agriculture, but also the sea. Templars constantly needed ships to carry money, animals, military equipment, manpower, and supplies from the West, where the money and goods were made, to the Holy Land and the East, where they were desperately needed for the Crusades. Certain Templar ships were also used to provide safe transport for Christian pilgrims—this was not only reliable, but also, in the long run, cheaper for the Order than hiring a commercial vessel. Templar ships were not warships, but more often, simple galleys that were constantly on the seas, on the move, and not staying in any one location for a long amount of time. In a climate where great danger—even piracy—was rampant on the seas, one can easily understand why a medieval pilgrim would choose to travel with the Templars, if at all possible, when considering various travel options. But the Templars themselves consistently needed to transport many badly needed supplies, manpower, and products to both eastern and western ports, so they, too, were equally concerned about security issues, perhaps not unlike international travel today.

In the East, both horses and food were regularly imported from Europe, as were other pack animals such as mules, for example. A steady supply of horses, which were very valuable and expensive, was crucial for the Templars in battle. From the early part of the 13th century, the Templars had their own ships and were beginning to build their own fleet, but they did not have an admiral per se until 1301. In Europe, they also had their own ports, such as La Rochelle, and at key ports in the East such as Acre, they had large shipyards as well as a number of buildings. Templar ships were privately run as individual units under Templar brothers who were experienced sailors, although technically, the Order itself owned the ships (which were often galleys). Similar to the Templars, their fellow Christians, the Hospitallers, also had built many castles and other fortresses in the Holy Land. As history has shown, by all accounts the Templars were extraordinary warriors on land in many battles—called

"Christ's militia" by many at the time—but the Hospitallers were especially adept at naval warfare in the Mediterranean, dubbed the "navy of Christ." As life on the high seas in medieval times was treacherous to say the least, they often found themselves having to defend their ships by using similar means as their enemies. The Hospitallers were renowned for their maritime skills, more than any other medieval military religious order, and similar to the Templars, they also required ships to carry money and supplies from the West to their brothers in the East, where they were badly needed for the Crusades. Uninterrupted maritime commerce was absolutely crucial, and in order to get goods and supplies to Christian sources, the ships had to be strongly defended. Pirates were a nightmare for everyone on the medieval high seas—Muslim, Christian, or otherwise—and similar tactics were known to be used by both sides at times. Especially as they were based on the island of Rhodes, and later, Malta, the Hospitallers in particular had to become exceptionally skilled at naval warfare in the Mediterranean. (see **Admiral**, **Templar**; **Acre**; **Assets**; **Hospitallers**; **Jolly Roger**)

Married brothers
(see **Confrere**)

Marshal
The Marshal was the chief Templar military officer responsible for the individual commanders and the horses, arms, equipment, and anything else involving military operations, a key responsibility. He also had authority in obtaining, ordering, and distributing supplies, critically important at the time of the Crusades. His office was an important one, as no Templar charge in battle was undertaken without his orders, and he also had the distinct honor of carrying the Templar's famed black-and-white standard, the beauseant, in battle. Taking it from the Undermarshal, he would then appoint a special sub-unit of 10 knights, under their own commander, to protect him in battle. Sometimes, there was also a Gonfanier, a banner-bearer, who would carry the standard in battle, under the Marshal's specific direction. (see **Organization of the Templar order**; **Beauseant**)

Martyrdom
Martyrdom is a key concept underlying the entire ethos of the Templar order, as to be a martyr for Christ on the battlefield was seen as a supreme honor before God. In evidence of this, the Knights Templar often

preferred to be beheaded, rather than convert to Islam, a courage that even their enemies, the Saracens, noted. They also were never allowed to leave the battlefield, no matter how difficult, if the beauseant was still raised; again, something that their fellow Christians as well as their enemies noted at various times during the Crusades. The courage and discipline of the Templars' as a unified fighting force was extraordinary, by all accounts, and their willingness to die for their beliefs was also symbolized via the red cross on the knights' mantles.

In some battles during the Crusades where Templars had been captured, Saladin was known to have made special efforts to single out the Templars and the Hospitallers for harsher punishments, as they were said to have fought the hardest. In addition, in their houses the Templars tended to clearly prefer saints who had been martyrs, such as St. Catherine of Alexandria or St. George. The Agnus Dei symbol on their seals, illustrating the sacrificial Lamb of God, also shows how highly the Templars valued martyrdom. (see **Agnus Dei**; **Red cross**; **Organization of the Templar order**; **Saints, Templar veneration of**)

Mary Magdalene, St.

In assisting with the major revision of the Templar Rule in 1129, Bernard of Clairvaux commended to the knights upon the reception into the Order many things, including mention of "the obedience of Bethany, the Castle of Mary and Martha." As we know, Bethany is mentioned in Bible, where it is described as the home of siblings Mary, Martha, and Lazarus, and where, according to John's gospel (12:1–8), Jesus was anointed by a woman named as Mary of Bethany who used precious spikenard, a very expensive oil, an event that stunned the other disciples present. One may recall there are several anointing scenes in the New Testament, and although many of them do not specifically name the woman, or call her Mary of Bethany, a number of theologians and researchers have postulated that she might, in fact, be Mary Magdalene. In Matthew 26:6–13, the anointing takes place at Simon the Leper's house in Bethany, by an unnamed woman; in Mark 14:3–9, this key event also occurs at Simon the Leper's house in Bethany, and also by an anonymous woman; and in Luke 7:36–50, the scriptures state that the event takes place at Simon the Pharisee's house (no location specified), and again, by an unnamed woman, described as a sinner.

The historical records show that the Knights Templar certainly did venerate St. Mary Magdalene, of course, as all devout Christians then— and now—do. Although the central Templar (and part of the Hospitaller) archive is believed to have been destroyed by the Turks on Cyprus in 1571, and few medieval records remain about specific Templar worship practices, we do have the key translation of their medieval Rule, which carefully outlines the strict code by which every Templar had to live his daily life. Yet the Rule—specifically, section 75.10—only makes specific reference to St. Mary Magdalene in the general list of the feast days to be observed, along with a number of other saints, so it does not indicate any special reverence for her as a saint beyond what would have been normal practice for medieval Catholic Christians at the time. Her specific feast day (22nd of July) is referred to in the Rule, and it was an important date in the annual Templar calendar, as were the other saints' days listed. However, to date, no actual historical documentation exists to prove that Bernard of Clairvaux ever meant "St. Mary Magdalene" when "Our Lady, the Blessed St. Mary" is referred to at various junctures throughout the Rule, and nearly all of the donations of land and other assets were made to the Templars specifically on behalf of the Blessed Virgin Mary, as she was widely known to the be patroness of the Order. Scholars are unanimous on this point, and until further records would surface to counter this stance, it cannot be assumed that the Templars preferred St. Mary Magdalene over any other female saint, although, again, they certainly highly venerated her openly, especially on her feast day, July 22. Perhaps new archives or records from the medieval period may surface in the future to clarify such matters.

From the historical record itself, it is clear that the Templars tended to put much emphasis on female saints who had been martyrs—such as St. Catherine of Alexandria, who is referred to in the Rule, section 75.17. The Templars venerated a number of saints' feast days and fasted on many others, and it is rarely acknowledged today outside of scholarly circles that they were also known to have highly venerated the Maccabees, the Jewish warriors who, according to the Old Testament, also had been martyrs for their cause. As knights in the Crusades, the Templars placed a special premium on martyrdom, and so it may not be surprising to find such an emphasis in the Rule itself, or to discover that one of their key mottos was Psalm 115: "Not unto us, O Lord, not unto us, but unto Thy Name be the Glory." The red cross on their mantles was also symbolic of martyrdom, as was their popular choice of the Agnus Dei, the Lamb of God, on many of the Order's seals. The Templars also highly venerated another now-famous martyr, St. George, of whom we know they had a statue at their castle at Safed in Galilee. They also claimed to possess the relics of the fourth century female martyr, St. Euphemia of Chalcedon. The Rule lists a number of specific saints that were venerated by the Templars, including St. Mary Magdalene, but does not single any one of them out for preferential treatment, tending to focus far more on Our Lady as patroness.

Regarding Bethany issues per se, it is rather interesting to note the distinct absence of either St. Lazarus or St. Martha in the list of Templar feast days in the Rule; yet, of course, there is a direct reference there to St. Mary Magdalene. Although the New Testament says nothing specifically about the life of St. Lazarus after the crucifixion, a number of legends do connect him to the region of southern France in various ways—as is also the case with Mary Magdalene. The Knights Hospitaller, medieval lepers in general, and a number of leper hospitals and hospices in the Middle Ages all claimed St. Lazarus of Bethany as one of their major patrons and honored his feast day on the 17th of December. The medieval Order of St. Lazarus was founded in the late 11th century with their Infirmary of St. Lazarus, an important early infirmary and leprosarium, which was located outside the walls of Jerusalem. They also followed the rule of St. Augustine, as did the initial Templars prior to the Council of Troyes in 1129. In the 13th century, the Order of Lazarus was confirmed by the papacy in 1255; they transferred their activities from Jerusalem to Acre, and, similar to many chivalric and military religious Orders at the time, gradually diminished in power after the fall of Acre in 1291.

St. Martha of Bethany, the sister of Lazarus and Mary in the New Testament, has a feast day of July 29th in the West, but in the eastern church she is celebrated on June 6th, along with the other *myrrophores*, the key women who brought special spices and oils to anoint the body of Jesus at the tomb. Very little is known about her life outside of the New Testament, and, perhaps predictably, a number of medieval legends have connected St. Martha with Provence, specifically Tarascon. Here, she was said to have tamed a dragon by subduing him with holy water and wrapping her sash around his neck, before leading him to Arles, where he was killed. But the Templars did not seem to show any particular reverence at all for either St. Lazarus or St. Martha, at least judging from the Rule itself. St. Mary Magdalene, however, is specifically named in the Templar Rule and was venerated by the Order on her feast day throughout its duration inside the Templar houses—per instructions in section 75 of the Rule. However, similar to a few of the other saints, she is not listed in section 74, which explains all of the feast days and fasting days that the Templar brothers should celebrate and observe, no matter where they were based, whether in the East or in their western preceptories.

So according to Templar Rule sections 74 and 75, where it specifically lists the saints and their feast and fasting days to be venerated by members of the Order, we have evidence that St. Mary Magdalene was venerated in Templar houses and preceptories, especially on her feast day of July 22 as part of the Templar annual calendar. However, there is no evidence that she was also venerated on a regular basis elsewhere by Templars, such as on a battlefield in the Holy Land, for instance, as were a number of the other saints that are listed in both sections 74 and 75. No existing documentation has surfaced that states the Templars ever believed that Jesus was married, and their Rule does not state this. It may also be of interest that the Templar Rule in section 122 clearly states how highly they valued their precious relic of a piece of the True Cross, giving specific precautions about guarding it, and so on, and they also claimed to possess a relic of the Crown of Thorns, both rather orthodox choices for medieval Christians at the time. It was the Hospitallers—not the Knights Templar—who claimed to possess a relic of Mary Magdalene.

One might surmise that given the premium placed on martyrdom by the Knights Templar as a whole, there may have been another way the Templars could have venerated St. Mary Magdalene, other than as a mere penitent saint in their yearly calendar. For example, a Templar knight could contemplate a skull or head, prior to his martyrdom for Christ in battle, in the ancient tradition of *memento mori*—a Latin term for "remember that you will die." This old tradition of meditating upon one's own death was based on the biblical injunction of Ecclesiasticus 7:40, which states: "...in all thy works, be mindful of thy last end, and thou wilt never sin." However, although the Danse Macabre ("Dance of Death") became a popular symbol used in medieval documents or buildings after the Black Death—after the Templars had been suppressed and disbanded in the 14th century—that image involved the whole skeleton and several figures, including Death himself with his scythe, as opposed to one person contemplating a single skull as a meditative aid, as is the case with memento mori.

The Franciscans, and later, the Jesuits, were known to use a skull at times for serious meditation. In later centuries, in certain Masonic traditions, the candidate was asked to first meditate on the idea of his own life—and death—prior to his initiation in a special small room called the Chamber of Reflection. Here, seated at a table, he was to write his own philosophical will, which would later to be read out in the lodge. Among the various symbols and objects present in the room, was a skull. Although various accusations were made against the medieval Templars at their trial about a so-called head, or heads, the accounts do not at all agree, nor do they describe a simple skull per se, as would be the case in the tradition of memento mori. So that is not the same tradition, as has sometimes been assumed.

The medieval Knights Templar never venerated a skull in relation to St. Mary Magdalene—there is no evidence for that—but in later centuries, long after the Templars were suppressed, many art historians have noted that such imagery was a favorite theme of Renaissance (and later) period paintings of Mary Magdalene, where she is often portrayed with a skull. But this is far more likely due to her association with Golgotha, the place of the skull, as she was seen to be a direct witness of the Crucifixion, rather than anything to do with the Templar order or a popular medieval theme, such as the Danse Macabre. But although there is no historical documentation to date that connects this relic specifically to the Templar order, there is indeed one famous association of a skull and Mary Magdalene that can still be seen today—the gold-encased skull reliquary of St. Mary Magdalene at the Basilica of St. Maximus la Sainte-Baume in Provence.

Although the Templars themselves never claimed any specific relic of St. Mary Magdalene, their rival order, the Hospitallers, did. They claimed to possess a relic of the finger of St. Mary Magdalene encased in a special silver reliquary. This relic was donated to the church of the Hospitallers in Aix in 1286, by Hospitaller brother William of Villaret, then Prior of Saint-Gilles (later to become Master of the Order), and is listed along with other precious items, such as a gem-encrusted silver cross, an image of St. Veronica, a precious missal, and so on. As 1286 was *before* the time of the suppression of the Templar order by papal bull in 1312, it was a Hospitaller relic and not merely a Templar one that had been later (post-1312) transferred to that Order. Perhaps in the course of time, more Templar archives will be discovered or translated to further clarify matters regarding St. Mary Magdalene; at present, however, all that can be said for certain about their Rule is that the Templar order, too, venerated this extraordinary saint, as many worldwide still do today, keeping her inspiring memory alive. (see **Mary Magdalene, medieval**

celebrations of; **Black Madonnas**; **Relics**; **Shrines**; **Pilgrimage**; **Saints,**
Templar veneration of; **Saints in medieval society**; **Rule**; **Women**; and
for further sources about pilgrimage and relics of specific saints, see
"Relics" and "Pilgrimage and Pilgrims" in the Recommended Reading
section)

Mary Magdalene, medieval celebrations of

There were many ways to celebrate the legacy of Mary Magdalene's
memory in the late Middle Ages and the time of the Templars (1119–
1312). We know that the Rule of the Templar order lists St. Mary
Magdalene's feast day—July 22nd—along with a number of other saints,
but it does not single any one of them out for special veneration, although Our Lady is the patroness of the Order. But she was also widely
venerated beyond the religious orders and churches, too.

Many church services and special prayers were said in honor of not
only Our Lady, but also St. Mary Magdalene in the late Middle Ages. But
it may not be fully appreciated today that St. Mary Magdalene in particular was also featured not only in various liturgical guild plays in medieval
times, but, also, at special fairs in her honor that were held on the 22nd of
July. A saint's feast day was celebrated in many ways in medieval Europe;
in addition to a number of religious services at a church, chapel, or cathedral, specific fairs and festivals were often held on this day, too. For
example, in Fife, Scotland, a well-known St. Magdalene's Day fair was
held on July 22. In England, France, and other countries, many fairs were
generally held, especially in the month of May, but in Mary Magdalene's
case, July was featured most often, as her feast day was on the 22nd.

In addition to being venerated by medieval religious orders, including the Knights Templar, St. Mary Magdalene was also the patron saint
for some guilds, and certain chapels and buildings were named after her
as well. In central Edinburgh, for example, the famous Magdalen Tower
dates back to 1541, but was originally built on the site of a previous church
there called Maison Dieu, dedicated to St. Mary Magdalene. A prosperous merchant named Mitchell (or Michael) Maquhane had a great interest in advancing the cause of the Hammermen—the metalworkers'
guild—in the city and left some money for this purpose at his death. His
wife, Janet Rynd, added further funds and the project was expanded to
include a small almshouse; a tower was added in 1626 and later a bell and a
clock. The only remaining pre-Reformation stained glass windows in all
of Scotland are to be seen in this extraordinary chapel today. It also has

a fascinating history involving the first national assembly, the Coventanters, and other religious groups. Various place names or residential districts were often named after Mary Magdalene in many places; in Edinburgh, for example, Magdalen Bridge and Magdalene Burn derive their names from a medieval chapel of St. Mary Magdalene, which stood some 200 yards east of the mouth of the burn, an area also known as Magdalen or Maitland Water. The early spellings of "Maidland" (1488), "Medlen" (1661), and "Maitland" referring to this area all reflect the medieval pronunciation of "maudlin" for Magdalene. Of course, Oxford and Cambridge both have Magdalen colleges, and many other chapels and churches were also named after St Mary Magdalene all over Europe and beyond. So fairs, festivals, place names, and so on were certainly popular ways to honor the memory of St. Mary Magdalene in the Middle Ages, in addition to important church services and prayers. The Templar Rule states that St. Mary Magdalene was venerated along with other saints in Templar houses, with specific mention of her feast day, July 22nd. (see **Mary Magdalene, St.**; **Black Madonnas**; **Saints, Templar veneration of**; **Saints in medieval society**; **Rule**; **Women**; for further sources about pilgrimage and relics of specific saints, see "Relics" and "Pilgrimage and Pilgrims" in the Recommended Reading section)

Masons
(see **Guilds, medieval**)

Master, Templar preceptor
A Master was the most important and influential official of a specific Templar province. There were Templar Masters for the major regions of Apulia, Aquitaine, Aragon and Catalonia, the Auvergne, Cyprus, England, France, Germany/Bohemia/Poland, Hungary and Slavonia, Normandy, Poitou, and Portugal. The Grand Master of the Order of the Temple had authority over the entire Order Itself, however. (see **Organization of the Templar order**; **Rule**; **Grand Master**)

Mills
Mills were particularly profitable for the Order. The Templars produced much grain on their lands, such as wheat, barley, or corn, for example, and wherever they did so they needed mills to grind the grain. On the whole there were few mills in the 12th century, so the Templars were in a position to charge a fee to others for the use of their mill. An important

source of Templar income, mills were mostly water-driven. Localized records often list what mills, if any, a Templar province possessed. For example, part of the English order's possessions were five Templar mills in London, and two in Temple Cowley, Oxford, among other locations throughout the country. There were also many other places in western Europe where the Templar order had mills; but, understandably, they were highly prized by the Order. (see **Assets**; **Farms**)

Mining

In certain areas, depending on the locality and its geographical conditions, the Templars are known to have occasionally participated in coal mining and the extraction of ores, such as silver, gold, and copper. Although it was one possible source of income for the Order, mining was not as important or wide-ranging as some of their other agricultural and farming enterprises, such as sheep farming, for instance. (see **Assets**)

de Molay, Jacques

Probably the most famous Templar Grand Master, Jacques de Molay was the last Grand Master of the Order of the Temple, who was burned at the stake on the orders of the French king Philippe IV in March of 1314. He was the 22nd Grand Master of the Order and served his term as Grand Master from 1293 to 1314. He exemplified good leadership in defending Palestine against the Syrians, and even after the devastating battle for all Christendom, the Fall of Acre in 1291, de Molay still tried to organize new forces to recapture what they had lost; he had certainly not given up by any means. Historians know that de Molay entered the Order of the Temple in 1265 at Beaune, in the diocese of Autun, and that he was received by Humbert of Pairaud, the Master in England, and also by Aimery of La Roche, the Master in France. Scholars maintain that his roots were most likely from Burgundy—probably the village of Molay in Franche-Comte. Unfortunately, perhaps similar to the Order itself, little is known for certain about his earliest years due to the relative scarcity of surviving records.

However, following the sudden arrests of the Templars in France in 1307, and the traumatic years of inquisitional hearings and trials, after the suppression in 1312, the elderly de Molay still remained in prison. (see **Trial**)

But in what, by all accounts, was a final and extraordinary display of courage, both de Molay and Geoffrey de Charney, the Preceptor of

Normandy, recanted their confessions before a stunned crowd in Paris, with de Molay declaring, in part: "Before heaven and earth and with all of you here as my witnesses…. I declare, and I must declare, that the Order is innocent. Its purity and saintliness is beyond question."

But the final words of the verse chronicle attributed to the 14th century medieval chronicler Geoffroi de Paris, a work whose author clearly witnessed the execution of de Molay in person, are also quite revealing, as scholars have noted. Given the earlier recanting of the confessions of de Molay and de Charney—which shocked everyone present, as to be a "relapsed heretic" was yet another crime—and witnessing their burning at the stake near the point where the Pont Neuf joins the Ile dela Cite from the Left Bank, the chronicler ended his report of the entire matter with these words:

> One can easily deceive the Church,
> But one can never in any way deceive God.
> I shall say nothing else
> Whosoever desires may add more.

Clearly, the trial of the Templars was controversial then, as it often is now, as its memory lingers on into our own century some 700 years later. (see **Trial of the Templars**; **Grand Master, order of the**; **Clement V**; **Philippe IV**; **Heresy**; Appendix B; and for further sources, see "Jacques de Molay" and "Trial of the Templars" in the Recommended Reading section)

Molesmes, Robert of

Robert of Molesmes, who belonged to the same family as Bernard of Clairvaux, was a late 11th century abbot of a monastery at Molesmes, south of Troyes, in Champagne. Robert and his monks at Molesmes were known to have lived a very strict, austere monastic life according to the Rule of St. Benedict. At Easter of 1097, Hughes I (count of Champagne) and his associates visited Robert at Molesmes, and, as some theologians suggest, may have been a possible factor in the later split between Robert's especially austere group and another faction of monks at Molesmes who refused to obey his especially severe regimen, preferring to keep their titles and observe somewhat more liberal policies. Due to the difficulties of this situation, a year later, in 1098, Robert and his group of monks—including St. Alberic and Stephen Harding, both of whom would later play key roles in the Cistercian order—got permission to leave Molesmes and found a new monastery. Leaving Champagne for Burgundy, they founded a monastery at Citeaux, the "mother" of all later Cistercian monasteries and center of the new Cistercian order. Its constitution, the *Carta caritatis*, was presented to Pope Calixtus II in 1119, the same year the earliest Templars presented themselves to Baldwin II in Jerusalem. St. Bernard played a key role in this effort and the Cistercian constitution was codified between 1119 and 1165. In the spring of 1099, the same monks who had remained at Molesmes and adamantly refused to live by Robert's strict regime went to Pope Urban II in Rome to complain. They said their monastery now had no abbot or other significant staff and that they wanted Robert back. Obviously, this was a totally different stance from their earlier position. Some historians believe Hughes I may have been involved, or that the powerful archbishop of Lyons may have had something to do with his decision. In any case, the pope wrote to the church authorities in Lyons and ordered Robert to be sent back to Molesmes from Citeaux.

After this event, Robert seems to have acquiesced to the more liberal regimen at Molesmes, though he had sharply disapproved of it before. In the spring of 1101, Hughes I again visited Molesmes; his brother, Stephen de Blois, had returned from the Holy Land in 1098, a couple of years before. After this 1101 meeting, it is interesting to note that the entire Citeaux monastery was then moved half a league south from its original location, ostensibly for better access to water. Stephen de Blois subsequently returned to the Holy Land, where Baldwin I, the king of Jerusalem, favorably received him. Robert of Molesmes later founded other monasteries, even after he was ordered to return to Molesmes. (see **Cistercians; Citeaux; Clairvaux Abbey; Bernard of Clairvaux**)

Montaigue, Pierre de
The 15th Grand Master of the Order of the Temple, Pierre de Montaigue served from 1219 to approximately 1232. Before he became Grand Master, he had been the Master of the Templar province of Aragon. He was originally from the Languedoc, at Vivarais. (see **Aragon; Grand Master;** Appendix B)

Montesa, Order of
After the suppression of the Templars in 1312, the Order's lands in Valencia in the kingdom of Aragon (now a part of modern-day Spain) were given to the Order of Montesa, by specific arrangement of the pope.

A number of Templar knights joined the new Order of Montesa, which was specially founded by James II of Aragon after the suppression, in order to receive the Templar properties in his kingdom virtually intact. In 1317, the Pope decreed that both Templar and Hospitaller lands and properties in Valencia would be given to the Order of Montesa; however, in an effort to be fair to the Hospitallers, he also said that the Hospitallers would then receive the remaining Templar lands in the kingdom of Aragon. However, the Order of Montesa was not actually formed in a fully administrative sense until two years later, in 1319. It adopted the rule of the Order of Calatrava and was under the spiritual guidance of Santas Creus, a Cistercian monastery, in Catalonia. In 1587, it was incorporated into the Crown of Aragon, and, later, in 1851, a diocese was created for all of the Spanish Orders at Ciudad Real, which survived until the Spanish Civil War. (see **Christ, Order of**; **Calatrava, Order of**; **Aragon**; **Trial, aftermath of**)

Montbard, Andre de
The fifth Grand Master of the Order of the Temple, Andre de Montbard was from Burgundy and served for a two-year period from 1154 to 1156. He was also the uncle of Bernard of Clairvaux, a key part of the network of the interrelated families that were highly significant regarding the origins of the Templar order. (see **Origins of the Templar order**)

Motto, Templar
The key motto of the Knights Templar was from Psalm 115: "Not unto us, O Lord, not unto us, but unto Thy Name be the Glory." (see **Martyrdom**)

Muslims
(see **Saracens**; **Saladin**; **Ayyubids**)

N

Naples, Philippe de
Originally from Picardy, but born in Neapolis, Syria, Philippe de Naples was the seventh Grand Master of the Order of the Temple and served from 1169 to 1171. (see **Grand Master**; Appendix B)

Naval warfare
(see **Admiral, Templar**; **Maritime trade and ports**)

Navigator, Henry the
(see **Order of Christ**)

New Temple (London)
(see **Temple Church, London**)

Nine Worthies
After Godfroi de Bouillon died in 1100, he was succeeded by his brother Baldwin I, who gladly accepted the title of King of Jerusalem. Godfroi has since become a figure of powerful legend in his own right, as an especially courageous leader of the First Crusade. In later medieval poetry he was commemorated as a descendant of the Swan Knight. He was also included among the famous Nine Worthies, who were considered to have been the greatest warriors in history. Three were selected from the Old Testament, three were Pagans from the ancient world, and three were Christian rulers—Godfroi, King Arthur, and Charlemagne. The Nine Worthies were featured on many medieval tapestries; for example, those that the Burgundy nobles commissioned from Arras and Tournai. Many medieval paintings and tapestries featured scenes from the Crusades, and at least 15 tapestries feature Godfroi de Bouillon. (see **Bouillon, Godfroi de**; **Arthurian knights**; **Grail romances**)

Nizari Ismailis

There is evidence of medieval Templar links with the Muslim world, especially with the Nizari Ismailis, a religiopolitical Islamic group that still flourishes under the leadership of the Aga Khan. The Nizari Ismailis, also known in medieval times as the Assassins, were well trained as devout holy warriors, as were the Knights Templar. Christian crusaders had some contact with the Assassins at the beginning of the 12th century, even before the official emergence of the Templar order in 1119. The medieval mission of Hassan-i-Sabbah, Arab chronicler of the Crusades, to the Ismailis of Syria resulted in early European contact with the Assassins during the Crusades. The mythical "Old Man of the Mountain" made famous by Marco Polo's accounts was in fact the Syrian chief of the Order. The earliest documentable contact between the Assassins and the crusaders took place in September 1106. Despite some major losses, the Syrian Assassins were still able to expel crusader troops from various castles and strongholds, something that the Seljuk Turkish princes had been unable to do.

In the beginning of the 14th century, the world explorer Marco Polo fueled European fascination with the Assassins when he compiled many legends about them into a collection, adding embellishments of his own. In the classic account of his travels, Polo described tales of "a magnificent enclosed garden hidden at Alamut in which all details corresponded to Muhammad's description of Paradise," Since then, legends about both the Templars and the Assassins have been plentiful. (see also **Saracens; Tancred**)

Old Man of the Mountain
(see **Nizari Ismailis**)

Omne Datum Optimum
Following the leadership of Hughs de Payns, under Robert de Craon's term of service as the second Grand Master, the Templars received their famous papal bull from Pope Innocent II: *Omne Datum Optimum*, or, "Every Best Gift." This effectively made the Order answerable only to the pope, and therefore free from all other ecclesiastical and secular demands. Prior to this time, the Order had to obtain its chaplains from outside the Order, and only then, after they were appointed by local bishops, were they allowed to conduct all religious services in Templar houses and commandaries. Now, however, with the advent of *Omne Datum Optimum* in 1139, the Templars could also have their own chaplain-brothers. Succeeding popes reaffirmed *Omne Datum Optimum* and added other privileges to it, including the right to build their own churches and cemeteries. (see **Craon, Robert de**; **Organization of the Templar order**)

Order of Christ
(see **Christ, Order of**)

Order of Montesa
(see **Montesa, Order of**)

Order of Santiago
(see **Santiago, Order of**)

Order of the Hospital of St. John
(see **Hospitallers**; **Krak des Chevaliers**; **St. John's Co-Cathedral**)

Organization of the Templar order

The memory of the Knights Templar as famed monastic warriors of the Crusades has certainly resonated throughout the centuries. Today, their image has come to us as especially devout and courageous warrior-monks. But although the Templars were a medieval military religious Order that uniquely combined the roles of knight and monk in a way the Western medieval world had never seen before, what is not always appreciated is how tightly organized they were as an Order and how strictly they adhered to their daily Rule. Today, we might think of the Templar organization more as a specialized "spiritual special forces for Christ," rather than praying monks in a monastery. The Order of the Poor Knights of Christ and the Temple of Solomon, later simply called Templars, were renowned for never leaving the battlefield, so extraordinary was their dedication and courage.

At their peak in the 12th century, the Templars became the largest, richest organization the Western world had ever seen, something akin to a wealthy modern-day multinational corporation. The Templars played a key role in introducing to medieval western Europe the prototypes of some of our modern-day banking practices, such as traveler's checks and the safe deposit box. Yet, the Knights Templar were more than merely spiritual special forces for Christ or warriors on the battlefield. They were also highly practical, being diplomats and trusted advisors to kings and popes; special guardians of a number of royal treasuries; maritime and seafaring experts; major property developers; caretakers of land and animals; agriculture experts; and business experts in commerce, trade, markets, and fairs. The Templars rapidly became one of the wealthiest and most powerful organizations the Western world has ever known.

During the 12th and 13th centuries, the Order acquired extensive property not only in the West, especially France, but also in the crusader states of Palestine and Syria. It developed an extensive network of hundreds of preceptories and commanderies throughout Europe and the Latin East. Aristocratic families, kings, and soldiers assisted the Order by giving them thousands of properties, such as churches, farms, mills, villages, monasteries, ports, and so on. Within a mere 10 years or so of their official founding, the fledging Order held donated lands in nearly every part of western Europe and beyond—a truly spectacular rise to power that has hardly been seen before or since. And the more popular they became, the greater their wealth and the number of new recruits, and, perhaps inevitably, the envy of many as well.

The ultimate extent of the Templar empire at its height was probably unknown, even to certain kings. Templar wealth was spread widely across numerous commercial activities and subsidiaries and supported by diverse elements, so it would have been hard to specify the precise location and form of all their assets at any one given time. With such a large empire, the Order was similar to a modern-day multinational corporation with branches in many countries. However, much of the Templars' wealth that had been donated by specific individuals was required to remain in their treasuries and could not be moved without the owner's permission, similar to a safety deposit box at the bank today. Obviously, the Templar order was highly varied in its activities.

Its administration was structured hierarchically, as were many other medieval military orders and religious groups. The Grand Master was based at the Order's headquarters in the Holy Land, along with the other major officers, each of whom had his own staff. In its western preceptories, the Order's extensive territories were divided into provinces. Each of these was administered by an area commander who, in turn, oversaw the Masters who were responsible for running individual houses in the province. The main function of the western European Templar houses was to provide manpower, money, and equipment for their brothers fighting in the East. A system of chapter meetings kept the officers of both East and West in contact with each other. Given its huge size and territories, the Order dealt with the challenges of multiple languages among its members.

The five most important offices of the entire Order—the Grand Master, Seneschal, Marshal, Commanders, and the Draper—constituted the major officers of the Order, although there seem to have been local variations regarding the distribution of duties among them. Under these major five officers were other Templar commanders with specific regional responsibilities, such as the commanders of the cities of Jerusalem, Tripoli, and Antioch, for example. There was also an Infirmarer, who ran the infirmary for aged brothers, but the Order did not have a hospital at its central convent for poor pilgrims and the needy. Templar brothers were also strongly encouraged to give alms to the poor, and as the Order did possess some hospices in the West, medical work was primarily done by the Hospitallers and other religious orders, as the focus for the Templars was the battlefield. Daily administration of the Order's regional houses was governed by various officials called *bailies*, and the officer in charge was called the *baili*. The Order consisted of a great variety of positions performing many different functions; sometimes, as with private consultants today, it would even hire some people from outside the Order. The influence of the Templar order at its height was monumental, but, as history has shown, eventually their great wealth and power made them a major target of the French king Philippe IV and Pope Clement V, who colluded in their downfall and the final suppression of the Order by papal bull in 1312. (see **Rule**; **Grand Master, office of**; **Seneschal**; **Marshal**; **Commander**; **Draper**; **de Molay, Jacques**; for further sources, see "Organization, Structure, and Rule" in the Recommending Reading section)

Origins of the Order

The early Templar order largely consisted of members from certain old Burgundian and Flemish families, based around the area of Troyes in modern-day Champagne. As there was a dire need for more policing of pilgrim routes by the early 12th century, one of the major reasons given for the emergence of the Order in 1119 involved the protection of Christian pilgrims. William of Tyre states that the Order of the Temple officially began when two French knights, Hugh de Payns and Godfroi de St. Omer, led seven others to the Patriarch of Jerusalem, Warmund of Picquigny, and took vows of poverty, chastity, and obedience. Initially, they were referred to as *Milites Templi Salomonis*, or "Poor Knights of Solomon's Temple," later shortened to Templars. The original nine knights included the scions of several noble families: Hugh de Payns was a vassal of Hughes I, count of Champagne, as was André de Montbard, the uncle of Bernard of Clairvaux; Godfroi de St. Omer, of Picardy, was a son of Hughes de St. Omer; two members of the ruling family of Flanders were also part of this initial group, listed as Payen de Montdidier and Achambaud de St.-Amand. The others were Godfroi, Geoffroi Bisol, and two Cistercians named Gondemar and Rossal. The Templars were assisted by both King Baldwin II, ruler of Jerusalem, and Warmund of Picquigny, patriarch of Jerusalem, when they initially presented themselves in Jerusalem. At this time, the Hospitallers were already caring for sick, exhausted pilgrims in their medical convent in Jerusalem, and, as fellow Christians, scholars believe that they naturally welcomed the initial Templar presence.

In two of the four charters drafted in the Kingdom of Jerusalem before 1128, the Templars are specifically referred to concerning the affairs of the Hospitaller order, whom the Church had already recognized by 1113, but the Hospitallers did not become a military religious order themselves until later in the 1130s. King Baldwin II give the Templars exclusive accommodation in his palace on the south side of the "Lord's Temple," near what is known today as the Dome of the Rock. This palace was called the al-Aqsa Mosque, and in earlier years, crusaders had dubbed it "Solomon's Temple." Historians maintain that both the King of Jerusalem and the Patriarch of Jerusalem definitely assisted the first nine Templars from the beginning, helping them obtain food, shelter, and supplies. Recent academic research suggests that there may have been more than only nine knights in the early years up to 1129, the Council of Troyes, but overall, evidence is scarce about these initial early years. Scholars believe that the overall number of Templars did not start to increase until around 1129; certainly, by the 1170s, documentation shows about 300 knights in the Kingdom of Jerusalem alone, so the Order had grown substantially by then. Mainly due to the lack of consistent documentation about their earliest years, there has been much speculation about what activities the first Templars may have been involved in; that is, whether it be their stated purpose of guarding the pilgrims' routes, or perhaps other activities in the Temple Mount vicinity. As the medieval chroniclers' accounts about the earliest Templars unfortunately do not always agree with each other, there is no evidence to say anything for certain about the Order's earliest years. The current scholarly assessment is that there is simply not enough evidence or eyewitness testimony to state anything definitive, especially regarding the Order's first nine years in Jerusalem from 1119 to around 1128.

The chronicler William of Tyre, writing as late as 1185, took a rather clear view that the original nine knights were seen as the equivalent of regular canons or priests living in a religious community. Fulk de Chartres, royal historian of King Baldwin II, noted that the Christian Franks did not have enough resources to maintain the Temple of Solomon properly for a period of years, and that eventually the building became quite delapidated, which seems to support a pious, struggling image for the early Templars; yet, even though he was on the premises of the Temple Mount area, curiously, he does not even mention the original nine Templars in his account at all!

Unfortunately, other than the rather vague accounts of William of Tyre and a few other chroniclers, we have no specific details about how the Order started. However, the Order was certainly in full operation by at least 1120, as records show that Fulk V, the Count of Anjou, stayed at the Temple and joined the Order as an associate member while on pilgrimage in Jerusalem in 1120–1121. The Hospitallers and the Knights Templar followed the liturgy of the Holy Sepulchre in their church services, and the seal of the Master of the Temple shows the symbol of the dome of the Holy Sepulchre. The early Templars also lived by the Augustinian rule, as it was not until the Council of Troyes (1129) that they received their new Rule, with great input by the powerful Cistercian abbot Bernard of Clairvaux. Ultimately, at present, little can be said for certain about the earliest years of the Templars. Documentation becomes much more readily available following the Council of Troyes in 1128–1129, after the Templars' were officially given their Rule and official papal recognition. (see **Hugh de Payns**; **Bernard of Clairvaux**; **Montbard, Andre**; **Patriarchate**; **Canons of the Holy Sepulchre**; **Cistercians**; for further sources about the beginning of the Order, see "Origins of the Order" in the Recommended Reading section)

Our Lady
(see **Blessed Virgin Mary, The**)

Outremer
A French word for the Levant, meaning "across the sea," used in writing about the history of the Crusades. In Templar history, it refers to the eastern territories where the knights were fighting in the Holy Land and its environs.

Paris, Matthew

Matthew Paris was a Benedictine monk of St. Albans Abbey in England. His medieval chronicles are among the most important accounts of the 12th and 13th centuries. Often colorful, lively, even opinionated at times, they nevertheless provide us with some of the most accurate portrayals of events, people, and places of this period in the late Middle Ages. As he traveled widely, visiting a number of kings and powerful nobles, he often obtained more information than other chroniclers at the time, as he was granted special access to important places and documents that other chroniclers were not privy to. Obviously, the general time frame of his works includes the period of the Order of the Temple (1119–1312), so some of Paris's chronicles inform his readers about the Templars and the events in their lives. True to his style, he would often present a mixed picture in his accounts, sometimes praising the knights and, at other times, strongly criticizing them. Even so, his accounts are still among the most valuable chronicles for Templar historians to study today.

Matthew Paris was also a talented artist who illuminated his manuscripts with beautiful maps, sketches, and drawings. Sometimes a witty and humorous touch comes through in his works—for example, he even included a sketch of the pet elephant of King Henry III, which was certainly an exotic rarity in medieval England. His most famous work was titled *Chronica majora*, and his details in these accounts are some of the most important historical records of the Middle Ages. He also wrote many biographies and histories of places, including a history of St. Albans Abbey. He died at St. Albans in 1259, so he never knew of the later 1307 arrests and trial of the Knights Templar.

Patriarchate

One of the five major Episcopal Sees of the Christian church in the ancient and early medieval world—Jerusalem, Rome, Antioch, Alexandria, and Constantinople. Each of these were ruled by a Patriarch. It was to the Patriarch of Jerusalem, Warmund of Piquigny, that chronicler William of Tyre informs us that the first nine Templars pledged their vows of poverty, chastity, and obedience to, promising to devote themselves to God's service. (see **Origins of the Templar order; Canons of the Holy Sepulchre**)

Payns, Hugh de
Hugh de Payns was the first Templar Grand Master and he served from 1118 to 1136. Unfortunately, there seems to be little detailed information about his early involvement with the Knights Templar. It is believed that he came from the village of Payens, or Payns, about 8 miles north of Troyes, and he is said to have been a vassal of Hughes I, whose court was centered at Troyes, and who we know took part in the First Crusade. He was also related to Hughes I, being of a cadet branch of the dynasty of the Counts of Champagne. Nothing for certain is known of his wife or her lineage. Some believe he had a son (others say nephew) named Theobald, who became the abbot of St. Columbe-de-Sens in 1139.

Hugh de Payns did not assume the office of Master of the Temple until 1125, some seven years after the initial emergence of the Order in 1119. Medieval chroniclers' accounts of the details of his life are rather vague, so he remains somewhat of an enigma today. Some scholars contend that his name was Hugh de Pagens. Others assert that it was more likely Hugh Peccator (Hugh the Sinner), the author of a letter that was specifically addressed to "the knights of Christ in the Temple at Jerusalem." Yet one still cannot be certain, however, as the name on the manuscript is not clear and the letter has no date. (see **Origins of the Templar order; Hughes I, Count of Champagne; Grand Master, office of; Organization of the Order;** Appendix B; and for further sources about the beginning of the Order, consult the "Origins of the Order" section in the Recommended Reading section)

Penn, William
(see **All Hallows by the Tower Church**)

Perigord, Armand de
The 16th Grand Master of the Order of the Temple, Armand de Perigord was from the house of the Count of Perigord, Guyenne, France, and served from 1232 to 1247. He died in battle near Acre in October of 1247. (see **Grand Master, office of;** Appendix B)

Philippe IV le Bel

Also known as Philip the Fair, Philippe IV le Bel was the French king who was in power at the time of the arrests, trial, and downfall of the Knights Templar. He has often been dubbed "the most notorious figure in Templar history"; yet, to be fair, although he did have a most definitive role in the Order's downfall, he was by no means the only governmental authority who was detrimental to the Templars during their trial. Philippe IV lived from 1268 to 1314, and served as king of France from 1285 to 1314. His aim was to establish France as the most Christian kingdom in all Christendom and, as many historians have noted, himself as the "most Christian" of all Christian kings. His grandfather was Saint Louis IX (1226–1270). Philippe was the second son of Philip III the Bold (ruling from 1270–1285) and his first wife, Isabelle of Aragon. He came to power in 1285 when his older brother Louis died. A year before, he had married Jeanne, an heiress of Champagne and Navarre. He is also well-known for his vociferous attack on Pope Boniface, who reigned from 1294 to 1303, as Boniface was an ambitious pope who wanted to ensure that the pope was the ultimate figure in all of Christendom. Philippe IV undoubtedly felt considerably threatened by this, and so accused Boniface of a number of crimes, including heresy, Black Magic, and the like—charges that would sound strangely familiar in October of 1307, when Philippe IV had the French Templars arrested. Historians maintain that this earlier event involving Pope Boniface in September of 1303 seems to have set a definite precedent for Philippe to later pursue other groups, especially the Knights Templar, a complex situation involving a number of factors, people, and motives. He also expelled the Jews from France in 1306, creating even more ill-will.

By 1307, the Templars were the most powerful and wealthy international Order—and accountable only to the papacy, not a king. Many historians believe that their wealth was certainly a major factor in why Philippe targeted the Order in France; but it was not the only one, however. In some collusion with a weakened Pope Clement V, Philippe was unquestionably a key player, spearheading the downfall, arrests, use of torture, and imprisonment of the Knights Templar. In fact, it is known that Philippe IV made a personal effort to be present on May 12, 1310, in Paris at Port St. Antoine, specifically to witness the burning of 54 Knights Templar at the stake. This event occurred at a crucial juncture in the trial against the Templars, as it was two and a half years after the initial arrests in October 1307, and was also two years before the final suppression of the Order. Historians note that when many of the other Templars who were still languishing in the dungeons of the Inquisition, facing further grueling interrogations, heard this horrific news, it significantly damaged their morale.

Although Philippe IV had largely succeeded in destroying the Order, to his chagrin, when the final papal bull of suppression was issued in 1312 by the pope, the Templar order itself was found not guilty as the charges were "not proven." A further major disappointment for him undoubtedly came with a subsequent papal bull issued shortly thereafter, in which the pope determined that all of the Templar order's assets would be transferred over to their rival order, the Knights Hospitallers, rather than to a king or any secular ruler. Philippe IV died on November 29, 1314, at the age of 46. As historians have long noted, the last year of his reign was particularly difficult, with a number of serious monetary and domestic crises. After his own death, his three sons died fairly soon afterward—without children—thus ending the line of the Capetian kings. Legend has it that not only other heretics, but the expelled Jews, too, had predicted "great misfortunes and dangers" for Philippe IV in his life. Enduring legends also claim that the last Templar Grand Master, Jacques de Molay, had supposedly uttered a powerful "curse" against both king Philippe IV and Pope Clement V as he was burned at the stake, asking that they join him in a year to account for their deeds before God. Ironically, although both king and pope did die within a year of de Molay, there is no historical evidence that their deaths were necessarily connected to that of de Molay. While we may never know about the curse, it is unfortunate that the historical legacy of the life of Jacques de Molay has often been overshadowed by legends of a supposed "curse" on Philippe IV, which, in the minds of the public, has often served to obscure his genuine earthly achievements as Grand Master of the Templar Order. Philippe IV has gone down in history, among other factors, as the bane of the Knights Templar. But perhaps most ironic of all, with historical hindsight, is the fact that the king who had so desired to be the "most Christian" of all, was the same king who orchestrated the downfall and destruction of the very knights who had so courageously fought, won, and died in many battles against the Saracens for Christendom. (see **Trial of the Templars; Charges; de Molay, Jacques; Clement V; Heresy;** Appendix D; and for further details and academic sources about the trial and role of Philippe IV, see "Trial of the Templars" in the Recommended Reading section)

Philosopher's Stone

It has sometimes been suggested that the Knights Templar may have found the Philosopher's Stone, or had it as a relic, something for which there is no documentable evidence. However, no group exists in a total vacuum, as it is also a part of its society and time. Today, post Harry Potter, many envision it as a red luminous stone, pulsating and powerful, a goal or prize after an epic battle between good and evil. Yet, the concept of the Philosopher's Stone is very old indeed, embodying a complex system of thought and tradition—far more than a mere physical object.

The Philosopher's Stone was an integral part of the philosophy of alchemy, which was studied by theologians and philosophers in Paris and other European locales in the late Middle Ages. The Templar order (1119–1312) existed in the late medieval period, a time when the philosophy of alchemy was again resurfacing. In certain European Christian circles, the concept of Christ increasingly being seen as an "elixir" of the soul and as the "salt of the earth" was being widely discussed. The Philosopher's Stone is central to the philosophy of alchemy, also called the "Royal Art," or the "Great Work." Alchemy was an ancient form of philosophical thought. It is best known in the popular mind today as attempting to turn base metals into gold, and for trying to discover a cure for diseases and a way of extending the human life span.

The search for the Philosopher's Stone is also seen as a major part of one's spiritual quest in alchemical thought, and is not merely a material process alone. However, alchemy is also much more than this; in fact, it is an extensive philosophy that has long been interrelated with other disciplines, including natural philosophy, medicine, astrology, metallurgy, and hermeticism. In ancient times, alchemy was widely studied. By the late Middle Ages, the time of the Knights Templar, many prominent intellectual giants in the West, including key theologians in Paris such as Thomas Aquinas and Albertus Magnus, studied certain alchemical philosophical tracts alongside their theological manuscripts, so important was the influence of alchemical thought at the time.

The word *alchemy* is largely known to the West due to its connection with the philosophy that resurfaced in 12th century Europe via contacts with the Arabic world largely through medieval Spain, but it is thought that the origin of the word possibly refers to Al-Khem, relating to Egypt. But the study of alchemy and alchemical processes is quite universal, with evidence from ancient India, China, Persia, Egypt, and others, describing specific experiments with mercury, salt, and sulfur, for example. However, although there is no evidence that the Templars were ever practicing alchemists, as has sometimes been put forth, they were living at a time and in an overall climate where alchemical philosophy was being taken quite seriously by the major medieval theologians of the day, particularly in Paris. There were also some medieval thinkers who were beginning to envision Christ in terms of a "Christian Philosopher's Stone," as the ultimate spiritual elixir that could transmute one's soul from darkness to light to eventually unite with God. Similar to many in late medieval times, the Templars were generally not literate individuals, so they would not have been able to read such manuscripts themselves.

Transmutation, or change from one state of existence into another, is a key concept in alchemy; for example, the process of lead changing into gold, or, for one to move from sickness back to health again. The transmutation of metals was said to be accomplished by a specific powder or elixir, often called the "Philosopher's Stone," which would cause the changes to occur. The alchemists, after a profound examination of natural processes and the secrets of nature, arrived at a view that involved two polarities of nature; one being mercury, the volatile intellect, and the other, sulfur, connected with the soul. Paracelsus added a third principle, salt, which as a solid, corresponds to that of the body. To the alchemist, these Paracelsian "Tria Prima" are not only chemical substances, but spiritual forces as well. According to Aristotle, the qualities of heat, dryness, coldness, and moisture were joined with the "prima materia" to develop into the four elements. Many experiments were done by alchemists, with the goal being transmutations. Such states of change were sought after by medieval alchemists, as is well known, and such experiments continued into later times, with certain alchemists having royal patrons.

From an early period, the Egyptians were known to be skilled workers in metals and, according to Greek writers, they were familiar with their transmutation, using quicksilver in the process of separating gold and silver from the native matrix. The resulting oxide, a black powder, was believed to possess marvelous powers. Salt, mainly because of its curative properties, was also viewed in Christian terms as the "salt of the earth" and as the "salt of wisdom." The very earliest Greek text that involves alchemy, "Physika kai Mystika" (Of Natural and Hidden Things), divides the Great Work of alchemy into four phases according to the colors it produces: a blackening (nigredo), whitening (albedo), yellowing (citrinitas), and reddening (rubedo). This early division has survived through the centuries in alchemical philosophy. Familiar names to us today in the West, such as Roger Bacon, Sir Isaac Newton, Ramon Lull, Robert Fludd, Nicolas Flamel, Paracelsus, and John Dee, were all involved in alchemical experiments and philosophy. Scholars largely agree that alchemy had "something" to do with the development of the eventual science of chemistry—however vaguely—but hermetic philosophers claim that some of the early underlying principles in chemistry may owe more to elements of ancient alchemical thought than is generally acknowledged today. Yet, little can be said for certain, as many medieval alchemical tracts were of necessity, written in obscure language and symbolism during a time of heresy; subsequent interpretations of them remain unclear.

Although the concept of Christ as the ultimate "spiritual elixir" was known to appeal to a number of devout Christians in late medieval times, there is no evidence that the Templars were ever practicing alchemists, as such activities would have been strictly forbidden by their austere Rule and policies. Yet, no doubt they would certainly have understood the concept of "transmutation" of one's character, as the Rule infers that a novice must transform himself from his earlier life prior to entering the Order into a higher form before being fully invested as a knight of the Order.

Pilgrimage

Following improved efforts to make travel safer for Christian pilgrims, by the 13th century in particular, a rapidly increasing number of Christian pilgrims, nobles, and merchants embarked on a greater number of pilgrimages. Far from merely booking a holiday to visit sites as many do today, pilgrimage to a Gothic cathedral, shrine, or tomb was another kind of travel, a more solemn spiritual odyssey, to someone in the High Middle Ages. It was not only a religious quest, but also a solemn *requirement* by the Church that was well understood in medieval times. Taking a pilgrimage was a serious commitment and called for much sacrifice, from whatever level of society one came. Travel was often very risky, expensive, and time consuming, so pilgrims preferred to travel in groups by land, and often, if going by sea for a significant leg of the journey, by assistance from the Knights Templar on their ships. It could easily take 10 *months* just to get from East Anglia in England to Venice, Italy—here one would then take a boat by sea to the Holy Land, which one would not see for at least another six weeks. Unlike modern times, one could never be certain he or she would see their relatives or friends again.

Pilgrimage was a major part of medieval life and was actively encouraged by the Church. Such "journeys of faith" took men and women thousands of miles from home for months at a time, so they were a popular activity for everyone at all levels of society, time and resources permitting. Pilgrims would often have as many as five symbols: a red cross on their mantle, the gray hat marked with a cross, in many cases a beard, a flask, and a donkey and a driver.

Pilgrimage is a key part of our image of life in the Middle Ages. Great importance was placed on the *next* life in the hereafter, as, after all, to a medieval pilgrim, Man's existence here on earth was merely temporary in any case. Pilgrims saw themselves as a "pious guest" here for the time being, before he or she was called away by God to his final resting place. Even Jesus himself was portrayed as a pilgrim, such as the imagery in the Church of Santo Domingo de Silos on the famous road to Compostela.

The motives of medieval pilgrims were many and varied. Some were moved by genuine piety. Others, such as criminals, had pilgrimage imposed on them as a legal measure by the authorities in atonement for their sins. For those who were sentenced to a pilgrimage, the penitent was required to take an oath before the authorities, swearing to purge himself accordingly, and was then given a safe-conduct document, similar to a type of passport. This listed the details of his crime, which had to be shown—and stamped—by the religious authorities at the various places he was ordered to present himself along the route and at his final destination, where he must again report before proceeding to the shrine to make his offering and beg for pardon. Essentially, this was akin to a medieval probation system, whereby a person was required to report at certain times and places, yet he was not actually in prison. He or she would also have to wear a distinguishing article or symbol while on pilgrimage, by which all could recognize him for his crime along the way; so, for instance, heretics were sometimes required to wear a black garment with a white cross on the front and back, while those who had committed a capital crime might have to wear chains around their necks, arms, or waist. If one would encounter such a person on the trail, he or she could not fail to notice. Pilgrimages became very popular by the 13th century, so much so that at one point, the French council took measures to forbid pilgrimages to Rome for a time, due to fears of temporary depopulation. But by and large, the main purposes of a pilgrimage were the seeking of the union of one's soul to God, paying respect to a venerated religious figure, usually a saint, to which one would pray for a miraculous cure for himself or a loved one. The Knights Templar, like a number of other military and/or religious orders in the Middle Ages, also assisted in shipping pilgrims and goods to and from the Holy Land, in addition to guarding the routes to Christian sites in Jerusalem. They thus provided safe and secure passage for many pilgrims. (see **Pilgrims**; **Shrines**; **Relics**; **Pilgrim badges**; **Saints in medieval society**; and for further sources and information, "Pilgrimage and Pilgrims" in the Recommended Reading section)

Pilgrim badges

Many mementos and trinkets such as small flasks were available to pilgrims; for example, sold in booths leading up to a cathedral itself. But especially valued were the official pilgrim badges, each unique and special for a particular shrine. They were collected by pilgrims who could then definitively prove that they had really been to Jerusalem, Rome, Compostela, and so on. Of course, a number of pilgrims arrived on Templar ships, or were assisted by Templars along the highways and byways leading to Jerusalem and other key cities for pilgrims. Medieval pilgrims would put their badges on their hat or cloak, so, naturally, the more one had, the more of a status symbol they became. The most well-recognized pilgrim badge travelers brought back from Jerusalem was the palm of Jericho symbol. From Compostela, it was the scallop shell. Treasured tokens from Canterbury took many forms, such as a picture of St. Thomas wearing his bishop's mitre or an image of the head of St. Thomas or his gloves. St. Thomas was quite popular on the Continent, too, as about 70 examples of Canterbury pilgrim's badges have also been found at the French Gothic cathedral shrines of Mont-Saint-Michel, Rocamadour, and Amiens. As the Knights Templar in the West assisted pilgrims and transported them to and from the Holy Land, they would have definitely recognized such pilgrim badges and the symbols on them. But the Order did not manufacture pilgrim badges.

As time went on, unfortunately, some pilgrims gradually tried to abuse the official pilgrim badge system of the Church, to the chagrin of the authorities. As everyone wanted to say they had been to a particular site, there developed a brisk trade by the unscrupulous in certain areas of selling fake pilgrim badges—a situation of great concern to the church; yet they found it impossible to stamp out the practice. In some cases there were frequent complaints about beggars picking up a cockle-shell from a beach and pretending to have been to Compostela, or of newly released criminals who specialized in masquerading as pilgrims on the roads of Christendom. In 1388, Richard II of England decreed that anyone claiming to be a pilgrim had to produce a proper letter of passage stamped with a special seal and if they did not and were able-bodied, then they were to be arrested. This was similar to a medieval version of identity verification today. Other cathedral shrines had to fight hard to preserve the uniqueness of their special symbol, similar to our concept of a trademark today. For instance, Pope Innocent III ruled in 1199 that only the Basilica of St. Peter in Rome should have the monopoly over the production of and selling of pilgrim badges showing St. Peter and St. Paul. Anyone else who was caught doing this faced severe penalties. So while pilgrim badges were often an integral part of a pilgrimage, and the Templars were known to assist many pilgrims through the years, the Order itself did not make or sell badges, as has sometimes been erroneously assumed. (see also **Pilgrims**; **Pilgrimage**; **Shrines**; **Relics**; and for additional sources, see "Pilgrimage and Pilgrims" in the Recommended Reading section)

Pilgrims

Pilgrims and pilgrimage had a role in the rather enigmatic, early origins of the Knights Templar. Following the First Crusade in the late 11th century, increasing numbers of Christian pilgrims risked their lives and flocked to Jerusalem from all over Europe to see the holy sites. Judging from eyewitness accounts, protection of pilgrims in the Holy Land was genuinely needed by this time, and was one of the major justifications for the founding of the Templar order. One such traumatized pilgrim in the first decade of the 12th century reported that it seemed as though Muslims lurked day and night in caves throughout the mountains between Jaffa and Jerusalem, ready to ambush Christians journeying to and from the coast. Similar frightening accounts kept arriving in Europe on a consistent basis, creating great concern for the welfare and security of travelers. Droves of pilgrims encountered a number of dangers, even health hazards. In the early 12th century, extra men and equipment were rarely available to patrol the pilgrim routes to Jerusalem or to escort new arrivals from the ports. In his now-famous account of 1102, the Norse pilgrim Saewulf wrote an eyewitness report of the terrible conditions that he encountered on his journey to Jerusalem, stating that Saracen robbers were regularly attacking, robbing, and killing pilgrims. He said conditions were so horrific that no one even wanted to stop to bury the dead; further, he describes how shocked he was when he saw many unburied corpses piled up along the route that had already been gnawed by wild animals for some time. Unfortunately, there was no organized system in place to provide food, drink, or shelter for pilgrims along the way, so by the time one arrived at Jerusalem, he or she was often exhausted, hungry, distressed, or ill.

But not all medieval travelers were pilgrims on a religious journey. The reputation of merchants along the way was constantly under attack in places, and travel for them, too, could also be quite dangerous. In some areas, they would also come into contact with pilgrims coming to or from a shrine or church. Medieval traders would often make long, perilous journeys to deliver and sell goods in other places, and would have special "safe houses" in the important foreign business centers such as Venice, where they could rest in safety. Similar to pilgrims, they, too, had to often take special precautions to guard their goods and person(s). Even though Christian pilgrimages to Jerusalem had come under Islamic rule previously (and to their credit the Islamic rulers, in accordance with the Prophet's instructions, did allow Christians to practice their religion without interference), there were still bands of robbers who terrified pilgrims en route to Jerusalem. Ironically, once the Christians had gained control of Jerusalem in 1099, the experiences of many pilgrims worsened no doubt due to the inevitable Muslim retaliation. In short, an already tense situation became intolerable. And finally, one might say, "the final straw" occurred on Easter in 1119, when the Saracens killed 300 pilgrims and took 60 prisoners. Obviously, the leaders of Christendom wanted to quickly respond to this escalating crisis. So the idea of an institution that combined a devout way of life with a military function, spearheaded by Bernard of Clairvaux, was very appealing. In 1119, the Order of the Poor Knights of Christ and the Temple of Solomon officially emerged, for the stated purpose of protecting pilgrims to the Holy Land. Among other things, the Templars were to protect pilgrims in the Holy Land and defend the Christian holy places there against any threats, such as the Church of the Holy Sepulchre and other key sites. In the Hierarchical Statutes of the Templar Rule, section 121 states that the Commander of the City of Jerusalem should have 10 knights under his direct command to lead and guard the pilgrims who come to the river Jordan, as many Christians had done for purification and prayer for many centuries. Given how dangerous travel was at the time, one can see why one of the earliest issues surrounding the formation of the public emergence of the Order in 1119 was the safety of pilgrims, Christian sites, and routes. (see **Origins of the Templar order**; **Pilgrimage**; **Shrines**; **Relics**; **Saints, Templar veneration of**; for further sources see "Pilgrimage and Pilgrims" in the Recommending Reading section)

Plessiez, Philippe de

The 13th Grand Master of the Order of the Temple, Philippe de Plessiez was from Anjou, France and served from 1201 to 1209. (see **Grand Masters, office of**; Appendix B)

Polycarp, St.

The Templars believed that they possessed a relic of the head of St. Polycarp, among others. One of the most important second century Christians, St. Polycarp (c.69–c.155) was said to have been a disciple of John the Apostle. He became bishop of Smyrna and staunchly defended orthodox Christian belief against the heresies of Marcion and Valentinus, one of the most influential of the Gnostics. He was later martyred at the age of 86; his feast was widely celebrated in Christendom on February 23rd. (see **Relics**)

Ports

(see **Admiral, Templar**; **Maritime trade and ports**; **Acre**)

Prayers

Prayers in a Templar house would begin very early, around 4 a.m., when the knight would rise for the day's first religious service called Matins. During this service, he would be required to recite 13 Paternosters (Lord's Prayers) and prayers to Our Lady. As the Rule states, the prayers to Our Lady were to be said first in the house every morning, followed by the other prayers. Matins was then followed by Prime, at 6 a.m., and the hearing of Mass. Prime was followed by Sext at approximately 11:30 a.m. By the time the Templars were ready for their first meal of the day, they would have already recited a total of at least 60 Paternosters, 30 of which were spoken for the living and another 30 for the deceased. After the afternoon meal, they were to meet in the chapel to give thanks. Next came Nones at 2:30 and Vespers at 6. Vespers was followed by the evening meal, which was eaten in silence. Compline was the last order of the day, and then the brethren would gather for some communal drinking, which was usually water, but on certain occasions, with permission of the Master, a bit of diluted wine would be permitted. Silence was an absolute requirement, especially from Compline in the evening until Matins the following morning at 4 a.m. Life in a medieval religious order was strict, and the Templars were no exception. Much of their day consisted of regular intervals of prayer, as laid out in the Rule itself. When the Templars were not at prayer or war, they were usually found doing agricultural pursuits in their western European preceptories, working in the fields or doing other essential tasks, as they were "never to remain idle" under any circumstances, as that was seen as the perogative of secular knights, not those of the Templar order. Unquestionably, the day of a Knight Templar was a life of the most extraordinary kind of daily sacrifice, as required by their Rule, and this was made clear at their initiation. Few today could withstand such a regimen for a long period of time. At the trial of the Templars, a number of the prayers called on not only God and Christ, but also the Blessed Virgin Mary, as she was the patroness of the Order. (see **Rule**; **Organization of the Templar order**; **Saints, Templar veneration of**; **The Blessed Virgin Mary**; for further sources about the structure and procedures in the daily life of the Templars, see "Organization, Structure, and Rule" in the Recommended Reading section)

Preceptory
Every Templar province consisted of baillies, the administrative and economic areas of the Order. Within each baillie were the enclosed living quarters, their church, cemetery, barns, mills, farm land, preceptories, and sheep flocks, for example. Some baillies had more than one preceptory in them, while others had only one or two, depending on the size and needs of the Order in that area. For example, in medieval England, there were Templar preceptories called Temple Bruer, Temple Garway, Temple Rothley, New Temple (known today as Temple Church, London), and many others. As the Order was huge at its height and its influence extended internationally, the Templars had preceptories in many countries and territories, both east and west. (see **Baillies**; **Organization of the Templar order**)

R

Red cross

The red cross was a symbol of martyrdom, added to the mantles of the Knights Templar in 1147, when Pope Eugenius III issued his papal bull regarding this and other matters. Although a cross is referred to in this bull, the exact design of the cross is not specified. Generally, the Templars did not use crosses that were unique only to them, as they were also used by other religious communities as well, so it cannot be said that the Templar order had only "one type" of official cross. However, one of the more commonly employed designs was the croix pattee—a four-sided cross with equidistant arms that "splay" out at the ends. Occasionally, the Greek cross, which has straight arms that do not splay or flare out at the ends, was used by the Order (and others at the time) as well, but not as often. The traditional Latin cross, perhaps the most familiar sign of Christianity in the modern-day West—where the vertical axis is longer than the horizontal axis—was not used on the mantles of the Knights Templar. From the time of the Second Crusade, following the bull of Pope Eugenius III, Templar knights would also sometimes feature a red cross on their black-and-white shields. But the striking appearance of their trademark white mantles and red crosses charging in battle in unison, was, by all accounts, quite something to behold.

However, Christian military religious Orders' insignia did not appear the same, either within the Order itself, or externally. This was partly to distinguish one Order from the other on the battlefield, for example. For contrast, the Templar knight-brothers were distinguished by their white mantles with red crosses and the Order's sergeant-brothers wore black or dark brown mantles with red crosses; but their rivals, the Knights Hospitaller, wore black mantles with white crosses. One of the other Christian military religious orders that existed around the same time, the Teutonic knights, had black Latin crosses on their white mantles and surcoats. (see **Martyrdom**; **Eugenius III, Pope**; **Mantles**; **Draper**; **Decoration**; **Organization of the Templar order**; **Hospitallers**)

Relics

In the Middle Ages, the real power of holy miracles was believed to not only come from God, but also to be present in a relic. A relic was allegedly a part of the body of Christ or of a specific saint or martyr; it could also be any object that had been connected with that saint's life as well. These precious objects were stored and very carefully guarded in the shrines of many Gothic cathedrals and monasteries. For example, a relic could be part of saints' clothing, their bones, special objects in their possession during their life such as a Bible, or a piece of the True Cross. Of course, the most precious relics were those associated with the Holy Family itself. Especially prized were those relating to the Crucifixion, such as various fragments of the True Cross, the Crown of Thorns, nails, even drops of the Holy Blood in glass vials. Kings, too, would often feature relics in their building projects, such as the monumental effort made by Louis IX of France when he built the Sainte-Chapelle in Paris in the 1240s, also intended as a reliquary for part of the True Cross, part of the Crown of Thorns, and other precious relics he had obtained from King Baldwin in Jerusalem. Historians note that a number of relics and other religious objects from trade with the East were brought back by the returning crusaders, such as the Knights Templar or the Hospitallers.

The Knights Templar believed that they had a cherished piece of the True Cross in their possession, as exemplified by section 122 of the Hierarchal Statutes of the Templar Rule, where it specifically refers to the Order's precious relic of the True Cross, stating that when the knights should have to transport their relic of a piece of the True Cross by horse, the Commander of Jerusalem and 10 knights should carefully guard it day and night, and should camp as close to the relic as they possibly can during their journey. Section 75 of the Templar Rule informs the reader about the specific saints' feast days that should be observed by Templars in their houses. A few of these relate specifically to relics—the dates of May 3rd, the commemoration of the finding of the True Cross by Helena, the mother of the Roman emperor Constantine, and also that of September 14th, a feast day commemorating the Exaltation of the True Cross.

However, the relic of the True Cross that the Order had in their possession was later captured by the Saracens at the battle of Hattin in 1187, and was naturally seen as a great loss by the Order of the Temple. An old legend claims that a Templar ran away and escaped with it and desperately buried it in the sand, only to return later, when he could not precisely locate it. Legends aside, history has shown that the Templars had definitely lost their most cherished relic at this time. Also in the East, the Order claimed to have had a relic of the Crown of Thorns, which, on Holy Thursday, the Order's priests were known to raise up for all to see. At Acre, the Templars also had a unique cross relic, made of what they believed to be a piece of wood from a bathing tub of Christ, which reputedly had great healing powers; many from far and wide were known to have come to the Templars' church to be healed.

Similar to all religious orders in medieval times, the Templars also venerated a number of saints' relics; in particular, records show that they highly valued the relics of what they believed to be the heads of two female saints—that of the fourth century martyr St. Euphemia of Chalcedon, at Castle Pilgrim in the Holy Land, and the head of one of St. Ursula's maidens, at Paris. However, there is no historically documentable evidence that the Knights Templar ever possessed the Shroud of Turin, the Ark of the Covenant, or a Holy Grail, as has sometimes been alleged. But from their Rule and other documents, it is known that the Templars were certain they owned a genuine piece of the True Cross, the head of St. Euphemia, a piece of the Crown of Thorns, and other precious relics, including a vial of the Precious Blood. Of course, other orders at the time also possessed various relics, and unfortunately, due to the destruction of the central archive and other records, the full picture regarding the Templars in particular is incomplete. In some areas, as in the Murcia region of Spain, for instance, the Knights Templar were the custodians of the Cross of Caravaca.

Yet, it is important to realize, however, that the Templars' (and later, Hospitallers') specific claims to the relics of St. Euphemia, for example, have in the course of time been shown to have not been authentic after all—in spite of their own certain belief in medieval times, even testifying to this in a defense at their trial—as, in fact, many claims had existed to the relics of St. Euphemia. Today, the body of St. Euphemia lies intact in the patriarchal church of St. George (Istanbul). It is known that later, by

1560, the Hospitaller order claimed to have a part of the body and also the head of St. Euphemia in a silver reliquary. From their trial, it is evident that the Templars also strongly believed that they possessed the head of St. Polycarp. And per further trial records, they also definitely possessed a now-famous head of another female saint, kept in their Paris treasury, on which was written "Head no. 58." Scholars today believe that this head was one of St. Ursula's maidens; the cult of St. Ursula and her maidens was very popular in late medieval times.

Although a muddle of inconsistent testimony can be gleaned from Templar trial records (retrieved from members of the Order while under great duress or torture), about a mysterious head said to be a "Baphomet," no specific evidence appears in either the Templar Rule or in other medieval period Templar documents. Scholars disagree about this term or object and what it may signify, or, indeed, whether it even existed as an "object," as it may have, instead, signified "Wisdom," a theory put forth by biblical scholar Dr. Hugh Schonfield some years ago. But since medieval times, nearly all writings about a supposed head of Baphomet come from far later times (the 18th, 19th, or 20th centuries), and not from authentic original medieval period documents. Regarding St. Mary Magdalene, the Templars did not claim her relics, but their rival Order, the Hospitallers, did; their records from 1286 list a relic of a finger of St. Mary Magdalene in a silver reliquary, among other items, that were donated to their Order. Also, as 1286 was before the suppression of the Templar order, this was indeed a Hospitaller relic, as it was in their possession prior to 1312.

After the suppression of the Order in 1312, Templar relics and archives, as well as the Order's lands, money, properties, and other assets, were eventually turned over to the Hospitallers. But by the 16th century, particularily when the Turks attacked Cyprus where many of the Hospitallers' records were stored, many Hospitaller (and remaining Templar) archives were lost or destroyed in 1571, scholars maintain. This tragic loss, coupled with the loss of other Templar archives in earlier times has, unfortunately, since that time, left a rather large gap for much speculation. Until more historical documentation is found and surviving documents are fully translated, further conclusions about Templar relics cannot be drawn. However, the Templar Rule does make it clear that the knights highly valued what they believed to be a genuine relic of the True Cross in the Order's possession, a rather conventional choice for those who would later be accused of blasphemy and heresy. (see **Shrines**; **saints, Templar veneration of**; **Templecombe**; **Pilgrims**; **Pilgrimage**; **Pilgrim Badges**; **Saints in medieval society**; **Polycarp, St.**; **Mary Magdalene, St.**; and for further sources, see "Relics" and "Pilgrimage and Pilgrims" in the Recommended Reading section)

Richard I ("the Lionheart")

Although there is no evidence that King Richard I ("the Lionheart") was ever a Templar himself, as has sometimes been claimed, historians know that he often had Templars at his court, and also, in his entourage while returning to Europe from crusade in the fall of 1192. On this fateful journey home, he was suddenly ambushed and captured by the troops of the Austrian duke Leopold V, with whom he had fiercely quarreled on several occasions while on crusade. Exactly what they argued about is not clear, but historians maintain that it was most likely over whose standard could be raised where on the battlefield; others have made the equally plausible suggestion that there may in fact have been far more to it than merely this single issue. In any case, Richard I was then turned over by Leopold V's men to the German emperor Henry VI in January 1193, and was imprisoned for ransom—an extraordinary event that surprised many at the time, as a *king* was held prisoner. He was held for 150,000 marks, a massive fortune in those days, and measures were immediately taken in his realms to collect it; naturally, this situation was rather traumatic for England in particular. It was decided that the ransom was to be collected on all property and income of the laity and clergy in Richard's territories, and all privileges were suspended including those held by the Knights Templar, who, similar to others at the time, also had to pay a tax on the lands they held as a knight's fee. As the Templars had many assets and lands, this fee was expensive. It has sometimes been suggested that perhaps the Templars were somehow involved in the collection of the ransom in England, but no evidence has been found of this. After much sacrifice by many individuals, especially in England, the huge ransom was finally paid and Richard I was released. After he died in 1199, he was succeeded by his equally temperamental brother, King John. Immediately, the Templars were quick to ingratiate themselves with him as they understandably wanted to resume their official privileges and other benefits that they had enjoyed under Richard's regime. Certain aspects of Richard's captivity, including details about the accounting records, are still rather unclear, and the precise location of his imprisonment in

Germany was not known for some time. (see **Acre**; **Thomas of Acre, Order of St.**; **Saladin**; for further sources, see "Crusades and the Military Orders" in the Recommended Reading section)

Romanticization of the Templars
While there were a number of military religious orders in the High Middle Ages, probably no other medieval chivalric order has had such a mythic hold on the popular imagination as the Knights Templar. Yet, the image many think of today when the word *Templar* is mentioned is that of a rather romanticized white knight with a red cross on his mantle, carrying sword and shield, guarding a secret Grail or rescuing a maiden. Much of this is undoubtedly due to Hollywood films or novels through the years and to various stories about Arthurian Grail knights. Ironically, they are not the same as the Knights Templar, with whom they are often confused, as strictly speaking the Templars were Christian military-religious knights who lived by an austere monastic Rule and the Arthurian knights primarily feature in Grail romances and are often portrayed as secular as much as they are as Christian. Yet, the often entirely romanticized image of a Templar knight today, although familiar to many, is not based at all on the hard, day-to-day reality that was actually the life of many of the medieval Templars on the battlefield in the Holy Land, or in the fields and stables of their commandaries in the western European countries. For example, there is no historical evidence that a Templar knight ever wrote a Grail romance, or that the Templars found a physical "Grail" object; however, one might define that most elusive of vessels. Perhaps the incessant romanticization of the Templars ultimately says far more about our modern-day world in the 21st century rather than about the Middle Ages per se; it seems our modern-day world wants the Templars to be what many—in the 21st century—want them to be, not what the historically documented information about the genuine medieval Order actually reflects. Granted, that the original medieval Templar archives were destroyed and/or lost on Cyprus in 1571 does not help, as well as the fact that some other Templar archives were lost or have parts missing; all of that has left a massive "gap" that has understandably invited much speculation, some of which is quite thought-provoking. Many questions certainly remain, and it may take some time to completely unravel certain areas of Templar history, but historians have to work with what documentable evidence they have, whether it is written or archaeological. Yet, of course, not all Templar archives were lost, however, as a number of genuine medieval Templar documents have been found scattered in

various archives, and often need to be translated. Admittedly, to many, such surviving archives may seem far less "glamorous" than treasure maps, for example, as the genuine records often tend to feature more mundane subjects such as supplies, accounting records, or sheep farming, matters that concerned the daily life of those in the historical Order itself.

That said, it is always possible, as in any field, that new documents or new discoveries may occur in the coming years. Who knows what they will reveal? It may well be that in the future, truth really will be "stranger than fiction," as the old saying goes. But until then, historians must work with the genuine documents that have managed to survive the ravages of time.

The popular "mythos" of the Templars clearly lives on, but so does their historical memory, that of the genuine medieval Order of the Temple. (1119–1312). Let us hope that in the future more historical documents and archives will be discovered or translated, shedding further light on the historical Templars and their legacy.

Roncin

A roncin was a horse whose use was primarily that of a pack animal for daily work or chores in Templar daily life, as distinguished from the elite horses used in battle; a roncin is mentioned in the Rule on several occasions. (see also **Turcoman**; **Rule**; **Horse racing and jousts**)

Rosslyn Chapel

A beautiful, ornate 15th century medieval chapel 6 miles south of Edinburgh, the capital of Scotland, Rosslyn Chapel is an important building of the late medieval and early Renaissance period. It is perhaps known today as one of the key film sites for *The Da Vinci Code*. Renowned for its solid stone-barrelled roof, ornate stone carvings, and stunning setting in the Scottish Borders, it is often incorrectly assumed to have been built by the Knights Templar, or to be a Templar site, which it is not. In fact, the headquarters for the medieval Scottish Knights Templar order was at nearby Balantradoch, a village now called Temple.

The foundation stone of Rosslyn Chapel was laid on September 21, 1446, the feast day of St. Matthew. The original name of Rosslyn Chapel was the Collegiate Church of St. Matthew. Spanning a 40 year period, at the direction of Sir William St. Clair III, the last prince (Jarl) of Orkney and the Chancellor of Scotland, Sir William, his team of specialists, as well as many stonemasons, both local and foreign, worked exclusively on building this masterpiece. The chapel's founder, Sir William, was not a

Knight Templar, as the Templar order had been officially suppressed in 1312, and the foundation stone for Rosslyn was not laid until work began in 1446—some 134 years later.

Stone barreled roof carvings, Rosslyn Chapel
Photo courtesy of Simon Brighton

Rosslyn Chapel has long been renowned for its famous stone carvings, which are some of the finest in Europe, and many of which relate to the symbolism of angels, stars, a cornucopia of vegetation, Christian saints, the Old Testament, the biblical Apocrypha, and a number of other traditions, including indigenous Scottish lore and ancient Pagan symbolism. Historians maintain that Rosslyn Chapel as we know it today is part of what was originally intended to be a larger cruciform building with a tower at its center, a collegiate church edifice that was ultimately never completed. The chapel is in fact very compact, as it has many ornate carvings all within a relatively small space, as compared to, say, a large Gothic cathedral, something that many visitors immediately comment on. Its three large pillars near the high altar area of the chapel, especially the ornate Apprentice Pillar, have for various reasons of interest to Freemasons and other groups worldwide for centuries.

Sir William, the brilliant founder of this magnificent chapel, appears to have been the primary architect, overseer, and Master of Works of this project, taking the utmost care regarding the building's design—he is said to have personally examined each carving in wood before he allowed it to later be carved in stone. His "right-hand man" was undoubtedly Sir Gilbert Hay, a learned figure of the time as well. After Sir William died in 1484, he was buried in the chapel's vaults, as were other members of the St. Clair family through the years. Unfortunately, as there are no surviving original designs of the chapel or notes, several claims, suppositions, and theories have added to the "intrigue" of Rosslyn Chapel. It has been suggested as a possible repository for many artifacts, including the lost Scrolls of the Temple, the Ark of the Covenant, the Holy Grail, and the genuine Stone of Destiny, for example; however, all of the theories put forth so far remain as speculation.

While most of the carvings have clear-cut explanations within a medieval or Renaissance context, a few remain rather enigmatic, partly because some are unfortunately badly eroded due to the ravages of time and are unclear, and/or because some of the iconography in the chapel can properly be interpreted in a number of different ways, a problem that frequently occurs in medieval architectural buildings in general. Its carvings must also be viewed within the overall context of late medieval symbolism, history, politics, the founder's vision, as well as taking into account local Scottish folklore and symbolism. A complex building with

Green Man, Rosslyn Chapel
Photo courtesy of Simon Brighton

many facets, it has long been noted that Rosslyn Chapel has the largest number of Green Man carvings of any medieval chapel in western Europe. A symbol of growth, abundance, fertility, and the cycles of the seasons, the Green Man was originally an ancient Pagan symbol that was later adopted for use in many medieval Christian buildings, including churches and chapels. More than 300 in number, the Green Man carvings at Rosslyn are not identical, and occur throughout the interior of the chapel as well as on the exterior, and, incredibly, there are even a few on the roof as well.

The Agnus Dei (Lamb of God) symbol, for instance, is also present as one worn carving in Rosslyn Chapel. Although this key Christian symbol does occur in a number of Templar buildings on the Continent, and on the medieval seals of some Templar Masters, it is often forgotten that the Lamb of God symbol also occurs in many other medieval non-Templar church buildings as well. It has long been an important Christian symbol of martyrdom in general, so it is not particularily unique to Rosslyn. But its presence here does not make Rosslyn Chapel a Templar building. In fact, as a number of carvings in the chapel also relate to others throughout the building, Rosslyn Chapel cannot—and perhaps never could be—merely put in a "box"; it is far too extraordinary for that. As is the case in many medieval churches, no one carving can truly ever be seen merely on its own, as one has to examine the whole context in which it occurs; this cannot be emphasized enough.

Apprentice pillar, Rosslyn Chapel
Photo courtesy of Simon Brighton

Serpent-dragons at the base of Apprentice Pillar, Rosslyn Chapel
Photo courtesy of Simon Brighton

It has also been suggested that the Mason's Pillar and the ornate Apprentice Pillar, for which Rosslyn is famed worldwide, represent the two pillars of Boaz and Jachin, which stood at the inner hallway of

Solomon's Temple in Jerusalem, and that Rosslyn Chapel may be a reproduction of that temple. Others believe the plan of Rosslyn Chapel is based instead on Herod's temple and its plans; others believe far more emphasis should be put on the second temple of Jerusalem of Zerubabbel, a Jewish guard of the Persian king Darius at the time of the end of the Babylonian captivity of the Jews in the first century. Their argument that Rosslyn may in fact be an allegory for Zerubabbel's temple is based on the fact that the only written words carved in the entire chapel are those spoken by Zerubabbel in the biblical apocryphal book of I Esdras chapter three: "Kings are strong, wine is stronger, women are stronger still—but, strongest of all, is Truth."

According to this I Esdras account, Zerubabbel, unlike the other guards present—had, at the request of King Darius, wisely answered a series of difficult questions, after which he was allowed to lead his suffering people, the Jews, to their freedom after decades in captivity. King Darius and his army had invaded Babylon in 590 B.C. in Jerusalem, and the Jews had long been suffering in exile in Babylon; and now, Zerubabbel in his infinite wisdom, as I Esdras informs the reader, had so impressed the conquering king that Darius finally allowed him to lead his people to their freedom, back to the Holy Land to rebuild Jerusalem and especially the Second Temple, which is referred to in this account as "the House of the Lord." I Esdras does not give any specific dimensions or measurements for the Second Temple, and does not specifically claim that this "Temple of the Lord" was a copy of the original design of King Solomon's temple. These verses are in I Esdras, chapters 5 and 7, where it also states that it took 18 years to build the Second Temple; but, again, as specific measurements are not given in this account, theoretically, the appearance of the Temple could possibly take a form different from that of the original design of King Solomon's Temple. There is also an account about Zerubabbel in the works of Josephus as well; and, at a later time, the Second Temple was significantly enlarged by King Herod, but the third temple was never completed, as no new temple was ever built on the original site on the Temple Mount platform in Jerusalem.

Advocates of the Zerubabbel theory maintain that it appears as though the founder, Sir William St. Clair, may have possibly identified with, or envisioned himself in the role of Prince Zerubabbel. Others believe that the inscription from I Esdras at Rosslyn may be connected specifically to the Royal Arch ceremony of Freemasonry, yet some knowledgeable Freemasons have informed this author that the Royal Arch ceremony itself was not created or written down until 1740—nearly 300 years after Rosslyn Chapel was begun—and that when Masons designed the ritual at that time, they did not use that particular section of I Esdras. In any case, Masonic and other researchers today are conducting further groundbreaking research on all of these theories, and we await their conclusions. Parallels have been drawn between the story of the Apprentice Pillar and the murder of Hiram Abiff, master mason at the building of the Temple of Solomon, who was struck down by a blow to the head, similar to the image of the "murdered apprentice" in Rosslyn Chapel. However, as with much of the symbolism in Rosslyn, such legends of a talented builder being murdered by a jealous master are not necessarily unique to Rosslyn Chapel, as they are also found in other medieval buildings as well, such as Rouen in France. A number of Masonic historians today maintain that there is actually no specific Masonic symbolism in Rosslyn Chapel at all, yet others disagree; so the debate continues.

"Murdered apprentice" carving, Rosslyn Chapel
Photo courtesy of Simon Brighton

Due to all of the various theories and interest in the chapel, many wonder as to whether or not an actual excavation will be done, and if so, when. The answer to this question has been explained by the Director of the Rosslyn Chapel Trust, who has stated that due to the Scottish law of the "Right of Sepulchre," a rather lengthy legal procedure would have to be followed in order to secure the necessary permission to dig on the church grounds by the authorities. Meanwhile, the focus is on preservation of the building, and not on excavation, at least for the near future. Many other fascinating aspects exist about Rosslyn Chapel and remain to be further explored but, by all accounts, nearly everyone agrees that, if possible, this magnificent chapel and its beautiful surroundings should be seen at least once in a lifetime. Perhaps the stellar imagery of this extraordinary chapel will be clarified in due course, as will a number of the other carvings, as time unfolds. Rosslyn Chapel is also an active Scottish Episcopal church today, but, it must be clearly stated that Rosslyn Chapel is not a Templar site, as the medieval Scottish Templars had their headquarters at nearby Balantradoch, today the village of Temple. In fact, both sites can be visited on the same day if one plans the journey carefully. Many are, and will be, engaged in further research about this extraordinary building and its environs for some time to come. But regardless of one's views, for many, Rosslyn Chapel will always remain a special "legacy of wisdom" in stone, a beacon of hope in a troubled world. (see **Temple, Balantradoch**; **Guilds, medieval**; **Freemasonry**)

Interior facing east, Rosslyn Chapel
Photo courtesy of Simon Brighton

Rule, Templar

The Rule is the most important document detailing the daily life of a medieval Templar. During the 12th and 13th centuries, the Order of the Temple developed a detailed set of regulations, a process that went through several stages after the Council of Troyes in 1129. Written in French, it included a translation of the original Latin Rule that would not have been readily comprehensible to many Templar recruits, as they were generally not literate individuals, but their chaplains were. The Rule had seven main sections: the Primitive Rule, Hierarchical Statutes, Penances, Conventual Life, the Holding of Ordinary Chapters, Further Details on

Penances, and Reception into the Order. Scholars believe the original manuscripts of the Latin Templar Rules were probably destroyed at the time of the 1307 arrests in France. Unfortunately, none of these documents have survived, so historians must work from extant translations. The Primitive Rule was the result of the deliberations of the Council of Troyes (1129) and was based to an extent on previous practices.

At the time of the Council, the Templars had been following the Rule of St. Augustine, however, this changed in 1129 with the direct influence of the Cistercian abbot St. Bernard of Clairvaux. The Cistercians were reformed Benedictines, and although they are not identical, one finds a number of similarities between the Rule of the Templars and the Rule of St. Benedict. However, Bernard's specific influence is unmistakable, as other aspects of it were specifically modeled on the Cistercian Rule. In 1119, again under Bernard's influence, the Cistercian constitution was also sent to the pope for approval—the same year the early Templars first presented themselves to King Baldwin II in Jerusalem. Bernard was heavily involved in church politics and the affairs of both organizations, and both were dedicated to Our Lady, whom Bernard greatly revered. By the mid-1160s, the Rule had also expanded into a military manual, although the knights' spiritual life and obligations were always the first priority. Any monastic order requires strict rules to live by in daily life and the Templars were no exception.

There were strict penalties for a number of issues and these are outlined in various sections of the Rule. Major punishments, especially the specific humiliation of losing one's mantle for a year and a day, were used when necessary. This was a terrible penalty in the Order, a symbol of great embarrassment and shame. If for whatever reason a particular knight-brother would lose his habit, he would also be immediately stripped of his prestigious white mantle, all of his weapons, and his horse(s). Then, for a specific period of time, as specified by the Rule and/or the Master, the knight would be forced to eat from the floor, do the most menial of tasks, and be generally separated from his brethren. Such penalties applied to things such as losing a horse through neglect, loaning Templar assets without the permission of the Order, and the like, but if a homosexual relationship was in evidence, he would then be expelled from the Order, the harshest of all penalties.

Ironically, however, although the inquisitors tried to use the charge of homosexuality as a major accusation during the Templar trials, there is very little historical evidence that it often occurred in the Templar order, unlike some of the other religious orders at the time. Knights were even required to sleep with candles burning at night to avoid the lust that darkness would supposedly bring; this was a common practice in many medieval monasteries. Other transgressions of the Templar Rule could result in outright expulsion from the Order, too, such as murdering a Christian, informing outsiders of what went on in chapter meetings, committing any act of heresy, plotting any false charges against a brother, leaving the Templar house for more than two days without permission, and leaving the battlefield while the black-and-white beauseant of the Order was still raised.

Many of these rules were similar to those of other military religious orders of the time, such as the Hospitallers or the Teutonic Knights, but the Templars were known to have had a particularily austere Rule. If for any reason a Templar was permanently expelled from the Order, he was *required* to join another religious order in an effort to save his soul. Overall, the Knights Templar remained true to their Rule. The history of the Templar order includes no lurid public sex scandals, unlike some of the other medieval religious orders at the time. Ironically, before the trial that took place between 1307 and 1312, the Templar order had not even been accused of outright heresy, again unlike other orders, though there were the occasional errant individuals, as with any large international organization. In fact, the Templars were generally viewed as more chaste than other religious men. Even non-Templar witnesses at the trial in Cyprus testified that the Templars were devout Christians, never missing mass, and so on.

Undoubtedly, the strict Rule and daily regimen required of Templar knights greatly contributed to their becoming one of the world's most formidable fighting forces of all time. But few today in our modern-day world could likely withstand such strict living conditions for a prolonged period of time, as did the Templars. (see **Organization of the Templar order; Food; Haircut; Decoration; Mantles; Prayers;** for further sources, see "Organization, Structure, and Rule" in the Recommended Reading section)

Sable, Robert de
The 11th Grand Master of the Order of the Temple, Robert de Sable was originally from Maine, France and served from 1191 to 1192/3. (see **Grand Masters**; Appendix B)

Safe deposit
In the 12th century, loans to crusaders were one of the Templar orders' most common financial transactions, but by the 13th century, the Templar empire had grown so large and powerful that their loans became a key part of the entire western European financial system. In a dangerous world, Templar commandaries and preceptories were regarded as the safest places by far to securely store important documents such as wills, treaties, and charters, or to store money, gems, coins, and family heirlooms, before one would set out on crusade or a pilgrimage. This applied to nobles and kings as much as peasants going on crusade, as nearly everyone at all levels of society preferred to leave their valuables with the Templars, where they were assured that they would be kept safe and in good condition for years. Crusaders and pilgrims traveling to the Holy Land in particular also tended to make sure that their earthly affairs were in order before they left, in case they died or became seriously injured and never returned home again. Today, we generally leave our valuables in a locked bank safe deposit box before a long journey; in the High Middle Ages, one would leave them with his local Templar house.

The Templars' wealth was distributed throughout their vast empire, similar to how corporations and banks operate today—that is, major urban offices usually have more assets than smaller branches in outlying areas, so many of these assets are put to use in other investments. However, much of the Templars' wealth from individuals could never be moved at all, due to their strict policy of storing one's money and goods in a secure box within their treasuries, where it could never be accessed without the owner's permission. In principle, this is very similar to the modern bank policy regarding safety deposit boxes. So much of the assets of the Order from their other business enterprises—and not the valuables deposited with them by individuals—made up their liquid capital.

Similar to any sound business organization, the Templars never kept all of their wealth in one place; in fact, such a practice is not advisable even now, much less in the dangerous political and economic climate of medieval Europe. The Templars were especially adept at finance, enterprise, and investment, and had the manpower, land, ships, and fortitude to carry it out; they diversified their holdings, as did a number of other religious orders of the time. Unquestionably the wealthiest organization in western Europe at that time, the Templars were ultimately answerable to no one but the papacy itself, a situation that undoubtedly contributed to the growing envy of them from the French king Philippe IV, who was instrumental in their downfall and, with the help of the pope, arrested the Templars in 1307. After the suppression in 1312, the major assets of the Templar order were turned over to their rival Order, the Hospitallers (including relics, land, and other valuables). But as the central archive of the Order has not been found with details of financial assets and transactions, especially in the Holy Land and its environs, this has unfortunately left a gap, leading to much speculation as to the specific whereabouts of their great wealth. Historians maintain that the central Templar archive disappeared, probably destroyed by the Turks' savage attack on Cyprus in 1571, as many important Templar and Hospitaller records were destroyed at this time. Yet other Templar records in European areas have been found more recently, but many still need to be translated, so hopefully more details will eventually emerge and be further clarified as scholars work on these manuscripts. (see **Assets**; **Loans**; **Treasuries, Templar**; **Commander, Kingdom of Jerusalem**; **Wool**; **Relics**; for further sources, see "Assets, Templar" in the Recommended Reading section)

Saint-Amand, Odo de

The eighth Grand Master of the Order of the Temple, Odo de Saint-Amand was from Limousin, France, and served from 1171 to 1179. He suffered an especially difficult end for a Templar Grand Master, as in 1179, he was captured and imprisoned by Saladin's men. Saladin then offered to exchange him for one of his nephews, who at the time was a prisoner of the Templars. Utterly refusing to compromise and with extraordinary courage under the circumstances, Saint-Amand replied with his now famous words: "A Templar has to either conquer or die, and only then may he give for his ransom his dagger and his belt." He languished in prison for a few more months, but eventually died in the dungeons of Saladin. (see **Grand Masters**; **Saladin**; Appendix B)

Saint Catherine's Church, Cornwall

St. Catherine's Church is located in the tiny hamlet of Temple, on Bodmin Moor, and stands on the site of what was the earlier Templar chapel. Also dubbed "Temple Church, Cornwall," it formed part of the medieval Preceptory of Trebeigh and was a lonely, remote church on desolate Bodmin Moor, far away from other Templar preceptories. It was not known to be particularily prosperous; it most likely was a key training center for Cornish knights. In 1150 the lordship of the manor of Trebeigh (Trebythe) was granted to the Order by King Stephen. Local tradition has it that pilgrims traveling from Ireland were in the habit of avoiding the hazards of sailing around Lands End, by going up the Padstow estuary, probably as far as Wadebridge, and then overland to the Fowey river. Padstow was an important port and Fowey was probably the busiest harbor on the south coast, from which many travelers from the West Country would have embarked for Europe. So, perhaps it was natural for the Templars to build their church and refuge on the moor to accommodate travelers who passed over this wild stretch of country on their way to the Holy Land. It is not known exactly in what year the 12th century church at this site, dedicated to St. Catherine of Alexandria, was built. It stands today on the site of the earlier Templar chapel. After the suppression of the Order in 1312, the church was eventually turned over to the Hospitallers. Although the church here is not the original Templar church, some stone carvings, including some crosses from the original church, can be seen embedded into the walls of the small house next to the church itself. (see Appendix E)

Saints in medieval society

Medieval society was very hierarchal, similar to a pyramid, with God at the very top; next were the saints. In the popular view, the saints performed a function similar to the Gods in Homer—alive, active, intensely interested in mortal affairs, each enjoying his or her own local cult centers, and intervening for the protection of their subjects—a kind of superior aristocracy. The saints who were seen as having a miraculous power, could intervene to protect their own, sometimes quite dramatically.

Under God and the saints, there were two divisions down to the rank of the masses—one was the *ecclesiastical*, with pope and bishops at the top, abbots and monks, archdeacons, cathedral canons, and more in between; the other were the more *secular* leaders, starting with the kings and emperors, then the princes and barons, knights and gentry, merchants and artisans. Finally, there were the peasants and slaves. Kings and barons lived in castles and palaces; peasants lived in huts and makeshift dwellings. Following a key tenet of Christianity, the churches and cathedrals were built as homes *for all elements of society*, and not only for the elite.

The Templars venerated a number of saints in battle, and in their many houses and commandaries, both in the Holy Land and in their western preceptories, as we learn from their Rule, in particular, sections 74 and 75. (see **Saints, Templar veneration of**; **Feast days**; **Rule**; **Gothic cathedrals**; **Shrines**; **Prayers**; **Relics**; **Pilgrimage**; **Pilgrims**)

Saints, Templar veneration of

Although the Templars, akin to many devout Christians in the Middle Ages, venerated a number of saints, by and large they tended to put far more emphasis on saints who had been martyrs, such as St. Catherine of Alexandria, for example, who is also referred to in the Rule, section 75.17. The Templars venerated a number of saints' feast days and fasted on many others; they were also known to venerate the Maccabees, the Jewish warriors of the Old Testament who had also been martyrs for their cause. As knights in the Crusades, the Templars placed a special premium on martyrdom, and so it may not be surprising to find such an emphasis in the Rule itself, or to discover that one of their key mottos was Psalm 115: "Not unto us, O Lord, not unto us, but unto Thy Name be the Glory." The Templars also venerated another now-famous martyr, St. George, of whom we know they had a statue at their castle at Safed in Galilee, for example. He, too, is also mentioned in the list of feast days observed by the medieval Knights Templar in their commandaries and houses, as taken directly from the Rule, section 75, which specifically outlines the feast days that were to be observed in the Templar houses: The nativity of Our Lord; the feast of St. Stephen; St. John the Evangelist; the Holy Innocents; the eighth day of Christmas, which is New Year's Day; Epiphany; St. Mary Candlemas; St. Mathias the Apostle; the Annunciation of Our Lady in March; Easter and the three days following;

St. George; Sts. Philip and James, two apostles; the finding of the Holy Cross; the Ascension of Our Lord; Pentecost and the two days following; St. John the Baptist; Sts. Peter and Paul, two apostles; St. Mary Magdalene; St. James the Apostle; St. Laurence; the Assumption of Our Lady; the nativity of Our Lady; the Exaltation of the Holy Cross; St. Matthew the Apostle; St. Michael; Sts. Simon and Jude; the feast of All Saints; St. Martin in winter; St. Catherine in winter; St. Andrew; St. Nicolas in winter; St. Thomas the Apostle. (see **Feast days, Templar**; **Saints in medieval society**; **Mary Magdalene, St.**; **Shrines**; **Relics**; **Rule**; **Prayers**; **Pilgrimage**; **Bernard of Clairvaux**)

Saladin

One of the most famous figures in the Crusades and a formidable foe of the Knights Templar, Saladin was the founder of the Ayyubid dynasty of Egypt and Syria, which restored Jerusalem to Muslim control in 1187 and later defended it against the Christian crusaders in the Third Crusade. His full name was Salah al-Din Yusuf ibn Ayyub, and he was known to his Muslim contemporaries as al-Nasir, "the Victorious," and was greatly respected in Europe. He was born in Mesopotamia in A.D. 1137 and was of Kurdish descent, rising to power in March of 1169, when he succeeded his uncle as commander of the Syrian troops. As history has shown, he was a remarkable warrior in many battles and a great leader of his armies; and, given the times, was also far ahead of many of his contemporaries in political judgment, personal morality, and leadership abilities. Certainly, Saladin was brilliant with battle strategy as well as being much more generous toward his defeated enemies than many of his rivals were. In addition, he is famous to many in the West today for the truce in September 1192 with Richard I ("the Lionheart"), in which Saladin remained in control of Jerusalem, but nobly agreed to allow Christian pilgrims access to the city and its key Christian holy sites, such as the Church of the Holy Sepulchre.

But regarding Templar history in particular, he was one of their most formidable foes, perhaps rather notorious on occasion for having all of the captured Templars beheaded, as they preferred to remain Christian rather than convert to Islam, particularily after the difficult battle of Hattin in 1187. One Muslim chronicler at the time, Ibn al-Athir, famously stated in his account that the Templars ("Dawiyya") and the Hospitallers ("Isbitariyya") were specifically singled out for ill treatment by Saladin amongst all of the prisoners only because they had fought more fiercely than all the other Franks. As not a single Knight Templar was willing to convert on a number of occasions, preferring instead to face martyrdom, this undoubtedly only served to further strengthen Saladin's resolve. His Ayyubid descendants were eventually sidelined by those of his brother, al-Adil Saif-ad-Din, but Saladin's legacy remains, many centuries after his death on March 3, 1193. (see **Ayyubids**; **Richard I ("the Lionheart")**; **Saint-Amand, Odo de**; **Saracens**; for further sources about the Crusades, see "Crusades and the Military Orders" in the Recommended Reading section)

Saracens

The Saracens were the Muslim enemies of the Christians at the time of the Crusades. Similar to the Knights Templar, they, too, were also strongly dedicated warriors, trained to be martyrs and to not fear death. Although the two faiths were often bitter rivals, a number of the underlying principles in their training were rather similar. By far the most famous leader of the Saracens at the time of the Templars was Saladin. Historians acknowledge that the Templar leadership regarded him with respect on a number of occasions, and the Muslims at times also referred to certain Templar leaders in equally respectful terms, even when both sides were fiercely at war. In fact, the Templars may have learned about mathematics, architecture, and building from their enemies. The Templars hired Arab scribes, as they were an obvious necessity on key diplomatic missions and in their wartime negotiations, and, as needed, the Grand Master had an Arab interpreter on his own personal staff. Complaints were occasionally made against some Templar Masters in the East that they had far too open communications with "heathens" (Muslims), even to the point where some of the Templars were said to have allowed Muslims to celebrate their religious rites in their homes. Unfortunately, such diplomatic measures later led to direct accusations of fraternizing with the enemy by the inquisitors. Yet, given the context of the time, especially during the 13th century, when much new knowledge was making its way from eastern to western Europe, astonishing many Westerners at times, it is not all surprising that the Knights Templar would have wanted to learn all they could about it. The Templars not only hired Saracen scribes when needed, but it is known that a few Templar Masters in European areas had ordered various translations of books of the Bible, including the book of Maccabees, to be made available in French, along with Arabic and Hebrew commentaries. Sometimes the Templars would also hire Saracens for tasks other than interpreting, as was the case on the island of Majorca, for example. Here, even after they had been warned about their associations with the Saracens, the Templars nonetheless still continued to employ Saracens to help them farm the land, much to the chagrin of the papacy. (see also **Saladin**)

Seals

The official seal of the Grand Master of the Order of the Temple featured the circular dome of the Church of the Holy Sepulchre on one side, and the symbol of two knights on one horse on the other. As the early Templars made their vows in Jerusalem, and were given accommodation by King Baldwin II on the southeastern side of the Temple Mount, and so on, it is perhaps not all that surprising to find the image of the Church of the Holy Sepulchre on the Order's seals. The original domes of both the Dome of the Rock and the Church of the Holy Sepulchre have been rebuilt since medieval times. The dome of the Church of the Holy Sepulchre was destroyed in a fire in 1808 and was later rebuilt, and the Dome of the Rock as we see it today was rebuilt in the 16th century. In addition to this large great seal of the Grand Master of the Templar Order, there was also a smaller one that portrayed the circular dome of the Holy Sepulchre.

It is important to point out that there was never only "one seal" or primary symbol of the Templar order. The image of two knights on one horse perhaps comes the closest—it is featured on many of the Grand Master's seals on one side, whereas the image on the other side would occasionally change, with minor variations, upon the installation of a new Templar Grand Master. Some military experts believe that the "two knights on one horse" symbol may be rather similar in its underlying concept to the "buddy-buddy" system used in some modern armies today, whereby soldiers operate in pairs. Some archaeologists maintain that this symbol goes back to Sumerian times. The Grand Master's official seal was made of silver or lead, and was kept locked at all times, only to be accessed by the Master and two other high officials, as the Rule makes clear. In the Order's headquarters in the East, it would have been stored in the treasury, under the care and protection of the Commander of the Kingdom of Jerusalem.

The provincial Masters of the Order also had their own seals that featured a variety of symbols throughout the life of the Order. Again, there was never only "one symbol" of a given provincial Master of the Order, as designs varied throughout the life of the Order, which spanned nearly 200 years. Examples of specific designs on Masters' seals include a variation of the Agnus Dei, the Lamb of God symbol, which was used primarily in England and Provence; an eagle or an image of the head of Christ, used in Germany; or the image of the dome of the Church of the Holy Sepulchre, which was used in southern France. Other symbols found on some Templar provincial seals include images of a castle tower, various crosses, doves, stars, a crescent moon, a tower with a pointed roof and a cross, and others. One of the more enigmatic symbols that has been found on a Templar Master's seal is that of Abraxas (see **Symbols**). The Master's silver seal was certainly an important object, as we learn from the Templar Rule, section 459, where it makes it clear that if any brother should break the Master's seal, he should be stripped of his habit. (see **Red cross**; **Agnus Dei**; **Symbols**)

Second Crusade

The Knights Templar first fought together in battle during the Second Crusade (1147–1149), in place of their usual duties of guarding pilgrims' routes and accosting Muslim bandits on the highways into Jerusalem, among other tasks, in their earlier years. Largely from this time, the famed image of the so-called "white knights of the Crusades," charging in unison under their black-and-white banner, was born. Certainly, the Templars were an extremely well-trained and disciplined fighting force, as not only their fellow Christians, but even their Saracen enemies, acknowledged on several occasions. Rallying as a totally dedicated, united force—and not merely as individuals—the Templars were known to never leave the battlefield while their famed black-and-white piebald standard, the beauseant, was raised. The Second Crusade is a complex event, but, briefly, the leader of the Second Crusade, King Louis VII of France, immediately recognized the extraordinary abilities of the Knights Templar and placed his army largely under their control and guidance, as did the Holy Roman Emperor–elect, Conrad III. Yet, even with the assistance of a fighting force as well-trained and effective as the Templars, the Second Crusade ended in failure when the crusaders were unsuccessful in their siege of Damascus and were forced into a humiliating retreat, with Conrad III returning home in 1148, and Louis VII a year later, in 1149. Regardless of this defeat, as history has shown, the Templars would later emerge victorious in other key battles. As an aside, one of the key supporters of the early Templars, the highly influential Cistercian abbot Bernard of Clairvaux, preached the Second Crusade in 1147 from Vezelay, today one of the key sites that claims relics of St. Mary Magdalene. (for further sources about the Crusades, see "Crusades and the Military Orders" in the Recommended Reading section)

Seneschal, office of
The Seneschal was an important office in the Templar order, as he was the Grand Master's deputy, or "right-hand man." Among other duties, he occasionally had the important honor of carrying the famed Templar standard, the beauseant, a black-and-white banner, into battle, but that was normally done by the Marshal, the chief military officer, or one of his subordinates. Chronicler Matthew Paris's 13th-century drawings show this banner as a simple oblong attached vertically to a pole or spear. The Templars were known to be very courageous in battle, and a knight could never leave the battlefield as long as their standard was still raised. Similar to the Grand Master, the office of Seneschal also had its own staff, horses, and supplies, an indication of its power and prestige. However, by the end of the 12th century, it seems that the office of Seneschal was no longer used, with the more generic term Grand Commander replacing it. (see **Organization of the Templar order; Marshal**)

Sergeants
Sergeants were not full knight-brothers of the Order, but key members who were one level below the knight-brothers in the Templar hierarchy, performing a variety of important tasks. They courageously served alongside the knight-brothers in many battles and were distinguished by their trademark black mantles with red crosses on them, as opposed to the white mantles with red crosses of their fellow knight-brothers. Occasionally, they would wear dark-brown mantles, but most often at this rank, they were black. Although the sergeants were also brave warriors on the battlefield in the East, they could also serve other functions as needed (for example, in the western European Templar preceptories as a notary or a gifted blacksmith). The sergeant-brothers were members of the Order itself and lived in Templar houses, distinct from many of the Confrere, who were associate members of the Order. (see **Knight-brothers; Organization of the Templar order; Draper; Confrere**)

Seven Liberal Arts
In the Middle Ages the seven liberal arts (sometimes called "sciences") were branches of the medieval curriculum that all liberi, or "free men," would study. They were the basis of education in the cathedral and

monastic schools, and later, the first European universities. The Church long remained divided on whether or not the so-called "Pagan learning" embodied in the seven liberal arts should be valued or largely tossed aside, but, ultimately, they decided, one might say, to "take the gold" of their predecessors. After all, many of the early Church Fathers knew Greek and studied these subjects, so it was felt that it would be better to assimilate this knowledge into the Christian educational curriculum.

The two parts of the curriculum were the *trivium* and the *quadrivium*. The trivium consisted of the subjects of Grammar, Rhetoric (Latin literature), and Aristotelian Logic, with the quadrivium comprised of Arithmetic, Geometry, Music, and Astronomy. In the late 12th and 13th centuries—the same time the cathedrals were built—a man who had studied the trivium at a university received a baccalaureate or Bachelor of Arts degree. Sound familiar? Today, we can be thankful for its medieval roots. Likewise, if a medieval student were to go on and study the more advanced subjects of the quadrivium, he would have then received his Magister Artium, or master's degree, allowing him to teach. Again, this structure is similar to that still in use today at many universities. For those who went on even further for doctoral study, they could choose to specialize in theology at a university such as Paris or Oxford, civil or canon law at Bologna, or medicine at Salerno. Graduates would receive a doctorate degree in their field of study, with some of these men choosing to teach at a university, while others opted for careers as physicians or ecclesiastical or civil lawyers, for example.

Perhaps contrary to the stereotype of the Middle Ages being nothing but a mere "cultural backwater," education was multicultural in the 12th century at many universities, especially Paris—where, for instance, alongside their Christian counterparts, such as the intellectual giants Albertus Magnus, Thomas Aquinas, Roger Bacon, or Boethius, one would also find the gifted Jewish scholar Moses Maimonides or brilliant Islamic philosophers such as Avicenna and Averroes. At this time, the influx of Islamic knowledge was coming into western Europe via Spain, and many Christians also knew about and studied these works, as exciting new translations from Arabic were coming more readily available. So this was the cultural backdrop of a key part of the time of the Templar order. Although many of the Templars were not particularily learned men on the whole, as they were first and foremost warrior-monks, some of them were from more noble backgrounds and they, or their families, had some contact with translators or scribes. Of course, by the early 13th century, the Knights Templar were accused of fraternizing with the enemy—the Saracens—but given the overall context of the time as well as their very real need to engage in diplomacy when negotiating terms with their enemies in the Crusades, this accusation can be seen in a more proper light. In addition, there was also a growing fear of the influx of Islamic knowledge into western Europe on the part of the Church, too, even dubbed "magic" by churchmen, especially after finding documents in the library of Toledo that had sigils on them, for example. So by the time of the targeting of Pope Bonifice by Philippe IV and, later, the sudden dawn arrests of the Knights Templars on October 13, 1307, it is not surprising that an occult-related accusation such as "magic" was also leveled at the Knights Templar, as it had been with other heretics as well. But the increasing influx of knowledge from the East and other distant areas into Europe in the late Middle Ages, as well as the further study of the seven liberal arts and geometry by many learned men of the day, including leading theologians, forever altered the landscape of western European education. But in certain quarters, as history has shown, it also brought with it increased fear of new knowledge, resulting in book-burning and destruction of a number of important texts and writings. (see **Geometry**; **Gothic cathedral architecture**; **Guilds, medieval**)

Shipley
St. Mary's Church, Shipley, near Horsham, England, was the largest Templar Preceptory in West Sussex. In approximately 1139, Philip de Braose (or Harcourt), son of Robert the Strong, gave the Shipley manor and its church to the Order of the Temple. Shipley was primarily and mainly an agricultural preceptory, and even today, this pleasant village remains peaceful and unspoiled. The major Templar-related remain to be seen here today is the austere, early Norman church of St. Mary. Long ago, as noted by George Tull, the Templars had a special enameled reliquary casket here, possibly from Limoges due to its style, that featured saints and the Crucifixion. Unfortunately, however, today there is only a replica of this priceless medieval treasure, as the original was stolen in 1976. The Templars were also known to have had lands nearby at Loxwood, Wisborough, and Bramber, and the chapel at Knepp. The last preceptor of Shipley was William de Egendon, 1304–1308, after which the lands were turned over to the Hospitallers, which was usually the case after 1307. St. Mary's at Shipley is still an active church today, and is well known for its Romanesque features as well as Templar heritage. (see Appendix E)

Shields

The Templars' shields in battle were generally black and white, similar to their famous banner, the beauseant, divided horizontally in thirds, with the top third the color black, and the bottom two thirds as white. At other times, they are portrayed as a large white shield with a large red cross on it, with no black in its design. However, sometimes the design could also be white at the top, including a small red cross in the center of that section only, and the remainder (the bottom two thirds), as the color black. As with its seals, there was no uniform policy regarding shields in the Order, and, similar to many military and religious organizations, the symbolism used tended to change over time. As the Templar order was officially in existence from 1119 to 1312, a period spanning nearly 200 years, there was some variation. (see **Beauseant**; **Red cross**; **Symbols**; **Seals**)

Shrines

In the Middle Ages, the Church greatly encouraged people to make special pilgrimages to holy places called shrines. These were often located in Gothic cathedrals and consisted of the remains of a saint or martyr. It was believed that if one prayed at these shrines, he or she might be forgiven for his or her sins and have a greater chance of going to Heaven. The closer a pilgrim could get to the saint's relics, the better. Others went to certain shrines known for their specific miraculous cures, desperately hoping that they, too, would be blessed. Pilgrims included those from all walks of life—from royalty to peasants.

One of the most popular medieval pilgrimage destinations was the Church of the Holy Sepulchre. In England, the most popular shrine was the tomb of St. Thomas Becket at Canterbury Cathedral. When Becket was scandalously murdered, local people managed to obtain pieces of cloth soaked in his blood. Rumors soon spread that when people touched this cloth, extraordinary cures for blindness, epilepsy, and leprosy were being claimed. Visitors from far and wide came to Becket's shrine, including royalty and those from the Continent. Another popular medieval shrine was at Walsingham in Norfolk, dedicated to Our Lady; this site was the most popular shrine of Our Lady, including, also, a Black Madonna as well. Many other medieval shrines were very popular, too, including Compostela, Vezelay, Chartres, Rome, and so on. Many miraculous cures were reported at such shrines. The precious wood, silver, or gold-encrusted reliquaries that contained the relics at shrines were also very important, as they were believed to hold in the power of the saint's relics to keep it from dissipating.

Those that have survived are now among the Western world's greatest objects of medieval art and many are still on display in Gothic cathedral treasuries. Exquisitely designed and adorned with jewels or precious stones, these special boxes or caskets containing relics were also carried into battle on important occasions, or carried through a town as part of a special church pageant or procession. The Knights Templar, for example, were known to carry their relic of a piece of the True Cross into battle on occasion, and other orders did so, too, such was the custom of the times. Although it was understood that the saint or martyr associated with a shrine was no longer living in the physical sense, in medieval times such sites were felt to be permeated with the highly charged spiritual energy of that person, that is, it was still vibrant and "alive," so to speak. Obviously, a cathedral's shrines were very valuable places—even priceless.

Churches and Gothic cathedrals often had at least one watcher at a saint's shrine who was its feretrar, or official guardian. Some shrine guardians also had their own assistants, due to the huge number of pilgrims on a daily basis, such as at Chartres; this situation is perhaps not unlike what some chapels and cathedrals are experiencing today in the wake of the modern-day *Da Vinci Code* phenomenon, with some sites now getting up to five times the normal number of visitors. The Templars, similar to many other devout Christians of their time, were known to have venerated saints and their relics, when and where appropriate, if not in battle. (see **Relics**; **Saints, Templar veneration of**; **Saints in medieval society**; **Pilgrimage**; **Pilgrims**; **Feast days**; **Mary Magdalene, St.**; **Pilgrim badges**; and for further sources pertaining to shrines, see "Relics" and "Pilgrimage and Pilgrims" in the Recommended Reading section)

Solerets
Solerets protected the legs and feet of a Templar knight, and were given to them by the Draper of the Order after their investiture, along with other items of their armor. (see **Draper**)

Song of Songs
Bernard of Clairvaux, one of the most powerful supporters of the early Templars, had a passion for Mary far beyond that of many saints before or since. Arguably one of the most gifted mystics of the Christian church's history, his numerous sermons and letters on the Song of Songs clearly illustrate his fervent devotion to her. The Song of Songs, often referred to as the Song of Solomon, was written more than 2,000 years ago, and is

in the Old Testament. Widely acknowledged as one of the greatest love poems of all time, it is set in a beautiful world of fertility and abundance, celebrating the joy of a young woman and her lover, and the heady experience of falling in love. It has often been described, for example, as the tale of King Solomon's love for the Queen of Sheba. Not merely a sensuous poem celebrating the delights of love between humans, it is also seen by scholars and theologians as an important spiritual analogy for our human longing for a union with God. It remains a major source of inspiration for poets and lovers and, even today, special passages are often read at wedding ceremonies.

Perhaps not surprisingly, the Song of Songs has been controversial at various times throughout the centuries; for example, Protestant Victorian sermons claimed it was lascivious and indecent in parts, but the early church authorities did not doubt its canonical validity, as it was highly valued as a spiritual analogy that was included in the Old Testament. The Song of Songs has been especially esteemed by Jewish mystics through the centuries, as well as by major Christian saints, such as Bernard, St. Teresa of Avila, and the poet St. John of the Cross, all of whom were especially known for finding major spiritual inspiration in the Song of Songs. Bernard himself was passionate about it and wrote 86 sermons on the first two chapters of the Song of Songs alone; his words reflect his allegorical interpretation of the Song's verses. But historically speaking, Bernard was only one in a steady stream of mystics through the centuries who had loved wisdom and especially appreciated the Song of Songs.

Such total love for God regarding the Song of Songs had also long been experienced by Jewish mystics, and a number of important medieval Kabbalistic commentaries were written about it. One of these was written by one of the famed 13th century Kabbalist luminaries of Gerona, Spain, Ezra ben Solomon. A leading light in his community, he wrote a commentary with Kabbalistic Tree of Life imagery regarding the Song of Songs, showing that its ostensible description of the passion of King Solomon for the Queen of Sheba was really about the ideal union between the creative energy of God in the upper Sephirot with the feminine principle of the Shekinah below. Again, we have an overall theme of the unity of both the masculine and feminine attributes of God. In the Song of Songs, the personification of wisdom is that of a black lady, the Black Shulamite, whose famous words resonate from its pages: "I am black and I am beautiful...." Much has been written through the years by theologians and scholars about this tradition of Wisdom of the Old Testament, of which the Song of Songs is but one example. Later, this Wisdom tradition was expounded on further by Gnostic commentators as well as Christian, Jewish, and Pagan philosophers. Russian Orthodox theologians have also written many works on this complex subject. Wisdom in Hebrew was defined as Chokmah, one of the 10 Sephirot on the Tree of Life. Bernard of Clairvaux was known to have attached much importance to safeguarding Jerusalem and to the concept of the heavenly Jerusalem, as we know, but he also found great inspiration in Song of Songs, the Hagia Sophia, Our Lady, and in the Wisdom tradition. His real goal, too, may well have been that of the spiritual Sion. (see **Bernard of Clairvaux; Black Madonnas**)

Sonnac, Guillaume de
The 17th Grand Master of the Order of the Temple, Guillaume de Sonnac served from 1247 to 1250. He was from Rouergue, Guyenne, France, and died on April 8, 1250, as he was attacked by the Saracens after the battle of Mansurah. His surname is sometimes also spelled as Senai in medieval archives. (see **Grand Master**; Appendix B)

Squire
Although not full knights in the Templar order, every knight-brother had his squire—an important role in the Order. Similar to the sergeant-brothers in the Order, squires, too, would wear a black or dark-brown mantle as opposed to the white mantle, which only the full knight-brothers were allowed to wear, as we know from the Rule. Horses were most essential for all the military orders, and especially for the Templars, who history has shown were very skilled at mounted warfare. Not only would the knight himself have to be ready for battle at any time, but his horses, armor, and equipment had to be well maintained. These were among the key duties of a squire and were absolutely essential. In battle, a knight's squire would go out ahead of him with the horse(s). When the Order was founded in the early 12th century, squires were not members of the Order at all, but outsiders hired for a set period. Only later was this policy changed. (see **Knight-brothers; Organization of the Templar order**)

Stained glass
For hundreds of years, visitors have marvelled at the extraordinary beauty and effect of medieval stained glass windows. Gothic architecture began in the 12th century with Abbot Suger, who, in his description of the ideal church, said he wanted to fill his Abbey Church of St. Denis, near Paris,

with "the most radiant windows." In short, *he wanted light*, and the more of it, the better. It has been commented on for centuries that when a visitor looks up at the stained glass windows in a Gothic cathedral, he or she often feels "pulled upwards," almost as to Heaven itself; the combination of the high nave and the stained glass windows creates this effect. The medieval designers of the cathedrals were well aware of this and valued the effects of light highly. Today, it is rather widely known that there are a number of frescoes with portrayals of Knights Templar on them at certain Templar sites, but there are also various images of Knights Templar in stained glass at certain locations; such as Lincoln Cathedral in England, or the Temple Grafton in Warwickshire. But although such windows feature the knights, it is important to recognize that the Knights Templar themselves did not create or design the windows, as is sometimes assumed.

Many today wonder why the Christian church has long emphasized stained glass windows and why certain symbols have long been enshrined in our memory through them. In contrast to the dark and somber Romanesque style that had gone before High Gothic design, Abbot Suger believed worshippers would feel uplifted and closer to God when surrounded by much light. From this one inspired wish, architects were inspired to provide the means—the now-famous "walls of glass" of the Gothic cathedrals. With the aid of the pointed arch and the flying buttresses, cathedral walls were strengthened to such a degree that spaces could be cut away for larger window casements, and thereby meet the terms of Gothic's prime directive—*more light*. The great height of Gothic construction came when the architect, stonemason, blacksmith, and glazier would all pool their resources together to create the luminous Rose windows of the era. Prime examples of these are the exquisite windows of Chartres Cathedral, for instance. But the technique was certainly well established in Europe by 1110–1130, when the monk Theophilus wrote his famous *Diversarium Artium Schedula*.

By the 12th century, complex techniques of stained glass manufacture had evolved, and this has remained rather constant, right up to the present day. As one might expect, religious figures from biblical stories were the focus on many of the subject matters of early stained glass windows. Some of the most stunning medieval cathedral stained glass is that of Chartres. To a medieval viewer of the stained glass windows, most of the themes, stories, and/or legends portrayed in the windows would have been second nature to them. Today, of course, we are far more unfamiliar with them, so the windows' narrative thread can easily be lost as we rely on a scene here or there to give us some sense of the story, rather than sense the whole. Following the narrative can also be difficult because medieval stained glass designers did not always arrange the sequences in a strict, logical order of events—for example, many windows start at the bottom and work their way through the narrative to the top—just the opposite of what one might expect today. Regrettably, most of us today have lost the ability to fully read the symbols and the stories displayed in the stained glass windows of cathedrals, or even their stone carvings, for that matter. In a sense, it is us who are now visually illiterate. It is we who have largely forgotten how important the world of *symbol* was in medieval times, as the emphasis in modern times has been almost exclusively on the written word. (see **Guilds, medieval**; **Geometry**; **Seven Liberal Arts**)

St. Mawr, Aymeric
(see **Magna Carta**)

Surcoat
Referred to in the Templar Rule, the surcoat was a piece of clothing that went over the body, similar to an overgarment. It was not identical to the mantles or tunics of the knight-brothers and sergeant-brothers in the Order.

Symbols
There were a number of symbols employed by the Templar order for various purposes, such as on its official seals, shields, gravestones, or as "graffiti" carvings on stone when they were imprisoned at Chinon or Domme. However, there was never any "one unified symbol" that represented the Order of the Temple throughout the entire life of the Order (1119–1312). But among those most commonly used were the symbol of the red cross, the black-and-white beauseant banner, as well as an image of two knights on one horse, which appears frequently on one side of the Grand Master's seals throughout the life of the Order. The Agnus Dei, the Lamb of God symbol, was an image that was frequently used by the Order in England and parts of France, and the dome of the Church of the Holy Sepulchre was also used on the Grand Master's seal a number of times. Other symbols used on the seals of the Order's provincial Masters include the star, doves, a lion, various crosses, the fleurs-de-lis, and a tower with a pointed roof and a cross, for example. Templar graves were

rarely adorned with much more than a sword; often, a cross with steps for its base would be used instead. A knight's name or the date of his birth or death were never carved on a Templar's gravestone, unlike what is often the norm today, as the Order itself took precedence over the individual's identity.

Example of the "Calvary step cross" symbol often found on Templar graves and dungeons

Photo courtesy of Simon Brighton

Rarely did the Knights Templar ever use the pentagram or a cup image in their preceptories, although the six-sided star is found among various other "Templar graffiti" symbols on the walls of the tower of Chinon Castle where the Templars were imprisoned. The Templars never used an image of the Shroud of Turin, the Ark of the Covenant, or a skull and crossbones image on their medieval period seals or carvings. A hand with a heart superimposed on its palm is found at Chinon and other sites, as well as a number of geometric grid patterns. Some Templar churches were round, incorporating a circular, and sometimes an octagonal symbolism, in them. But other orders and organizations, too, built round churches, so they were not unique only to the Knights Templar, as has been commonly assumed in the past.

But among the most interesting is the Gnostic symbol of Abraxas that is portrayed on a Templar Grand Master's seal in the Archives Nationales in Paris, which was used in a French charter in 1214, as pointed out by Sylvia Beamon in her research regarding the Royston Cave in England. This seal bears the words "Secretum Templi." Abraxas was also spelled as Abrasax in the early centuries A.D.; he was often known as Iao, a form of the Tetragrammaton, the letters used to represent the name of God in Judaism. He was sometimes referred to as Our Father and Lord of Hosts in some Gnostic writings. The Abraxas image, also called the Anguipede ("snake-foot")—the particular form used on this seal— portrays a male warrior with a rooster's head, human arms, and snakes as legs, who carries a shield and a "whip of Helios," identifying himself with the Bible's sun charioteer, Elias. On many Gnostic coins or gems the name Abraxas or Abrasax was often written below that of Yahweh or Jehovah. Experts maintain that Abraxas was also a common form of the Jewish Jehovah. It is seen, for example, on medallions of the second and first centuries B.C. Jesus called on Jehovah as his God in his last words on the cross, as reported by Matthew (27:46–49) and Mark (15:34–35).

Regarding its use on a Templar seal, it is unclear whether this image is merely decorative or whether it might in fact relate to the Order's treasury in some manner, as in ancient times, Abraxas gemstones were often used as magical protection devices in the Roman period, for in- stance. The symbol is also found on some medieval amulet stones, but this Abraxas figure is *not* the same as the 18th-century portrayals of what has been called Baphomet. Abraxas was the name of the god of the year in Greek Gnosticism, and scholars maintain that the word is probably comprised of the first letters of the Hebrew names for God. The seven letters of the name have a numerical value of 365. In spite of the Order's rather intriguing use of this Abraxas seal, however, this does not auto- matically mean that the entire Knights Templar order were Gnostics. On the contrary, they were never once accused of Gnosticism in their trial and there is no historical evidence to support such a conclusion. But given the vociferous nature of the inquisitional lines of questioning, as well as the use of torture, if they had had any evidence that the Templars were Gnostics, they would certainly have been charged as such.

There exists a great variety of Templar symbols from the medieval period, and not all of them have been found or cataloged to date. Clearly, as few definitive conclusions can be drawn, more detailed research needs to be undertaken in the future by archaeologists, art historians, and re- searchers to better clarify precisely what the symbols were, their proper context(s), where they were used, in what manner, and, if possible, what they may indicate. (see also **Seals**; **Agnus Dei**; **Red cross**; **Beauseant**)

Tancred

The earliest documentable contact between the Nizari Ismailis (dubbed "the Assassins") and the crusaders took place in September of 1106. Tancred, prince of Antioch, attacked the newly acquired Nizari castle of Apace outside of Aleppo. The Christians defeated the Nizaris. Tancred captured the new Syrian chief *dai*, Abu Tahir, "the Goldsmith," and forced him to ransom himself. In 1110, the Nizari Ismailis lost a second area of land to Tancred. Even so, in spite of this, the Syrian Assassins were able to expel crusader troops from various castles and strongholds, something that the Seljuk Turkish princes had been unable to do. Although technically before the time of the Templars, these early developments and conflicts involving the Nizaris set the stage for later situations that would directly affect the Knights Templar in their battles during the Crusades. (see also **Nizari Ismailis**; for further sources about the Crusades, see "Crusades and Military Orders" in the Recommended Reading section)

Temple (Balantradoch)

Often confused with nearby Rosslyn Chapel regarding medieval Templar connections, Balantradoch (now called Temple) was the genuine headquarters of the medieval Scottish Knights Templar order. The documentable history about the Order in Scotland shows that shortly after the first Templars returned from the Holy Land in the late autumn of 1127, Hugh de Payns and his colleagues visited a number of European kings and nobles to garner more tangible support for the new Order. David I, the king of Scotland in the 12th century, welcomed the new Templars and formed a Scottish headquarters for them, donating his lands at Balantradoch, a village about 4 miles from Roslin and 6 miles south of Edinburgh. The Balantradoch/Temple lands would have come under the jurisdiction of the Sheriff of Lothian, Sir William St. Clair, the fourth baron of Rosslyn. Unfortunately, none of the surnames of specific Templars in Scotland were written down for posterity.

A 12th-century Scottish version of the Latin Templar Rule still survives in the National Library of Scotland. Its title is *Regula Pauperum Commilitonum Christi Templique Salommonci,* and it was written by one Johannes Michaelensis, who describes himself as a resident of Albanensis. Alba was an earlier name for what is now called Scotland. The first historically documentable instance of the Knights Templar in Scotland appears in a charter in St. Andrews dated 1160, around the mid-12th century. Two of the witnesses listed on this charter are "Richard of the Hospital of Jerusalem" and "Robert, Brother of the Temple." The Hospitallers of the Order of St. John, were also introduced into Scotland at this time, again, primarily due to the support of David I. Historians note that it seems as though wherever the Hospitallers gained property in most major Scottish towns, the growth of the Templar order was also rather dramatic. Eventually, by around 1300 or so, more than 600 Templar properties were accounted for in the Order's holdings in Scotland alone. By 1312, when the Templar order had been suppressed internationally (although no Order of Suppression was legally issued in Scotland), the Order was essentially disbanded for all but administrative purposes. There is no historical evidence, however, that the Templars fought at the battle of Bannockburn, which has sometimes been alleged.

About one month after the official dissolution of the Templars in 1312, all the lands, preceptories, and other properties owned by the Templars in Scotland were to be transferred over to the Scottish Hospitallers. Unlike in some other countries, including England, Scotland's overall process of land transfer and assets, although amicable enough for the most part, seems to have taken much longer to finally resolve. With only one exception, there is no evidence of the Hospitallers attempting to obtain Templar property in Scotland, leading some to surmise that the Hospitallers worked together with the Templars in Scotland.

For a period of approximately 200 years, the Scottish Templar lands (*Terrae Templariae*) were maintained and administered by the Scottish Order of St. John (the Hospitallers), or, in some cases according to historical documents, by a *combined* Order called "the Order of St. John and the Temple." Properties were leased and a designated official acted as an overseer (the "Temple bailie") who also collected the rents. The "Temple bailie" would report back to the Prior of St. John at Torphichen.

*Balantradoch Church
ruins in graveyard
Photos courtesy of Alan
Glassman*

A charter of King James IV of Scotland, dated 1488, has the interesting title *Fratribus Hospitalis Hierosolimitani, Militibus Templi Solomonis.* In this charter, the king *reaffirmed* all the ancient rights and privileges of not only the Order of St. John but also the Templars. This may indicate that, as late as the 15th century, the Scottish Templars had some kind of legal existence. Obviously, the overall situation in Scotland was unique, as compared to the land transfer procedures operating in other countries at the time, so whatever occurred in Scotland after 1307, the year of the initial Templar arrests in France, there seems to have been a type of legal acknowledgement of the Templars up to the mid-16th century in Scotland. The two Scottish Templars who had been arrested and questioned after the suppression in 1312 were absolved and sent to Cistercian monasteries in the Borders. Many speculate that a number of other Templars in Scotland in 1307 must have either fled, or somehow disappeared from the public arena, yet no evidence has been found to confirm this. Clearly, much still remains unresolved about the details of medieval Templar history in Scotland. (see **Trial of the Templars**; Appendix E; for further sources, see "Trial of the Templars" in the Recommended Reading section)

Temple Bruer

Temple Bruer was an important Templar preceptory in south Lincolnshire, a key agricultural area for centuries. Comprising part of a huge Templar estate, the Preceptory de la Bruere, or the Heath, stood a little to the west of the old Roman highway in the area on Ermine Street. This area was quite remote and wild at the time of the Templars. The last English Grand Master, William de la More, was received into the Order at Temple Bruer. The foundation charter of 1150 shows an area described as "de terra vastate et brueria" on the plateau south of Lincolnshire. By 1185, after the Templars had

The cat-image carving, embedded into the altar area on Temple Bruer ground floor, Lincolnshire
Photo courtesy of Simon Brighton

come to the area, a village had grown up around their preceptory; the villagers were known to have paid the Knights Templar rents in money, hens, and produce. They also provided essential services for the Templars, such as cultivating the land, assisting with building, or tending the animals for the Order. As the wool trade was lucrative in late medieval times, this preceptory, too, had many flocks of sheep in particular. The original round church of the Templars is unfortunately no longer to be seen today, but, in 1726, it is known that the remains of the church and a round nave with a tower attached to it were still visible. But as is often the case when a hundred or so years have passed, only the tower is still left standing. This tower is 54 feet high and can still be seen today; it has a fascinating array of stone carvings and graffiti marks, some left by the medieval

Temple Bruer tower (front)
Photo courtesy of Eran Bauer

Templars at this site. Temple Bruer has been surveyed twice, in 1841 and also in 1901. Plans of the building during its many stages can be seen on the visitor display panels on the walls of the bottom floor interior of the tower, which illustrate how this rather haunting site has changed through time. Interestingly, Temple Bruer was also said to possess a portrait of the head of a man, similar to that at Templecombe in Somerset. There were said to have been four of them; it is not known what happened to this portrait. (see Appendix E)

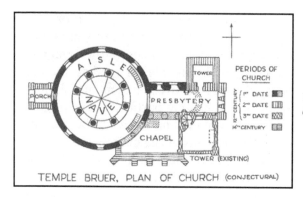

Temple Bruer floor plan
Courtesy of Eran Bauer

Temple Church (London)

Called New Temple in medieval times, the Temple Church in London was the headquarters of the English Knights Templar. Originally, the headquarters was based in the Holborn area circa 1128, at what is perhaps more familiar to us today as the site of the London Holburn tube station. Later, in 1161, the English Templar headquarters was transferred to the area now known as the Temple Bar area in London. One of the major Templar headquarters in all of western Europe in medieval times, the Temple Church was consecrated in 1185 in honor of the Blessed Virgin Mary on February 10, 1185, by Heraclius, the Patriarch of Jerusalem. King Henry II was also present at the consecration of Temple Church in 1185, so important was this event. Many Templar churches were round in design, similar to the Templar church here, in honor of the Church of the Holy Sepulchre in Jerusalem.

Temple Church, general view (London)
Photo courtesy of Eran Bauer

The effigies on the floor of the church generally commemorate patrons of the Knights Templar who are buried at Temple Church. For example, one prominent patron was William Marshal, earl of Pembroke (1174–1219), a friend of King John, who played a very important part in the negotiations for the Magna Carta in 1215. Ironically, few, if any, of these effigies are of actual Templar knights who went on Crusades, as is often assumed today; the effigies were placed in their present position largely during the restoration of the church in 1841.

Tomb of William Marshall, earl of Pembroke, who became a Templar on his deathbed; and his son, William
Photo courtesy of Simon Brighton

The Temple Church has a long and varied history. About 50 years after its consecration in 1185, the Templars faced much more challenging times. The Holy Land was recaptured by the Saracens, their extensive wealth made them a target of envious enemies, and, in 1307, at the instigation of Philip IV, king of France, with the collusion of the pope, the Templars were rounded up and arrested. Many historians today question a number of these charges and the extensive use of torture by representatives of the Inquisition. The final papal bull abolishing the Order took place in 1312. In England, King Edward II took control of the London Temple and its church. Eventually, he gave it to the Knights Hospitaller of St. John. King Henry III greatly favored the Templars, to the extent that he wished to be buried in their church. As a consequence of the king's wish, the choir of the church was pulled down and a far larger one built in its place, which is the choir that we see today. This was consecrated on Ascension Day in 1240 in the presence of Henry III. However, after Henry III died, it was discovered that he had changed his will, and instead he was buried in Westminster Abbey. At the time, the lawyers in London were looking for a home in order to attend the royal courts in Westminster, and the Temple was rented to two colleges of lawyers, who came to be identified as the Inner and Middle Temples, also referred to as the Inns of Court. These two colleges of lawyers shared use of the Temple church, and it became the college chapel of those two societies, which it still is today.

The 16th century brought with it many changes. During 1540, at the time of the Dissolution of the Monasteries by King Henry VIII, the Knights Hospitaller of St. John were also abolished and their property confiscated. The Temple again belonged to the Crown. King Henry VIII then provided a priest for the Temple Church, to whom he gave the title "Master of the Temple." In 1585, the second Master of the Temple, Richard Alvey, died. His deputy—the Reader, Walter Travers—expected to be promoted, but because of his extreme Calvinist views, this did not occur. Instead, a new Master, Richard Hooker, was appointed from Exeter College, Oxford, after which, one might say, matters became quite lively.

Each Sunday morning Hooker would preach his sermon, but each Sunday afternoon, Travers would contradict him with his Calvinist perspective. This tête-à-tête became known as the Battle of the Pulpit, with some saying that it seemed as though Canterbury was preached in the morning and Geneva in the afternoon! As a result of this rather epic battle with Walter Travers over a period of time, Richard Hooker then became recognized as the founding father of Anglican theology. By the close of the 16th century, the two Inns of Court had erected many fine buildings at the Temple, yet their position as tenants was not terribly secure. Understandably, in order to protect what they had already built up from any future whims of the Crown, they petitioned King James I for a more satisfactory arrangement. The result of this came on August 13, 1608, when the king granted them a Royal Charter giving them use of the Temple in perpetuity. But in modern-day parlance, there was one "hitch"— the two Inns of Court were also required to maintain the Temple Church in perpetuity, which were quite reasonable terms overall. In gratitude,

Outer courtyard view, Temple Church, London
Photo courtesy Simon Brighton

Outside view Temple Church, London
Photo courtesy of Simon Brighton

the Inns gave King James I a gold cup, which was later sold in Holland when his son, Charles I, needed more funds to keep his army in the field. This gold cup has now disappeared. So, the Temple and Temple Church are still governed by this original Royal Charter of King James I today. Temple Church was restored again in Victorian times.

In 1841, it was carefully restored by Smirke and Burton, being decorated in the high Victorian Gothic style. The idea was to bring Temple

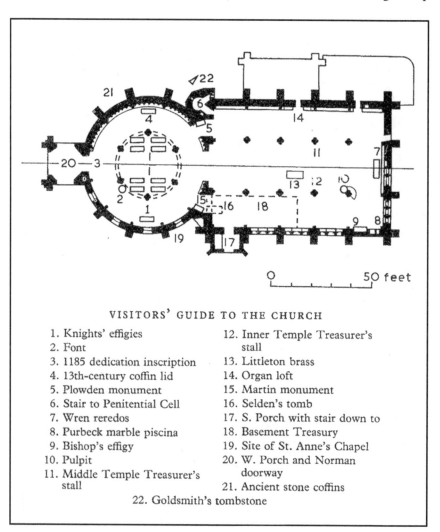

VISITORS' GUIDE TO THE CHURCH

1. Knights' effigies
2. Font
3. 1185 dedication inscription
4. 13th-century coffin lid
5. Plowden monument
6. Stair to Penitential Cell
7. Wren reredos
8. Purbeck marble piscina
9. Bishop's effigy
10. Pulpit
11. Middle Temple Treasurer's stall
12. Inner Temple Treasurer's stall
13. Littleton brass
14. Organ loft
15. Martin monument
16. Selden's tomb
17. S. Porch with stair down to
18. Basement Treasury
19. Site of St. Anne's Chapel
20. W. Porch and Norman doorway
21. Ancient stone coffins
22. Goldsmith's tombstone

Floor plan, Temple Church, London
Courtesy of Eran Bauer

Church back to its original appearance, but, unfortunately, nothing of this fine work remains today, as it was destroyed by fire bombs exactly 100 years after its completion, in 1941. After the 1841 Victorian restoration, a choir of men and boys was introduced for the first time, which became known as one of the finest choirs in London. In 1923, for example, Dr. G.T. Thalben-Ball was appointed organist and choirmaster, later becoming world-renowned, especially for the record made in 1927 of Mendelssohn's *Hear My Prayer* (by Thalben-Ball and the boy soloist Ernest Lough), which brought many visitors to the church from all over the world. This tradition of high quality music is still maintained today. In 1941, on the evening of May 10, air raids on London caused serious damage to Temple Church and the surrounding area. Restoration took a long time to complete, with the choir being the first area of the church to be rededicated in March 1954. The round church was rededicated in November 1958. But what may be one of the most notable features in the church today, the east window, was a gift from the Glaziers' Company in 1954 to replace the window that was destroyed in the war. It was designed by Carl Edwards and illustrates Jesus' connection with the Temple at Jerusalem.

The east window not only depicts scenes of Jesus' connection with the Temple at Jerusalem, but also features personalities associated with Temple Church over the centuries, most notably King Henry II, King Henry III, and several of the medieval Masters of the Temple. In one panel of this famous window, we see an image of Jesus talking with the learned teachers there, and in another, an image of him driving out the money-changers. Since its restoration in 1954, Temple church has resumed its role as the chapel and spiritual home of the Inner and

Statue outside the Temple Church, London, commemorating the Knights Templar
Photo courtesy of Simon Brighton

Middle Temples. Each Sunday morning, except August and September when the Law Courts are not in session, its world-renowned choir sings the morning service, either Matins or Holy Communion. It also still continues to attract many visitors from around the world, most recently it was a key part of a Hollywood film set for *The Da Vinci Code* in May of 2006. Outside the church, there is a monument commemmorating the Knights Templar, showing two knights on one horse. Yet, the full history and legacy of this important church, especially as it relates to the Knights Templar, still resonates on the site today, as many visitors attest to. (see Appendix E)

Temple Balsall

Temple Balsall is a remote village in the middle of the old Forest of Arden, southeast of Solihull. The name Balsall comes from an Anglo-Saxon word meaning watery pastures. It was spelled *Belesale* in the 1185 survey, and was gifted to the Templars in 1146 by Roger de Mowbray, a major patron who also went on three crusades himself, having been captured by the Turks on his last, when he was more than 65 years of age. The Templars ransomed him, but he died soon after this and was buried in Palestine. Temple Balsall had become an English Templar preceptory by 1226, and was the major headquarters for other Templar lands in Warwickshire—namely, those of Cubbinton, Harbury, Tysoe, Wolvey, Studley, Warwick, Chilver-scoton, Sherbourne, Fletchamstead, Temple Herdewicke, and others. It was quite a large complex, with domestic buildings including the Hall, the Preceptor's room built onto it, a pantry, buttery, kitchen, larder, bakehouse, brewhouse, and a dovecote. On the whole, Temple Balsall seems to have been a favorite place for the reception of new members into the Order for novice Templars in England. By 1312, the time of the papal bull that suppressed the Order, the lands of Temple Balsall had gone to the Knights Hospitaller. Few records have survived of their time of possession. The surviving Old Hall we can now see at Temple Balsall has an 18th century exterior, but the internal timbers are original, dated around 1180. The last church that the Knights Templar built in England is next door, called St. Mary's Church; it became a parish church in 1863. A panel in the stained glass east window shows a Templar Knight in armor and mantle, keeping watch over today's congregation. In the church at nearby Temple Grafton, Warwickshire, there is also a stained glass window featuring a Knight Templar. (see **Stained glass**; Appendix E)

Stained glass windows, Temple Grafton, showing Templars and Hospitallers protecting pilgrims and caring for the sick
Photo courtesy of Simon Brighton

Templecombe

Templecombe was the only Preceptory of the Knights Templar in Somerset and remains as an important Templar site to visit in the West Country area of England today. In 1185, the manor at this site was originally owned by Serlo Fitz Odo, and was then given to the Knights Templar order. After the arrests of the Templars in 1307, the lands were turned over to the Knights Hospitaller of St. John of Jerusalem. A 1338 inventory of the site shows 368 acres belonging to the manor. The Templar Preceptor was responsible for managing the Templar estates in the West Country, admitting new members to the Order, and training men and horses for service in the Crusades. Sadly, very little now remains of the original Templar Preceptory, as is often the case with medieval sites. But the major Templar-related site to see at Templecombe today is St. Mary's Church.

Templecombe village was once two different parishes—Temple Combe and Abbas Combe—which are now combined at the time of the Domesday records, the Vill of Combe was shared by the Benedictine Nunnery of Shaftesbury, which had been founded in A.D. 888 by Alfred the Great. His second daughter, Ethelgeda, was the first abbess at Shaftesbury Abbey, the major convent in England at the time. St. Mary's Church is believed to have been founded around this time, as its parent house was Shaftesbury. For many centuries, Shaftesbury Abbey had the right to appoint clergy at Templecombe. In 1539, during the time of the Dissolution of the Monasteries by King Henry VIII, it passed to Richard Duke, Esq., who held the manor.

St. Mary's Church, Templecombe, Somerset
Photo courtesy of Simon Brighton

In the existing church today, however, only the tower, the nave roof, and transept with piscina and font are genuinely old; the Normon font in Purbeck marble is one of the earliest features. Unfortunately, during World War II, four bombs were dropped by the Germans on the southern side of the church, which caused extensive damage to the roof, tower, and arches in the nave. But the most intriguing feature to be seen in the church today is a rather enigmatic panel painting of the head of an unidentified man. This painting, long believed by many to be a possible portrayal of the head of Jesus, was discovered in the outhouse of a cottage in West Court, off the High Street in Templecombe in 1945. The owner of the cottage is recorded as Mrs. A. Topp, but it was her tenant, Mrs. Drew, who actually discovered the painting. She happened to look up at the ceiling when inside the shed collecting wood for her fire and saw the strange image above. The painting had apparently been very carefully tied by wire into the roof and totally concealed by plaster. Some of the plaster had fallen away and revealed a face looking down. Naturally, she informed the rector, who took the painting away for proper cleaning and restoration. The painting was presented to St. Mary's Church in 1956, and has hung on the South Wall of the church ever since. However, no expert consensus has been reached about precisely who the depiction represents; the key hole and hinge marks on the panel suggest that it may possibly have been used as a door at some time. This life-size painting, medieval in style, was carbon-dated at A.D. 1280. The painting may have a possible connection with the Knights Templar, as it has been suggested that during the Crusades, they obtained the prized possession of the Holy Shroud, brought it back to Europe, and from it, copied their paintings. However, upon closer examination, this particular painting and its features do not match those of the Shroud of Turin, or any other artifact that has been found to date in any Templar properties that is similar. This has led some to believe that it is a portrayal of a man who may have still been alive and well, in other words, not crucified or deceased as had previously been assumed. But as others speculate, the painting may instead be a copy of the Mandylion of the Eastern Orthodox Church, also an important relic of Christendom.

Enigmatic panel painting, identity of subject unknown at present, Templecombe
Photo courtesy of Simon Brighton

The Shroud of Turin is a 14-foot length of linen bearing a full-length body, and not merely only the head, as this particular painting features. The Mandylion is generally believed to be a (now) lost cloth that bore *only the image of the face* of Christ that was apparently made when he was alive and well, not deceased, similar to the Shroud of Turin. Similarly, the Templecombe painting also bears only the image of a head, and not a full-bodied man, as with the Shroud of Turin. However, there is no concrete historical evidence that the Templars ever had the Mandylion, so, again, the image on this painting remains an enigma today. Professional art historians and restorers have studied the painting and have not come to any definitive conclusions about the identity of the man in question. Interestingly, as some point out, although the top portion of the panel is missing, the Templecombe painting does not appear to have included a halo. (see **Relics**; Appendix E)

Temple Ewell

The Templar preceptory at Temple Ewell was founded sometime before 1164. The Templars acquired the manor in 1163 and replaced the wooden Saxon church with a Norman stone building. It was given to them by William, the brother of King Henry II and Wm. De Peverell, Constable of Dover Castle. A survey of 1185 reveals a sizable estate of more than 300 acres. Matthew Paris, the medieval chronicler of St. Albans Abbey, commented that King John made his submission to the Papal Legate, Pandulph, on May 15, 1213, "in the house of the Templars near Dover," which may have been Temple Ewell, or, perhaps, in the ancient Round Church nearby, a Templar church, on the Western Heights. It is known that Ralph de Malton was the Preceptor here in 1309 and that Robert de Sautre was a Brother at Temple Ewell, but not much else is known for certain about the history prior to this. Unfortunately, there are no remains of the buildings above ground level, but an important excavation was done between 1864 and 1866, in which some medieval floor tiles and iron objects were unearthed. After the suppression of the Templars by papal authority in 1312, the Knights Hospitaller took over the manor at Temple Ewell. The Hospitallers also made some improvements to Temple Ewell church, which lasted until the major renovations of 1874. Remnants of the Temple Ewell preceptory remained above ground until 1740. (see Appendix E)

Temple Garway

Temple Garway was an important preceptory on the River Monnow, in the Welsh borders, located south of Hereford. Garway was originally a Welsh-speaking area called Llangarewi that later became English speaking. Temple Garway was founded by the Knights Templar around 1186, but the exact date is not known for certain; however, records show that King Richard I confirmed Templar ownership of Temple Garway in 1189 in honor of his father. St. Michael's Church is the oldest building in Garway village, having consistently served the Christian community for at least nine centuries. There have been at least three major building phases here:

Foundations of a round church at St. Michael's Church, Garway, Herefordshire
Photo courtesy of Simon Brighton

St. Michael's from the north, Garway
Photo courtesy of Simon Brighton

✦ 203

the earliest timber church, of which all traces have been lost; the Templar phase of the latter 12th century, and, following the suppression of the Templar order in 1312, later alterations were made by the Knights Hospitaller; and finally, after the Reformation, further additional modifications were made. So the church that stands on this site today is the product of many changes over time.

The medieval Templars built their round church here, and the ruins of its foundations can still be seen today. As with many modified medieval period churches, some of the original stones from the earlier Templar church were included in the mortar of the existing building; a number of interesting symbols are present on the outside of the church that are Templar-related, such as crosses, runic-like inscriptions, and so on. There are a number of symbols here relating to various traditions; those of particular Templar interest are to be found near the west door of the chapel, where the Lamb of God symbol, the Agnus Dei, can be seen rather high up on the wall, and those in what has been dubbed the "Templars' chapel" area, which can be found near the south chapel of the church. This area is of a 12th century date and existed during part of the time of the Templar order. Although it is probable that the carvings in this area may have been done by the medieval Templars, as there was

Green Man image, Garway
Photo courtesy of Simon Brighton

also an earlier church on the site before it was given to the Templars, there is actually no direct evidence to say for certain. However, as many have noted, it is quite intriguing to note the following symbols above the piscina in the south chapel: a fish, a serpent (some say an eel), a chalice, and a host. To the right above the west door are worn symbols of the Crucifixion that are also found in a number of medieval chapels, including the three nails, the Tau cross, a crown, a spear, a sponge on a reed, and a sword. Throughout the church, there are also some grave slabs that have been incorporated into the building, some Templar, some not. One of the grotesque capital images of the Norman chevron chancel arch (dated 1175–1180) is an image of what appears to be a "green man" with horns or pointed ears, or, what others insist is a "green cat" image, with foliage coming out of its mouth.

A dovecote tower also is present on the site, as is Church House Farm. In 1294, Jacques de Molay visited Temple Garway. Originally, its preceptory, living quarters, church, water mill, and other buildings—were part of the Templars' much larger 200 acres at this key agricultural site by 1308. Administratively, Templar Garway's influence extended as far as south Wales. After the arrests of the Templars here in 1308, and following the suppression of the Order by papal bull in 1312, Temple Garway was eventually turned over to the Hospitallers, who arrived in 1326. (see Appendix E)

Temple Rothley

Temple Rothley, an English Templar preceptory, stood between Leicester and Loughborough. The Templars already had land at Rothley by 1203, and they were given other lands in the area later. It is believed that the Templar preceptory was established about 1231, when Henry III granted the manor and Rothley church to the Templars. Later, the preceptory came to include lands in 13 neighboring areas, several mills, large pastures for sheep grazing, and five dependent chapels. Today, the site of the original preceptory is occupied by the Rothley Court Hotel; there is nothing left of the manor house at all. After 1231, history shows that Rothley Temple became a more major center of Templar activity, with estates from Ashby Folville to Wymondham in Norfolk. In 1285, Edward I gave the Templars the right

Interior of Rothley (Templar) Chapel, at north end of Rothley Court Hotel, Leicestershire
Photo courtesy of Simon Brighton

to hold their weekly market in Rothley village, and permission for an annual fair in honor of St. Barnabas. The original 13th century Templar Chapel at Rothley is certainly well worth a visit today. (see Appendix E)

Templar Chapel, Rothley,
Leicestershire
Photo courtesy of Simon Brighton

A later depiction of Knight Templar,
Rothley, Leicestershire
Photo courtesy of Simon Brighton

Teutonic Knights, Order of

Founded in 1190 and approved by the pope in 1199, the Teutonic knights were officially known as the Order of the Hospital of St. Mary of the Teutons of Jerusalem. They were organized to serve a hospital near Acre that was established by Germans from Bremen and Lubeck. It became a military Order in 1198; in 1230, it was asked by Duke Corrado of Masovia to fight against the pagan Prussians, in return for power over the regions subjugated. After the fall of Acre in 1201, the Order transferred its head-quarters to Venice, and then, in 1309, to Marienburg. Two distinct traditions within the order developed: one in Prussia and the other in Livonia. The Teutonic knights had numerous conflicts with not only Prussia, but also many of their neighbors as well, including Christians. In 1410, at the battle of Tanneburg, the Teutonic knights were defeated, and, by 1457, had lost almost all of their Prussian territory. They then moved their headquarters to Konigsberg; after this time, many of the knights became Protestants, with at least one of its Grand Masters becoming a Lutheran. The Order continued until 1923; today, it still exists as a religious order. The Templars were not particularily numerous in certain eastern European areas in the north until the earlier part of the 13th century; they did have some commandaries in Germany by the late 12th century, but not as many as in other areas. (see "Crusades and the Military Orders" in the Recommended Reading section)

Thomas of Acre, Order of St.
Founded in 1192 by King Richard I ("the Lionheart"), the Order of St. Thomas of Acre was organized as a house of canons to care for the sick. After the crusaders attacked Acre from 1189 to 1191, the chaplain of St. Paul's in England began to minister to the sick and wounded. After the capture of Acre, he built a small chapel funded by Richard I and founded a hospital for the care of Englishmen. Later, in the 1220s, it was transformed into a military order by Peter des Roches, bishop of Winchester. It adopted the rule of the Teutonic knights and received papal recognition in 1236, a key moment in its history. It was not a large or wealthy order such as the Knights Templar, although Templar members knew some of the members of this order following the fall of Acre in 1291. After that date, many orders, including the Templars, Hospitallers, and this one as well, fled to Cyprus. Gradually, the focus of the Order of St. Thomas of Acre shifted to London, where it established a school in the 16th century. It was dissolved at the Reformation. (see **Acre**; **Richard I ("the Lionheart")**; for futher sources about this and other orders in the crusades, see "Crusades and Military Orders" in the Recommended Reading section)

Tomar
This was the location of the headquarters of the Portuguese Knights Templar, and later, after the suppression of the Order of the Temple in 1312, of the Order of Christ. (see **Order of Christ**; **Trial of the Templars, summary of**)

Torroge, Arnaud de
The ninth Grand Master of the Order of the Temple, Arnaud de Torroge served from 1181 to 1184. Before he became Grand Master, he had served as the Templar Master in Aragon. His surname is sometimes also spelled

as Torroje. (see **Grand Master**; **Organization of the Templar order**; **Aragon**; Appendix B)

Tower of London

In addition to being one of the most fascinating historical sites to visit in London today, the Tower of London was also one of the key prisons in England where the medieval English Templars were held and interrogated. In London, Templars were also interrogated next door, on what is now known as the site of All Hallows Church, where they had an association with the earlier medieval church of St. Mary. (see **All Hallows by the Tower Church**; **Trial of the Templars, summary of**; Appendix E)

Treasuries, Templar

The Templars were known to have had tremendous stores of gold, silver, land deeds, gems, relics, and other valuables in their treasuries, a subject about which there has been a lot misconception and even wild speculation at times. They were indeed powerful in the financial sphere and lent great sums of money, not only to kings, but also to popes and prominent merchants. The headquarters of the Order was in the Holy Land, with the Commander of the Kingdom of Jerusalem being responsible for the treasury, among other duties; but, of course, every major Templar commandary would have its own valuables to store for safekeeping as well. For the most part, larger cities would have larger treasuries, such as Paris, but nearly all medieval contemporaries agree that the Knights Templar treasuries were by far the safest place to store one's money and valuables in, as the Templars were known to be extremely trustworthy and had a very good reputation regarding monetary affairs. A number of experts believe that some of the Templar business methods may well have been prototypes for some of our modern-day banking practices.

The Templars further refined the concept of a letter of credit, for instance. This was for a good reason, given how dangerous travel was in the 12th century. Bandits occupied every forest, even controlling many towns and villages. Tales of ambushes, even murders, of pilgrims abounded. It was frightening enough to get safely from one part of Europe to another safely, let alone consider transporting large amounts of money or traveling on further to the Holy Land to see the Christian pilgrimage sites, such as the Holy Sepulchre in Jerusalem. So, the Templars attempted to solve this problem for Christian pilgrims, crusaders, and others, as they already had a number of existing commandaries in nearly every major region. For example, if a merchant from England or France wanted to undertake a journey to the Holy Land or Rome, he would simply deposit a prescribed sum of money with the Templars in his own town before his departure, and, in exchange for the money, the Templars would give him a promissory note written in cipher—an item that would have been of no use at all to a potential robber. The traveler would then go on to Rome, unencumbered by the cash. Once he arrived, he would immediately go to the Templar headquarters in Rome, and on production of the note written in cipher and proof of his identity, he would be given his money in the local currency minus a small handling fee. Given the highly dangerous circumstances of travel in medieval times, his fee was certainly a good investment in terms of insurance for the safe arrival of the money. The handling fee was not interest, however, as the medieval Church strictly forbade the practice of usury.

Understandably, Templar policy was very strict about access to the treasury strong room(s); for example, in the Hierarchical Statutes of the Rule, section 81 states that even the Master himself could not hold the lock or key to the treasury on his own; section 83 says that when assets came to the Order from overseas, that is, to the Holy Land from the West, they should be immediately placed in the treasury by order of the Commander of the Kingdom of Jerusalem, and that no one may take or remove any of it until the Master has seen them and given his permission. The seal to the treasury was kept locked by three keys, for the Master and two other officials only. (see **Assets**; **Loans**; **Safe deposit**; **Seal**; **Commander, Templar office of**; for further sources about the assets of the Order, see "Assets" in the Recommended Reading section)

Tremelay, Bernard de
Originally from Burgundy, Bernard de Tremelay was the fourth Grand Master of the Order of the Temple; he served in the year 1153. (see **Grand Master**; Appendix B)

Trial of the Templars, summary of
The trial of the Templars is a very complex matter. Briefly, historical documents show that on September 14, 1307, the French king Philip IV's secret orders to his *baillis* and *senechaux*—his law enforcement authorities—were issued, instructing them to prepare for sudden dawn raids on every Templar they could find in France. The charges listed were horrific, even by medieval standards, and would result in one of the most notorious

trials in the history of Western civilization. Ironically, the king's order began with the now-famous words: "A bitter thing, a lamentable thing, a thing which is horrible to contemplate, terrible to hear of, a detestable crime." The trial of the Templars was not a single event, as has sometimes been assumed; in fact, it occurred as a series of councils held between the 1307 arrests and the burning of the last Templar Grand Master, Jacques de Molay, in March of 1314. History records that on September 22, the inquisitor-general of France, the Dominican friar Guillaume de Paris, wrote to the inquisitors in Toulouse and Carcassone, initially listing various alleged crimes by the Templars. He confidentially informed them of the coming arrests of the Templars and told them to get ready to collect the necessary depositions and evidence against the Templars. Though historians acknowledge that the French king and the pope had discussed the arrests of the French Templars in general, incredibly, it seems that the pope himself was apparently not directly informed about the actual arrests on that fateful day, October 13, 1307. In fact, the pope declared in one of his letters in 1308 that the king did not go forward with the October arrests of the Templars "through letters of the Pope," in other words, he had not been consulted about them. The prosecutors of the French king were never able to claim unequivocally that the pope himself had authorized the arrests on October 13, 1307, so initially at least, the 1307 arrests of the French Templars seem largely to have been at the instigation of King Philippe IV. Of course, this day—Friday the 13th, unlucky for some—has gone down in history and folklore as one of the most notorious dates of all to remember, perhaps reminiscent of the arrests of the Knights Templar.

Historians know that King Philippe was certainly envious of the Order's power and wealth, as were many others, but the entire matter of his many specific individual motivations is complex and research is still ongoing in these areas as more documents are translated by scholars. But it is interesting to note that the day before the Templars were imprisoned—the 12th of October—the Templar Grand Master, Jacques de Molay, had been honored as one of the pallbearers at the funeral of King Philippe's sister-in-law. It seems that he had been lured there and badly deceived, for the very next day he, along with every Templar that could be found in France, was shocked to find himself in prison. Clement V estimated there were about 2,000 Templars in France at the time, but this number included everyone from full knights to servants. On the 14th, the day after the arrests, the learned theologians of the University of Paris and the cathedral canons met at Notre Dame Cathedral in Paris, where the king's chief prosecutor Nogaret and others spoke to them regarding the events. On the 15th, the French public was invited to come to the garden of the royal palace, where they were to be addressed by the king's men and the inquisitors. Also at this time, all over France other local town meetings were held about the sudden arrests of the Knights Templar, as the knights were still quite popular with the public. These meetings served much the same purpose to help mold or shape public opinion as newspapers, television, or the Internet do today. There was much talk about the arrests and horrific charges. Many members of the public simply found it very hard, if not impossible, to believe that the Knights Templar could ever be guilty of such lurid crimes. After all, they had fought and won so many decisive battles for Christendom in the Crusades.

After this country-wide effort of influencing public opinion, King Philippe then sent letters to all the kings and princes of Christendom, attempting to elaborate on his views about the Templars' arrests and trying to enlist their support against the Templars in their own countries. Perhaps not all that surprisingly, as the charges seemed so unbelievable, his requests were largely rebuffed by other monarchs—in fact, a number simply did not believe him at first. Edward II of England and James II of Aragon, for example, refused to immediately arrest the Templars and even wrote letters to other kings and to the pope in defense of the Order. Meanwhile, grueling interrogations of the Templars in France began. The king's orders said that the Templars were to be terrorized by threats and torture even prior to their official appearance before the Inquisition. A number of the elderly Templars had not been fighting in the Holy Land, but simply had been working the land in their agricultural pursuits, and so on, and still found themselves in this traumatic, lonely situation in prison. Understandably, the younger knights could hold out somewhat longer in prison, due to their greater physical strength. Torture was the legal and accepted method of conducting interrogations, and the Inquisition exerted its brutality, convinced of its divine mission. The Templars were doomed from the start, it seems.

The aim of a medieval heresy trial was not to find out the truth, as we think of a trial today; instead, the emphasis was on proving the charges. One of the main types of torture was the notorious rack; there was also torture by fire, mainly by smearing fat on the soles of the feet and holding them up to flames. One unbelievable—but factual—account of this method comes from when a Templar priest's bones simply dropped out of his feet several days after enduring torture by fire. He then brought his bones to his hearing before the papal commission. Of course, the usual kinds of psychological tortures were also regularly inflicted, in addition to starvation or lack of water, and many Templars simply died in prison. But on October 24, 1307, the remaining imprisoned Templars heard the unbelievable news that their Grand Master Jacques de Molay had apparently admitted the Order's crimes to a prestigious assembly of legal scholars at the University of Paris. De Molay was an elderly man by 1307, and records from the trial hearings indicate that he often appeared quite confused and worn down by the pressure of his interrogations and of being imprisoned. Making matters worse, the day after de Molay confessed, 30 more leaders and other Templars did the same. Many historians maintain that nearly all of them were no doubt completely broken by torture and/or the pressures of the interrogations.

By early November, Hugh de Pairaud, Visitor of the Order and second-in-command to de Molay, also confessed, adding to the demoralization of the remaining imprisoned Templars. Most historians agree that torture was probably used. In all, 138 depositions survive from the interrogations held in Paris in the autumn of 1307. But as the interrogation press continued, the French king needed Pope Clement's power to legitimize his actions, as the Templar order was ultimately accountable only to the pope under papal jurisdiction. The pope wrote a rather angry reply to King Philippe for interfering with Church affairs, but as he was also greatly pressured from the French king on a number of fronts, Clement V finally succumbed, issuing a bull requiring the kings of England, Ireland, Castile, Aragon, Portugal, Italy, Germany, and Cyprus to arrest the Templars within their borders, *but* to do so in the name of the pope. He had been greatly offended by Philip's disregard for papal opinion, and though he could not reverse the king's action, he wanted to emphasize his own higher authority, which he seems to have valued over the fate of the Templars.

Historians surmise that the king no doubt would have preferred the trial of the Templars to conclude rather quickly, but when Clement intervened with his letter admonishing him regarding the proper procedures, it delayed the entire saga for years. Notably, the charges of heresy only affected the Templar brothers; the sisters, associates, and servants of the Order were not asked to testify at all in France, even though they could have given good, eyewitness accounts of what had gone on in the Order's houses. The investigators did not want their testimony. Very little third-party evidence was heard during the French trial; in other places, such as England or Cyprus, third party testimony was allowed and, tellingly, in those areas the general conclusion was that the initial charges were false. Gradually, as the years and hearings wore on, and due to much papal pressure for their souls, the kings in other countries finally arrested the Templars, but in some instances this took some time to occur. Indeed, it took seven years from the arrests until Jacques de Molay and his treasurer, Geoffrey de Charney, were burned at the stake in Paris in 1314.

But the final end of the Order became imminent on March 22, 1311, when a secret consistory of the Council of Vienne was convened—an important church council where the French king was also present. Pope Clement presented his bull *Vox in excelso* to the assembled cardinals and prelates. The Order itself was declared not guilty as the charges were unproven. Clement argued that by that time, after some seven years of hearings, the Templar order had been so badly defamed in the minds of the public and with other monarchs that it could no longer properly defend Christendom nor hope to gain good recruits in the future. Then, in early April 1311, the Pope read out the bull in public, and the dissolution of the Order was finally accomplished—ironically, an event that many a Saracen army had long hoped for. On June 5, 1311, the papal commission presented its findings to King Philippe IV, and a complete record of the hearings was prepared for the pope. The commission concluded that the case against the Order was unproven. That is, *the Order itself had not been found guilty.* But the question of the guilt or innocence *of individuals* was a different matter. At the Council of Vienne in October 1311, a number of the Church fathers supported the idea that the Templars should be allowed to make a defense of the Order as a whole. This infuriated both King Philip and Pope Clement, who wanted to wrap up the proceedings. Notably, none of the invited European royalty came and one-third of the invited clergy did not attend. Clement's main concern at this juncture seems to have been how to divide up the extensive Templar property, rather than how to defend the Order per se.

By May of 1312, another important bull in Templar history, the *Ad providam*, was issued by the pope, which decreed that all of the Templar properties, archives, and other assets be turned over to the Hospitallers. Four officials of the Order, along with other Templars, had been imprisoned from the time of the suppression in 1312. On March 8, 1314, these four officials were brought before a small group of French cardinals and theologians in Paris for a decree about their fate. This council condemned the four to perpetual imprisonment, assuming that this would largely end the entire matter; but they were wrong. In an extraordinary moment that astounded those present, Grand Master Jacques de Molay, and Geoffrey de Charney, his treasurer, bravely denied all confessions of guilt and defended the innocence and holiness of the Order. At this meeting, he was then called a relapsed heretic (another serious charge), as he had recanted his earlier confession. De Molay stated as part of his speech: "Before heaven and earth and with all of you here as my witnesses…I declare, and I must declare, that the Order is innocent. Its purity and saintliness is beyond question." Stunned and disturbed by this unexpected drama, the churchmen turned the two men over to the French authorities. King Philip then immediately had them both burned at the stake, without consulting with the pope. This final event took place on a small island in the middle of the Seine River opposite the royal gardens on March 18, 1314. One of the greatest ironies in Templar history is that the very knights who had fought so hard and won so many battles for Christendom, were later defeated and suppressed for complex reasons by their own church via the pope and the French king, an event that many a Saracen would have gladly welcomed. Perhaps as we now—in 2007— acknowledge the 700 year anniversary of the initial arrests of the Knights Templar in October of 1307, we can at least keep the spirit of their courage in the face of all obstacles alive for future generations. (see **de Molay, Jacques**; **Trial, aftermath of**; **Heresy**; **Charges**; **Philippe IV**; **Clement V**; and for further sources about the many issues pertaining to the trial, see "Trial of the Templars" in the Recommended Reading section)

Trial of the Templars, aftermath of

The papal bull *Ad providam Christi Vicarii*, issued on May 2, 1312, declared that because property owned by the Knights Templar had originally been donated for sustaining the crusading effort in the Holy Land, it should continue to be used for that purpose. So, all property and lands were to be transferred to the Order of the Hospital of St. John. The only exceptions were the Templar properties in Portugal, Castille, and Majorca, which were to be transferred to local crusading orders. This sounds simple enough, but in some cases these arrangements took quite some time to carry out. Templar knights who were still in custody would be allowed to live on what had been Templar properties, and those who had been absolved and reconciled to the Church were to be treated fairly and even given pensions. Many ended up joining other monastic communities, such as the Cistercians. Historians acknowledge that the worst fate meted out to the Templars had occurred in France. But contrary to popular belief, not all Templars were tortured in prison or burned at the stake. In fact, a number survived, although they had languished in various prisons all over Europe from 1307 until the time of the suppression; but the majority of Templars in prison were freed after 1312, after which they either were pensioned off or joined other orders. Yet, the situation for Templars after the 1307 arrests and the 1312 suppression of the Order was often quite different in countries other than France. Not surprisingly, where torture was used, the prisoners often confessed to the most charges. In places where no torture was allowed, they would be found innocent; this pattern appeared in nearly every country. Although unanswered questions remain about if, when, where, or how the medieval Templars may have survived, historians do have more information now than at any other time. Many theories exist about where the Templars may have fled to and/or what may have happened to their assets.

The Iberian Peninsula
(Aragon, Majorca, Castile, and Portugal)

As compared to the treatment of the Templars in France, on the Iberian peninsula it was less severe. After 1307, the Templars in Aragon took refuge in their castles and appealed to the Aragonese king and the pope, declaring their innocence. James II of Aragon strongly defended the Templars. He wrote to the pope and to the kings of neighboring Castille and Portugal himself, declaring that as his predecessors had believed the Order was without error and had always labored for the exaltation of the faith, he wanted more information before he took any action. He held out against the tremendous pressure exerted by the French king until late November 1307, when he finally ordered the arrest of the knights in his domain. Historians believe that he was most likely trying to appear to cooperate with Philip. He had the Templar castles attacked, but the Templars in Aragon put up a good defense, and the last Templar castle did not surrender until 1309. The Templars were imprisoned in Aragon but as little torture was used due to Aragonese law, none of the brothers confessed to any charges. Perhaps not surprisingly, when the French king and the pope heard about this, they were not at all pleased. The papal inquiry in Aragon didn't start until January of 1310, and although it is known that some torture was used in 1311 on eight Templars in Barcelona (on orders from the pope), still none of them confessed to any of the charges. The Templars were found innocent in Aragon and in 1312, the Church council at Tarragona released them all and gave them pensions.

Majorca was closely associated with the Aragonese crown, and apparently King James I of Majorca did not resist papal authority to nearly the extent that James II of Aragon did. Here, the Templars were arrested fairly soon after the November 22nd, 1307 orders they received in this region. In the kingdom of Castile-Leon, historians know that the Templars were arrested sometime during 1308, as two commissions were set up in August of that year. At Medina del Campo, the archbishop of Compostela questioned 30 Templars and three witnesses, but found nothing incriminating, as no confessions were made. After their acquittal, many of them lived as hermit monks in the mountains. In Portugal, the bishop of Lisbon conducted an inquiry at Orense, where some 28 Templars and six other witnesses appeared. Nothing incriminating was found, and as the provincial councils found no further evidence against the Templars in this area, no confessions were obtained in Portugal. Templar properties on the Iberian peninsula, especially in Portugal and Valencia, which was part of Aragon at that time, largely stayed in Templar hands. In 1317, 10 years after the arrests, the pope approved the founding of two new military orders: in Portugal, the Knights of Christ, which received Templar lands directly, and in Valencia, the Order of Montesa, began in July 1319, when James II of Aragon donated the castle of Montesa.

Italy and the Papal States

Overall, the number of Templars arrested in Italy seems rather small, as only seven papal and episcopal commissions were set up. Little documentation has survived, but historians know that hardly any witnesses were found for the inquiries, so it appears that a number of Templars were able to flee. In Lombardy, for example, the authorities refused to use torture, even against the orders of the pope, and the Templars were found innocent. In Venice, the state—not the Church—ran the investigation and the Templars were not arrested. In Ravenna, only seven Templars were brought before the inquiry, and they, too, were found not guilty. In Tuscany, the archbishop of Pisa and the bishop of Florence held inquiries in Florence in September of 1311. Here, as the use of torture was legal, some were found guilty; out of the 13 Templars questioned, six confessed.

Germany

In Germany, matters concerning the arrests sometimes became controversial as, by and large, the Templars were still quite popular with the public. This meant that the Inquisitors had quite a "PR problem" on their hands, one might say, in Germany. Much depended on the local rulers and their political inclinations; for example, at Trier, a number of witnesses were heard, and the Order was acquitted. The archbishop of Magdeburg was not at all favorable toward the Templars; he stormed one of their castles and imprisoned a number of them, including the Preceptor of Germany. This greatly angered the bishop of Halberstadt, a Templar ally, who, believing his rights had been infringed upon (as the castle was in his territory), excommunicated the archbishop. The Templars then escaped, and Pope Clement V was thus forced to intervene. He revoked the excommunication in September of 1310. But one of the most dramatic incidents connected with the Templar trials anywhere was that in Mainz, Germany, where the archbishop was conducting an inquiry of the knights. On May 14th, 1310, while the council was in session, the archbishop was suddenly confronted by the Templar Preceptor at Grumbach, who burst through the doors, accompanied by 20 of his fully armed knights. The archbishop, clearly frightened at this unexpected intervention, asked the Preceptor to be seated, and if he had anything to say to the committee. The Preceptor, Hugh of Salm, said he and his other knights understood that this council had largely been brought together on the orders of the pope for the express purpose of destroying the Order, and that it seemed that the Templars had been charged with a number of horrific crimes. This was harsh and unfair, he said, as they had been condemned without a proper hearing or conviction, and so they had now come to appeal to a futurep and all his clergy for justice. He also told the committee that the Templars who had constantly denied these terrible accusations had simply been burned at the stake. The archbishop, perhaps understandably, became fearful that there may well be a riot, and replied by saying that he would discuss the matter with the Pope. The council adjourned after this incident until the first of July. Later, his brother, Frederick, the Preceptor of the Rhine, also made additional comments, even offering to prove the Order's innocence by voluntarily submitting to a red hot iron test. Eventually, the archbishop of Mainz declared the Order innocent, a decision that Pope Clement later annulled. Many Templars in Germany were not even initially arrested. Some German Templar lands were turned over to the Hospitallers, but many were returned to the families who had originally donated them to the Order. In 1317, German Templars were allowed to join the Hospitallers, but others either fled or possibly joined other orders. Yet, much is still unknown for certain.

✦

England

King Edward II of England did not believe the charges against the Templars were true, so he did not immediately act against them, even though Philip IV of France was his father-in-law. Again, this greatly angered the French king. There is no evidence that Edward had any personal or political animosity against the Order per se. Similar to James of Aragon, Edward II also wrote to the pope himself, saying that such horrific charges were the work of the evil-minded; he did not believe that the Templars could be guilty of crimes of this gravity. However, Edward II received the papal bull *Pastoralis praeemienitiae* with its clear instructions to arrest the Templars. His own soul was at stake, so ,reluctantly, he finally acted; at this point, he seems to have turned against the Order more directly. The Templars in England were arrested and taken by county sheriffs to the royal castles in each area, such as Newcastle upon Tyne, York, Lincoln, Cambridge, Oxford, Warwick, or Canterbury. William de la More, Master of the Templars in England, was arrested at Temple Ewell and taken to Canterbury. English Templar estates were placed in the hands of special keepers. Yet, in certain areas, there were apparently a rather large number of knights "at large," so law enforcement authorities were ordered to round up any Templars that they saw in their territories. The sheriffs, however, were unenthusiastic, especially in York. In Kent, too, Templars were believed to have remained roaming "at large," some even in disguise. English law did not allow torture, which made life very difficult for the Inquisitors. The papal Inquisitors kept pressuring Edward II to allow the use of torture in an effort to get confessions in England. Although he initially resisted, finally, in December of 1309, he succumbed to their pressure and relented. But then another problem arose: No one was prepared to torture the brothers! This became a serious matter for the Inquisitors; so, in June of 1310, a letter was written to the archbishop of Canterbury by the Inquisitors, complaining that they could find no one to carry out tortures properly, and that the procedure ought to be by ecclesiastical law as in France. In other words, they wanted to use torture, as the French had done, but were prevented by English law from doing so. The Inquisitors went on to recommend eight ways to speed up the proceedings, the most extraordinary of which was the suggestion of sending all of the English Templars over across the Channel to the county of Ponthieu; however, this did not happen, as all of the English Templars ended up being tried only on England soil.

Even so, Edward II at this point seems to have made more of an effort to demand torture, probably due to further pressure from the French king, but he would only allow it according to ecclesiastical law. So, even though some torture was applied in England, it was apparently still not enough to satisfy the pope, as he seemed to have become rather desperate about the situation in England. Because events were not proceeding smoothly for the Inquisitors in England, they ended up resorting to the use of many witnesses from outside the Order. In France, where brutal torture resulted in many confessions, hardly any third-party witnesses were called, but, in England, there were 60, and of this group, only six of them were *not* ecclesiastics. All in all, 144 English Templars were questioned. At last, in London, three Templars finally confessed. But in the diocese of York no torture was used, so no brothers there confessed at all. The three in London who made the standard confessions to the charges were absolved and reconciled with the Church; and, as a nod of compromise to the pope in 1311, all of the English Templars declared that the whole Order was now so defamed that the members were unable to purge themselves, which, on the face of it, was quite true indeed. Nearly all of those remaining in prison in England confessed publicly that they abjured all heresies, and on the steps of St. Paul's Cathedral, they asked for penances, forgiveness, and absolutions, and for reconciliation with the Church. The elderly brothers asked for forgiveness in the chapel of St. Mary (Barking Abbey). Then, they were pensioned off and joined other monasteries. The Grand Master of the English Templars, William de la More, as well as Himbert Blanke, Preceptor of the Auvergne, who was in England at the time, both adamantly refused to ask for absolution for something they had not done. They refused to see the point of it, and languished in prison, with de la More dying in the Tower of London in February of 1311. But compared to the fate of de Molay and the Templars in France, their deaths were peaceful ones. In England it took much longer to sort out the complexities of the transfer of Templar properties. As Edward II had been using Templar lands to reward his friends and finance his Scottish campaigns, it was not until as late as 1324 before the title deeds were turned over to the Hospitallers. The Hospitallers had to go to the English Parliament as late as 1334 to confirm their right to the Templar lands, but even with this confirmation, they didn't get the title to the London Temple until 1340. Lengthy litigation continued with the families who had originally given the lands to the Temple and some lands were never transferred.

Scotland

Only two Templars were arrested in Scotland, and, ironically, both were English. One was Walter Clifton, who had been in the

Order for 10 years and was Preceptor of Balantradoch (Temple), the headquarters of the medieval Scottish Knights Templar; the other was William Middleton, who had also been at Balantradoch but was the Preceptor of Culter by then. They were called to answer the articles against them in November 1309 in front of the bishop of St. Andrews and the papal nuncio, John de Solerio. Both said that their receptions had been according to the Rule. Then, some 50 hostile witnesses testified against the Templars, including a number of heads of religious houses, friars, and rectors, the abbot of Dunfermline, the prior of Holyrood, Henry and William St. Clair of Roslin, who all said they heard things against the brothers' secret receptions and that their fathers said that the Templars had lost the Holy Land in 1291. For other details about the Templar order in Scotland and the land transfers after 1312, please see **Temple (Balantradoch)**.

Ireland

The Templars did not come to Ireland until the second half of the 12th century, along with a number of other Anglo-Norman, Welsh, Scottish, and French invaders. They founded commandaries and were given various lands. The earliest reference to Templars in the English royal administrative records for Ireland dates from the period of September 1220, when the government of Henry III instructed the Irish authorities to deposit proceeds with the Templars and Hospitallers, a function both Orders often performed throughout England at that time. Especially during the 1230s, the Templars in Ireland were mainly in cooperation with Henry III and his key officials in Ireland, and their role continued to grow from that point onward. The Templars were involved in the collection of a new customs duty in Waterford and with auditing accounts in 1301; this sort of activity was typical of their involvement in Ireland at the time. Templars arrested in Ireland were sent to Dublin Castle; perhaps rather ironically, most of their surnames were English.

Cyprus

Briefly, after the devastating loss of the Holy Land in 1291, Cyprus became the headquarters for the Templar order in the Latin East. But the political situation in Cyprus was a quagmire for the Templars, mainly because back in 1306, the Templars were instrumental in the overthrow of Henry II of Cyprus, after which the new ruler, Amaury de Lusignan, was installed. The Templars in the past had also supported the rival Angevins for the throne of the king of Jerusalem, so these decisions and other factors may well have had a direct impact on their tragic, final fate, some scholars believe. After the orders for their arrests came in 1307, all Templars everywhere were understandably concerned about their future, and Cyprus was no exception. History records that in May of 1308, the Master of the Order of the Temple in Cyprus, along with his two top officers, presented themselves before the governor of the island, declaring the innocence of the Templars. On June 1, 1308, the ruler, Amaury de Lusignan, attacked the Templar castle at Limassol. The Templars surrendered and were then arrested and imprisoned, with further hearings held nearly two years later—quite a long period of time. But all of the Templars still maintained their innocence. Then, on June 5th, 1310, Amaury was murdered, and from that point on scholars maintain that the Templars essentially lost their protector on the island. Henry II came back into power during this year, 1310, and he had the central Templar commandary on Cyprus destroyed, obviously in retaliation for the Order's support for his rival, Amaury. These actions then allowed Pope Clement V to instigate further proceedings against the Order, including torture, that contributed to their downfall on the island. (see **Trial, summary of; de Molay, Jacques; Heresy;** and for further suggested sources about these countries and other areas regarding the trial and its aftermath, please see "Trial of the Templars" in the Recommended Reading section)

✦

Troubadours

Troubadours were poets and musicians of the Middle Ages. They were instrumental in popularizing the chivalric ideal embodied in many of the

Grail romances and courtly love literature, and were also key "propagandists" for transmitting the values of the chivalric code. These gifted poets and professional entertainers were sometimes also key messengers, traveling from court to court with their lively tales and powerful songs. But they were not connected with the Knights Templar, as has sometimes been supposed. Flourishing mainly in the 12th and 13th centuries, they helped popularize composing poetry and song lyrics in the vernacular languages rather than merely in Latin. The term *troubadour*, strictly speaking, applies mainly to the Provencal poets; in northern France, they were known as *trouveres*, and, in Germany, as *minnesingers*. Although troubadours have often been thought of as minstrels, in fact, they were not the same, as troubadours were composers of intricate rhyming verses and songs, but rarely performed them; minstrels were talented performers but did not necessarily write their own material, as a number were illiterate. Troubadour songs often had special rhyming eight-line stanzas with one or two shorter stanzas, and were hardly ever longer than 60 lines. They would often sing of secular subjects rather than overtly religious ones, often about political themes as much as the love of a lady. In the late Middle Ages, a peak time for the troubadours on the whole, some troubadours would remain at a particular court or place; others, called *jongleurs*, would travel from place to place. Yet, although they were also prominent at the time of the Knights Templar, the Templars were not troubadours, as this kind of pursuit would have been viewed by the Order as a distinctly secular activity, something that their strict Rule did not allow. Templars were only permitted to sing hymns and other religious songs in their houses.

However, especially in the Languedoc area of southern France, many of the same patrons of certain troubadours were also supportive of the Templar order, and, before 1244, of the Cathars as well. Guiraut Riquier, the last troubadour, died in 1294. (see **Chrétien de Troyes**; **Grail romances**; **Arthurian knights**; **Chivalry**; **Knighthood, secular**)

Troy weight

Fairs such as the hugely popular Champagne fairs were major medieval commercial events and would be held over a period of seven weeks. The Templars were given special privileges and rights to trade at the fair, and merchants from far and wide would come to these fairs, keen to participate in the hustle and bustle of the marketplace and to buy, sell, or barter their goods. A number of economic historians maintain that the origins of the wide-ranging use of the "Troyes weight" measure in western Europe also have a direct connection with the medieval Champagne fairs. The troy weight today is still used in connection with dealings in precious metals; the term is derivative of Troyes, the capital of the province of Champagne. Historians believe that this system of weights was most likely initially brought to Europe from Cairo by various crusaders, and that it was then adopted as the standard of weight in the dealings of the fairs of Troyes. In time, the Templars gradually increased their share of the taxation levied on sales at these fairs, gaining specific rights on wool and yarn in 1164; on animals in 1214; and on tanning hides in 1243; interestingly, the tanning guilds sponsored some of the earliest Templar buildings in Paris. (see **Fairs, Champagne**; **Assets**; **Wool**)

Tunic
Referred to in the Rule, the tunic worn by a Templar had short sleeves and was worn over his shirt; later, by the late 12th and 13th centuries, it became longer. It is not the same as the mantle or surcoat of the Templars. (see **Mantle**; **Rule**)

Turcoman
An elite riding horse, as opposed to work horses and a pack animal called a roncin. (see **Roncin**; **Horse racing and jousts**; **Rule**)

Turcopole
A mercenary fighter of mixed race, a lightly equipped cavalryman with special skills in the Crusader states, referred to in the Rule on several occasions. They were overseen by the Turcopolier in the Templar order hierarchy. The word comes from a Greek term meaning "sons of Turks."

Tyre, Guillaume de
A medieval chronicler and one of a number of the major historical sources about the Knights Templar. However, he wrote as late as 1185 about the beginning of the Order, so he was not an eyewitness. Although many of the chronicles about the early years of the Templar order are interesting, they generally do not agree with each other as to the specific details about the Order's beginnings, so no firm conclusions can be drawn. (see **Origins of the Templar order**; **Paris, Matthew**; and for suggested sources about William of Tyre and his life, see "Tyre, William of" in the Recommended Reading section)

Vassel
In medieval times, one who would swear loyalty and military service to a feudal lord in exchange for land tenure, money, or other benefits.

Vichiers, Renaud de
The 18th Grand Master of the Order of the Temple, Renaud de Vichiers was from Champagne. Serving from the years 1250 to 1256, he previously served the Order as Preceptor of France and later, as Grand Marshal, before becoming Grand Master in 1250. (see **Grand Master, trials of**; Appendix B)

Women

Although the Rule of the Order clearly forbids the reception of full sisters in the Templar order, scholars acknowledge that in certain localities, the Order did indeed have women members. However, on the whole, as with many monastic organizations, any direct associations with women were viewed as "dangerous," to quote section 70 of the Rule. Section 71 goes on to reiterate that it is forbidden to kiss a woman, even if it be a widow, young girl, one's mother, sister, aunt, or any other woman. Templars could never under any circumstances strike a Christian woman (or man); if he did so, he could lose his habit. However, women were members of the Order—usually as associates—an affiliate status that was given to some men (for example, those who were married and wanted to assist the Order in some way, as married men could not be full knights in the Order due to the strict vow of chastity). Many women brought money, influence, and other valuable gifts in addition to important family connections. Sometimes the women lived on Templar property but in a house that was separate from the brothers. Many of the women on record as sisters (*soror*) or associates (*donata*) of the Order were members of Templar houses in Catalonia, one of the few places where extensive Templar records have survived. Perhaps in the future, scholars will discover other records in other locations, regarding further details and clarification on the presence of women in the Templar order. (see **Organization of the Templar order**)

Wool

The Cistercian monks, whom the Templars were associated, especially in France, were the most famous recipients of marginal land. They became renowned for making dormant lands become very fertile and productive, and similar to the Templars and other medieval religious orders, the Cistercians also had large flocks of sheep on their lands. Perhaps ironically for us to consider today, sheep were in fact one of the most brilliant investment concepts for the Knights Templar, as one of its most lucrative enterprises was the wool trade. Most of the wool generated from Cistercian or Templar sources from Britain and northern France ended up in the area around the city of Bruges, Belgium—long famed for its talented artisans and guild members, who could rapidly turn wool into beautiful cloth. Such cloth was very valuable and often fetched a high price at major medieval fairs, such as those at Champagne.

Templar financial transactions were involved in the wool trade in a major way, including the Champagne fairs, and the Templars were also responsible for shipping much of the wool on to key ports, such as Flanders. So sheep in the fields of England or France, for example, were valuable assets indeed, generating a healthy revenue for not only the Knights Templar, but also other religious monastic orders such as the Cistericians. The Templars had a special license to export and sell their wool. In attesting to the great value put on their sheep, the Templar Rule states in number 258 in its section on Penances that any brother who would give away an animal from either the sheepfold or the stable, that is, commit a theft, would then be in major jeopardy of losing his mantle altogether, quite a humiliating punishment for a Templar. (see **Assets**; **Fairs, Champagne**; **Farms**)

 # Appendix
A

Chronology of Events

Order of the Temple (1119–1314)

Templar events are in **bold**. Other events and people relating to the Church, cultural events, and the Crusades are included where relevant.

1118–31   Reign of Baldwin II, King of Jerusalem

1119   **Official public emergence and beginnings of the Order of the Temple; nine knights, led by Hugh de Payns, the first Templar Grand Masters, present themselves to Baldwin II in Jerusalem**

1119   Cistercian Order constitution, *Carta Caritatis*, presented to Pope Calixtus II

1119–27   **First nine Templar knights remain in the Holy Land**

1123   First Lateran Council extends Jerusalem privileges to Spanish crusades

1124   Crusaders control Tyre and occupy entire coast, except for Ascalon, which remains under Muslim control

1126   Death of Hughes de Champagne, recorded at Chartres

1127   **(autumn) The early Templars return from the Holy Land; beginning of the Order's unprecedented rise in power and influence**

1128   First Cistercian house established in Britain (Waverley, Surrey)

1128   Zengi becomes ruler of Aleppo and Mosul

1129   **(January) Council of Troyes; Rule of the Templar order established and official recognition of the fledging Order granted by Pope Honorius**

1129	William of Malmesbury completes *De Antiquitate Glastonie Ecclesie*
1130	**Bernard of Clairvaux completes "In Praise of the New Knighthood"; new Templar recruits from England and France sent to Jerusalem to help spread the Order's influence**
1130–53	Under the able leadership and powerful influence of Bernard of Clairvaux, the Templars created nearly 100 monasteries
1130	Zengi takes Hama and attacks Antioch
1131–43	Reign of Fulk of Anjou, King of Jerusalem
1132	Construction of the western facade and front nave of St. Denis Cathedral begins
1134	**Construction of the north tower of Chartres Cathedral begins; the Templars, Hospitallers, and the Canons of the Holy Sepulchre were each left one third of the kingdom of Aragon**
1135	Council of Pisa
1136	Geoffrey of Monmouth brings Arthurian literature to the world's attention with his Latin text *History of the Kings of Britain*
1136	**Robert de Craon became Templar Grand Master; serves until 1149**
1136–37	**Templars established in the Amanus March (north of Antioch)**
1137	Zengi, Muslim ruler of Aleppo and Mosul, captures Fulk, King of Jerusalem, then releases him
1139	Second Lateran Council
1138–42	Byzantine confrontation with crusader principality of Antioch
1139	**Templar castles in the Holy Land completed: Baghras, Darbask, Destroit, La Roche, de Roussel, Port Bonnet; in this year, Hugh de Payns, Grand Master of the Templars,**

died; Fulk takes over as King of Jerusalem from Baldwin II; and also, on March 29th, 1139, Pope Innocent II issues his bull *Omne Datum Optimum*

1140	Alliance of Jerusalem and Damascus against Zengi, Muslim ruler of Aleppo and Mosul
1140	Council of Sens
1142	Peter the Venerable commissions the translation of the Koran into Latin
1143	Death of Fulk of Anjou, King of Jerusalem; Baldwin III assumes the reins; also in this year, Celestine II, with the blessing of Innocent II, becomes pope
1144	Zengi of Aleppo wins control of Edessa on Christmas Eve, which sparks the Second Crusade; also in this year, Lucius II takes over from Celestine II as pope; later in 1144, he dies in battle
1145	Eugenius III becomes Pope after the death of Lucius II; and in December of 1145, proclaims the Second Crusade
1146	Bernard of Clairvaux travels extensively and preaches the Second Crusade
1146	Murder of Zengi, Muslim ruler of Aleppo and Mosul; his son, Nur al-Din, succeeds him
1147–49	Second Crusade
1147	**Pope Eugenius approves Templar usage of the red cross on their white mantles**
1147–70	Peak of career of Bernart de Ventadorn, renowned Languedoc troubadour favored in Eleanor of Aquitaine's court; influenced not only the Occitan tradition, but also French and German poetry
1148	Council of Reims
1148	(July) Louis VII of France, Queen Eleanor of Aquitaine, and Emperor Conrad III go to the Holy Land (Second Crusade)

1149	Baldwin III, with consent of the Patriarch of Jerusalem, gives Dietrich of Alsace the relic of Holy Blood collected by Joseph of Arimathea
1149	**Everard de Barres become Templar Grand Master; serves until 1152**
1149–50	**Gaza granted to the Templars**
1151	Death of Abbot Suger of St. Denis (1081–1151)
1150–1300	General time frame of the Cathars and Albigensians
1153	**Bernard of Tremelay becomes Templar Grand Master; serves for one year**
1153	Anastasius IV becomes pope
1153	**Death of Bernard of Clairvaux**
1153	Construction of Notre Dame Cathedral, Paris begins
1153	Ascalon falls to the Franks
1154	Nur al-Din takes control of Damascus in the Holy Land
1154	Henry II becomes king of England
1154	Baldwin III captures Ascalon
1154	The Great Schism between the Roman Catholic and Eastern Orthodox churches occurs
1154	Adrian IV becomes pope, after Anastasius IV
1154	**By this time, the Templars were safely transporting an average of 6,000 pilgrims a year to the Holy Land and were seen as not only devout, but also as powerful bankers, merchants, farmers, navigators, and diplomats by their contemporaries**
1154	**Andre de Montbard, uncle of Bernard of Clairvaux, becomes Templar Grand Master; serves until 1156**
1156	**Bernard de Blanchefort becomes Templar Grand Master; serves until 1169; in the period of his leadership, the "two knights on one horse" Templar seal symbol was initiated**
1156	Death of Peter the Venerable, abbot of Cluny

1160	**Grand-scale Templar round church founded in Tomar, Portugal, by Gualdim Pais, Templar Grand Master**
mid-1160s	**Hierarchical statutes added to the Templar Rule**
late 1160s	**Statutes on daily monastic life, chapter meetings, and penances added to the Templar Rule**
1162	**Amalric I assumes power as King of Jerusalem after Baldwin III**
1163–69	Nur al-Din's lieutenant, Shirkuh, wins control of Egypt; he dies two months later and is succeeded by his nephew, Saladin, who became the leader of the Saracens
1163–74	Reign of Amaury, King of Jerusalem
1168	Callistus III elected Pope
1169	**Philip of Nablus becomes Templar Grand Master; serves until 1171**
1170	Murder of St. Thomas Beckett, archbishop of Canterbury
1171–1220	Various major Grail manuscripts written in France, Wales, England, Germany, and Spain
1171	**Odo of Saint-Amand becomes Templar Grand Master; serves until 1179**
1171	Saladin proclaims overthrow of the Fatimid caliphate; as master of Egypt, finds himself in conflict with Nur al-Din
1174	Death of Nur al-Din; Saladin wins control of Damascus
1174	Canonization of Bernard of Clairvaux (later, in 1830, was nominated a Doctor of the Church)
1176	Saladin took the throne as King of Egypt and Syria (1174–93)
1174–85	Reign of Baldwin IV, king of Jerusalem; succeeds Almaric I
1179	Third Lateran Council
1179	Pope Alexander flees Rome; Innocent III becomes pope by less than the required two thirds majority

1181   Arnold of Torroja becomes Templar Grand Master when Odo de Saint-Amand was captured by Saladin's army while in the process of overseeing the construction of the Templar castle at Jacob's Ford; serves until 1184; Odo held in a prison in Damascus and died, having refused to comply with demands for his ransom

1183   Saladin wins control of Aleppo

1185–86   Reign of Baldwin V, King of Jerusalem

1185   Urban III succeeds Lucius III as pope

1185   **Gerard de Ridefort becomes Templar Grand Master; serves until 1189**

1186–94   Reign of Guy of Lusignan, King of Jerusalem

1187   Battle of Hattin; Jerusalem falls to Saladin

1187   Gregory VIII becomes pope, succeeding Urban III; killed in battle at Pisa; Clement III then becomes pope on July 6, 1187

1189   Richard I (the "Lionheart") becomes King of England, after Henry II

1189–92   Third Crusade

1190   Formation of the Teutonic Knights of St. Mary's Hospital at Jerusalem

1190   Chrétien de Troyes (Champagne) brings the Holy Grail, Perceval, and Lancelot to the attention of the world in his Grail romance *Perceval*

1190   Pope Alexander III pronounces the Cathars "anathema"

1190–92   Richard I arrives in Holy Land; Christians recover several cities, but not Jerusalem, from the Saracens

1191   **Templar headquarters in the Latin East moves to Acre**

1191   Richard I ("the Lionheart") meets Saladin at Battle of Arsuf

1191   Celestine III becomes pope; succeeds Clement III

1191   **Robert de Sable becomes Templar Grand Master**

1191   Announcement of discovery of King Arthur's tomb in grounds of Glastonbury Abbey in England

1191–92   **Templars occupy Cyprus**

1192   Joachim of Fiore, monastic scholar and mystic, founds the Florensian Order

1192   Richard I departs from Holy Land with his entourage, said to include Templars

1192   **Richard I captured on way home from Crusade by the troops of Austrian duke Leopold V, with whom he had quarreled; imprisoned and held for ransom by German Emperor Henry VI; privileges in Richard's dominions, including English Templars' privileges, suspended during this time**

1193   Saladin dies at age 55 in Damascus; succeeded by his brother al-Adil

1194   Beginning of the rebuilding of Chartres

1194   **Gilbert Erail becomes Templar Grand Master; serves until 1200**

1201   **Philip of Plessis becomes Templar Grand Master; serves until 1209**

1201   Fourth Crusade begins

1201   Around this time great tensions flared between the Templars and the Hospitallers, with Pope Innocent III eventually cautioning them that their primary focus should instead be on their Saracen enemies

1204   Rabbi Moses Maimonides dies. Conquest of Constantinople by Western crusading armies

1205   Beginning of Cathar massacres by the Inquisition

1206   St. Francis of Assisi begins his mission

1208   (March 10) Pope Innocent III calls for a crusade against the Albigensians

1209	Start of the Albigensian Crusade, Beziers, France
1209	Franciscan Order Rule approved by Innocent III
1210	**William of Chartres becomes Templar Grand Master; serves until 1218/9**
1210	John of Brienne becomes King of Jerusalem after Amalric II
1215	Magna Carta
1215	Fourth Lateran Council
1216	Dominican Order ("Black Friars") officially recognized by papal bull
1217–21	**Building of Atlit (Castle Pilgrim), a major Templar fortress in Holy Land**
1218–21	Fifth Crusade
1219	**Peter of Montaigue becomes Templar Grand Master; serves until 1230/2**
1220	Dominican Rule confirmed
1223	Second Franciscan Rule confirmed by papal bull
1224/5–74	Lifespan of St. Thomas Aquinas, theologian, natural philosopher, and poet
1227	Genghis Khan dies
1228–89	Crusade of Frederick II
1232	**Amand of Perigord becomes Templar Grand Master; serves until 1244/6**
1233	Beginning of the Inquisition; pope grants right to proceed to Dominican Order
1233–1315	Lifespan of the Blessed Ramon Lull, scholar, philosopher, alchemist
1239–40	Crusade of Theobald of Champagne
1240–41	Crusade of Richard of Cornwall

1241	Hospitallers negotiate the return of Jerusalem to Christian control
1241	Albertus Magnus (Albert the Great), Dominican, sent to Paris to study theology; intellectual, translator of texts, and alchemist; made bishop of Regensburg in 1260; teacher of Thomas Aquinas; died in 1280
1244	Franks lose Jerusalem in Holy Land
1244	(March 16) final siege of Montsegur; 225 Cathars massacred in *auto de fe*
1245	Oxford-based Roger Bacon, pioneer-teacher of the "new" Aristotle, science, and metaphysics, goes to Paris to teach; became a Franciscan c. 1250; wrote his *Opus Maius* in 1267
1247	**William of Sonnac becomes Templar Grand Master; serves until 1250**
1248–54	Crusade of St. Louis
1250	Battle of Mansurah
1250	(December 13) The death of Frederick II
1250	**Reginald of Vichiers becomes Templar Grand Master; serves until 1256**
1252	King Henry III of England accuses the Templars of "excessive pride"
1256	**Thomas Berard becomes Templar Grand Master; serves until 1273**
1257–67	**Additional penances added to the Templar Rule**
1260–1327/8	Time of Meister Eckhart, Dominican theologian, philosopher, mystic
1265–1308	Time of Johannes Duns Scotus, Scottish Franciscan theologian and developer of Aristotle's arguments
1265–1321	Lifespan of Florentine Dante Alighieri, author of *The Divine Comedy*
1266	Safed falls to the Turks

after 1268	**Catalan Rule of the Templars created**
1271	Languedoc comes under rule of French crown; travels of Marco Polo (1271–95)
1271–72	Crusade of Edward of England
1273	Rudolf of Habsburg elected king of Germany
1273	**William of Beaujeu becomes Templar Grand Master; serves until 1291**
1274	Council of Lyon
1274	Death of St. Thomas Aquinas
1277	Maria of Antioch sells her rights to the throne of Jerusalem to Charles of Anjou
1285	Council of Constantinople (Second Synod of Blachernae) discusses and rejects pro-Western interpretation of the Trinity as enunciated by the Patriarch John XI Bekko
1291	(April 6) Start of the siege of Acre
1291	**(May 18) Acre captured; death of Templar Grand Master William de Beaujeu**
1291	**(May 28) The Collapse of the Tower of the Temple**
1291	**(August 14) The Acre falls to the Mamluks; Templars evacuate Atlit (Castle Pilgrim) and Tortosa**
1291	**Theobald Gaudin becomes Templar Grand Master; serves until 1293**
1293	**Jacques de Molay becomes (the last) Templar Grand Master; later, burned at the stake in 1314**
1302	**Loss of Ruad and massacre of the Templar garrison there**
1305	Clement V becomes pope
1307	**Head of St. Euphemia kept in a silver reliquary in the house of the Temple, Nicosia**
1307	**(October 13) The dawn arrests of the Templars in France**
1307	**(October 27) The pope orders all Christian kings to arrest Templars; many European kings initially resistant**

1308	**Pope Clement suspends Inquisition of the Templars in France**
1308	**(August) About 60 Templar officials, including Grand Master Jacques de Molay and four other high officials, interrogated at Chinon Castle and plead guilty, hoping to be reconciled with the Church**
1309	**(August) Papal commission begins in France**
1310	**(February) Templar trial begins**
	(April) Philip de Marigny, brother of King Philip IV's chief minister of finance, installed as Archbishop of Sens
	(May) Provincial church council under Archbishop Marigny orders 54 Templars burned at the stake as "relapsed heretics"
	(also in May) Papal commission adjourned for five months
	(November) Templar defense collapses
1311	**Council of Vienne; Templar Order formally dissolved by pope's first bull, *Vox in excelso*, but charges against the Order "not proven"**
1312	**Pope's second bull, *Ad providam*, transfers Templar property to the Hospitaller order**
1314	**(March) Last Templar Grand Master, Jacques de Molay, and preceptor of Normandy, Geoffroi de Charney, burned at the stake; both publicly retracted their confessions and were nonetheless executed the same day in Paris**
1314	(April) Death of Pope Clement V
1314	24 June, St. John's Day
1314	(November) Death of Philip IV, king of France
1319	Order of Christ founded in Tomar, Portugal
1571	**Ottomans destroy much of the central Templar archive on Cyprus; many Hospitaller records also destroyed**

 # Appendix B

Grand Masters of the Knights Templar

1119–1136	Hughes de Payns
1136–1149	Robert de Craon
1149–1152	Everard des Barres
1153	Bernard de Tremelay
1154–1156	Andre de Montbard
1156–1169	Bertrand de Blanquefort
1169–1171	Philippe de Nablus
1171–1179	Odo of Saint-Amand
1181–1184	Arnaud de Torroge
1185–1189	Gerard de Ridefort
1191–1192/3	Robert de Sable
1194–1200	Gilbert Eral
1201–1209	Philippe du Plessiez
1210–1218/9	Guillaume deChartres
1219–1230/2	Pierre de Montaigue
1232–1244/6	Armand de Perigord
1247–1250	Guillaume de Sonnac
1250–1256	Renaud de Vichiers
1256–1273	Thomas Beraud
1273–1291	Guillaume de Beaujeu
1291–1292/3	Thibaud Gaudini
1293–1314	Jacques de Molay

Primary source: M. Barber. *The New Knighthood: A History of the Order of the Temple*. (Cambridge: Cambridge University Press, 1994). xxiii.

Note: Other accounts include Richard de Bures, 1245–1247

 # Appendix
G

Popes Contemporary With the Medieval Templar Order
(1119–1312)

Name	Years	Name	Years
Gelasius II	1118–1119	Celestine IV	1241
Callistus II	1119–1124	Innocent IV	1243–1254
Honorius II	1124–1130	Alexander IV	1254–1261
Innocent II	1130–1143	Urban IV	1261–1264
Celestine II	1143–1144	Clement IV	1265–1268
Lucius II	1144–1145	Gregory X	1271–1276
Eugenius III	1145–1153	Innocent V	1276
Anastasius IV	1153–1154	Adrian V	1276
Adrian IV	1154–1159	John XXI	1276–1277
Alexander III	1159–1181	Nicholas III	1277–1280
Lucius III	1181–1185	Martin IV	1281–1285
Urban III	1185–1187	Honorius IV	1285–1287
Gregory VIII	1187	Nicholas IV	1288–1292
Clement III	1187–1191	Celestine V	1294
Celestine III	1191–1198	Boniface VIII	1294–1303
Innocent III	1198–1216	Benedict XI	1303–1304
Honorius III	1216–1227	Clement V	1305–1314
Gregory IX	1227–1241		

 # Appendix D

Charges Against the Templars

Note: This list contains the major categories of charges, although by June of 1308, a total of some 127 charges had been drawn up against the Order; the following list contains the 10 major ones.

After a series of trials and hearings over several years in a number of countries, the final verdict on the Templar order was that of "not proven," as declared by Pope Clement V in his bull *Vox in excelso*, which he presented to the assembled cardinals and prelates at the Council of Vienne on March 22, 1312. In this bull, the pope basically said that while the evidence against the Order did not justify its definitive condemnation, by now, the entire proceedings had already so scandalized the Order, and the situation had so badly deteriorated due to the defamatory nature of the accusations and the trial itself, that no honorable man would want to join it; so, therefore, he recommended that the Order to be abolished. Many knights then joined the Order of Christ in Portugal and other orders after the suppression. Finally, in May 1312, a couple of months later, another papal bull, *Ad providam Christi Vicarii*, was issued, turning over all Templar properties and assets to the Hospitallers.

Please see the **Trial of the Templars** entry in the encyclopedia for a summary; for a list of further books and articles to consult about the specific details of the trial of the Templars in various countries, please see the "Trial" category in the Recommended Reading section at the end of this work.

1. That during the reception ceremony, or soon after, new brothers were required to deny Christ and spit on the cross, upon the command of those receiving them.

2. That they exchanged obscene kisses at their reception into the Order.

3. That their receptions and chapter meetings were held in secret at night, and that they were made to swear that they would never leave the Order.

4. That they had to swear to never reveal what was said at their reception.

5. That they adored a cat.

6. That they did not believe in the Mass or in other sacraments of the Church and that their priests did not speak the words of consecration in the Mass or consecrate the host.

7. That laity such as the Master or Commander of the Order could absolve them of their sins, rather than ordained priests.

8. That they practiced institutional sodomy.

9. That they worshipped an idol, a bearded male head, and said that the head had great powers. Each of them wore around their waist a cord that had been wound around the head.

10. That they used illegal means to acquire property and wealth, and that they also abused their duties of charity and hospitality.

Appendix E

Selected List of Templar Sites

Important Note: The following 54 sites are some of the more well-known or better-preserved places associated with the medieval Knights Templar. These sites may have once been a Templar commandary or preceptory, or, a chapel, barn, farm, or port that had an important historical connection with the Templar order (1119–1312). As there are thousands of Templar sites in total, this list is in no way intended to be a comprehensive one, but a general list of some of the better-preserved sites that can most easily be seen today by the modern-day visitor. Selected sites have been chosen for each country, in alphabetical order, and I have also included two sites in the Holy Land (Jerusalem and Acre).

Please note that a number of medieval Templar sites in many countries are still on private property, so they are not listed here. At other sites that were once relevant to the Templars in medieval times, there is often very little, if anything, left for a visitor to see today, unfortunately; so the main focus here is on the most accessible sites that are easiest to see in each country. When visiting these sites, please be considerate, and if possible try to support the local church, charity, or trust that is responsible for the upkeep of the site in whatever way you can. Your public support for such heritage organizations is a key reason why visitors can continue to see these sites today.

Enjoy your journey!

Belgium

+ *Templar House: Westvleteren* (Flanders)—A small Templar banking house and strongroom that was dependent on the larger Templar House of Ypres in medieval times.

Britain

+ *Temple Church* (London)—Called New Temple in medieval times, it was the headquarters of the English Knights Templar. There is also a monument outside Temple Church that shows two knights on one horse, in memory of the Knights Templar.

+ *All Hallows Church* (London)—This was where the Templars were held and defended themselves; the crypt also contains a Templar altar. The crypt also contains an altar with stones that were brought back from the east by the medieval Templars.

+ *The Tower of London* (London)—One of the prisons where Templars were interrogated.

+ *Cressing Temple* (Essex)—Has especially well-restored wooden Templar wheat and barley barns.

+ *Temple Garway* (Herefordshire)—The Templars' Garway church and site of Temple Garway preceptory; now called St. Michael's Church; fascinating stone carvings; remains of the former circular nave of the original Templar round church can be seen; dovecote.

+ *Temple Bruer* (Lincolnshire)—Interesting medieval tower still remains; was part of the Templar preceptory at this fascinating site; various carvings and medieval graffiti can be seen.

+ *Temple Rothley* (Leicestershire)—Templar chapel (c. 1240) is attached to the modern-day Rothley Court Hotel; some stone carvings and graffiti can still be seen.

+ *Shipley* (West Sussex)—St. Mary's church, Shipley, is one of the earliest Templar churches in Britain.

+ *Temple Ewell* (Kent)—Sts. Peter and Paul church; is also the adopted "guild church" for the Templar Pilgrimage Trust charity.

+ *Temple Church* (Bristol)—Some medieval remains can still be seen today; Bristol was an important medieval port for the Templars, second only to London; the train station name—Temple Meads—is in honor of the Knights Templar.

+ *Templecombe* (Somerset)—Enigmatic panel painting discovered here of the head of an unidentified man; this church in Somerset can easily be accessed when visiting the West Country and Bristol.

+ *St Catherine's Temple church* (Bodmin Moor, Cornwall)—12th century remnants of stones from the old Templar buildings can still be seen on the outbuilding next to the church; as Padstow and Fowey were important ports in medieval times, this site was most likely an important refuge on Bodmin Moor for pilgrims and travelers enroute to the Holy Land or the Continent.

+ *Llanmadoc* (Gower peninsula, Wales)—Very early Christian church, dedicated to St. Madoc; although not a Templar preceptory itself, this church was administered by Temple Garway; interesting stone carvings and crosses can be seen.

+ *Templar Church* (Temple, Midlothian, Scotland)—This was the site of the medieval headquarters of the Scottish Knights Templar; once called Balantradoch. Ruins of the Knights Templar church can still be seen today; is also near Edinburgh, the capital of Scotland, as well as the village of Roslin, where Rosslyn Chapel can be seen.

+ *Rosslyn Chapel* (Roslin village, Midlothian, Scotland)—Technically, not a Templar-related site historically (see nearby Temple, which was the Scottish headquarters of the Templars, mentioned above in **Templar Church**, above); however, Rosslyn is an important late medieval Scottish chapel with extraordinary stone carvings and was also a major film site for *The Da Vinci Code*; site close to Temple (Midlothian) and Edinburgh.

Croatia

+ *Vrana*—Fortress of the Templars still remains.

Cyprus

+ *Famagusta*—Templar church can still be seen here, alongside the Hospitaller church. Famagusta was the only deep-water harbor on Cyprus, and key to supplying men and equipment for battle to Outremer; also, the cathedral of St. Nicolas, completed in 1336 by the Lusignans, is now a mosque.

+ *Kyrenia castle*—This was the last prison where the major officers of the Templars were kept; it was later rebuilt by the Venetians; fairly well-preserved overall.

+ *Kolossi Castle*—Kolossi castle, built in the late 12th-century, is also known as the Templar Commandaria castle it is fairly well-preserved and near Limassol.

France

As there are an especially large number of Templar-related sites in France; here are a few of the better-preserved sites:

+ *Notre Dame Cathedral* (Paris)—Notre Dame de Paris is one of the finest Gothic cathedrals to visit today, with many important architectural features and carvings. Regarding Templar history, in October of 1307, from the steps of this extraordinary cathedral, the medieval theologians and cardinals announced the charges against the Templar order, to the shock and horror of the public.

+ *Jacques de Molay commemoration placque* (Paris)—Isle in the River Seine; the plaque here reads: "In this place Jacques de Molay, last Grand Master of the Order of the Temple, was burned on 18 March 1314."

+ *La Couvertoirade* (Aveyron)—Important site for both the medieval Templars and Hospitallers; a well-preserved castle, commandary, fortifications; La Couvertoirade was originally a village belonging to the Knights Templar, but after the suppression (1312) it was turned over to the Hospitallers; the buildings in this village are currently being further restored.

+ *Courva*l (Normandy)—Templar commandary.

+ *Gisors* (Normandy)—One of the major prisons where Templars were held; medieval graffiti/carvings on the walls.

+ *Caudebec* (Normandy)—Templar house, cross, and remains of a hospital.

+ *Metz* (Lorraine)—13th-century Chapelle des Templiers, with restored frescoes.

✦ *Domme* (Dordogne)—Another Templar prison; large amount of "Templar graffiti" found at this site.

✦ *Cahors* (Lot)—Vestiges of medieval Templar castle, chapel, and a church can be seen.

✦ *Loubert* (Gironde)—The Templar chapel of the House of Petit-Mas-Deu.

✦ *Arville* (Loir et Cher)—Located between Le Mans and Chartres, this is one of the best-preserved Templar commandaries to be seen in France today; the site includes a chapel, barn, fortified gate, bakery, and dovecote. There is also an excellent museum here, housed in the informative "Centre d'histoire des Ordres de Chevalerie."

✦ *Tour des Templiers* (Hyeres)—A Romanesque-style tower remains here that used to be part of the original House of Hyeres.

✦ *Toulon* (Provence)—Important Templar harbor and commandary; 12th-century Church of St.-Sauveur and Templar house.

✦ *Richerenches* (Provence)—Well-preserved Templar fortress and commandary; remains of city defense wall can be seen.

✦ *Collioure* (Pyrennes-Orientales)—Long a favorite of artists such as Matisse, this harbor and its beautiful beaches and scenery is still dominated by the sight of the medieval Chateau Royal, originally built by the Knights Templar in the 13th century, which now forms part of the harbor wall.

* Note: A recommended French language book to consult about many more French sites relating to the Knights Templar is *Les sites Templiers de France*, Editions Quest-France, 1997, by Jean-Luc Aubarbier and Michel Binet.

Italy

✦ *Siena* (Tuscany)—Templar church with some carvings; paintings in fresco.

✦ *Pilonice Paterno* (Umbria)—Well-preserved Templar site.

+ *Perugia*—Templar church of San Bevignate; has frescoes of Templars in battle.

+ *Ormelle*—Church with interesting frescos; was part of the former Templar commandary.

+ *Tempio di Ormella di Oderzio* (Veneto)—Church with well-preserved frescos and three Templar crosses.

+ *Piazza Armerina* (Sicily)—Templar tower and cloister.

Middle East

+ *Acre*—(St-Jean d'Acre) Crypt of St. John with some subterranean remains; Acre was a key fortified city and harbor in the time of the Templars and was the location of a devastating battle for the Templars ("Fall of Acre") in 1291; although most of the original Templar site here is now submerged, more remains are being excavated by archaeologists today.

+ *Jerusalem*—Temple Mount area and Church of the Holy Sepulchre, among others in this important city.

Poland

+ *Chwarszczany*—Templar commandary of Quartschen and its chapel.

Portugal

+ *Almurol*—Templar castle.

+ *Pombal*—Well-preserved Templar fortress, built by Gualdim Pais, Master of the Templar order in 1161.

+ *Tomar*—Castelo de Tomar ou dos Templarios, a Templar castle founded by Gualdim Pais, Master of the Temple, and became the headquarters for the Portuguese Knights Templar; later, after the suppression of the Templars in the early 14th century, it became the central convent for the Portuguese Order of Christ.

Slovenia

+ *Dora*—Church of St. Mary the Virgin, a Templar church.

Spain

+ *Barcelona*—The chapel of the Church of Santa Maria del Palau, on the northeastern corner of the Temple quarter, east of the cathedral, is the only real surviving part of the original Templar building left; there are some carvings over the doorway.

+ *Granyena* (Catalonia, in medieval Aragon)—In 1131, this castle was donated to the Templars by Ramon Berenguer III, count of Barcelona and associate confrere of the Order.

+ *Peniscola*—Templar castle.

+ *Ponferrada* (Leon)—Castillo de los Templarios.

+ *Tarragona*—Templar castle.

+ *Xivert*—Templar fortress.

Recommended Reading

Note for teachers, librarians, and researchers: 12 key Templar subject areas for further study are typed in **bold**; books and articles for recommended reading on that specific topic follow.

Although a great variety of books are available on the Templars today, judging from the many inquiries that I regularly receive, a phenomenal number of librarians, teachers, and researchers worldwide are now seeking specific advice about which *academic sources* are best to consult about certain research areas relating to the medieval Templar order. As such sources may not always be as familiar, or as easily accessible to non-academics, in an effort to meet this need and to further assist librarians and researchers, I have included academic sources from not only the usual fields of Medieval History or the Crusades, but also some from a few of the other key disciplines of the period, such as Religious Studies, Archaeology, Architecture, Economics, Political Science, Pilgrimage, and others, as relevant.

Please note that these recommendations apply only to the specific period of the historic medieval Knights Templar order (1119–1312). Full bibliographic details for suggested books and periodical and journal articles are provided here, as well as in the full Bibliography at the end of this book. For articles in edited volumes, only the articles that relate to the subject of the Knights Templar that I am recommending are listed specifically here.

Architecture/Archaeology, Templar

Books

Andrews, D. *Cressing Temple.* Chelmsford: Essex County Council, United Kingdom, 1993.

Boas, A.J. *Crusader Architecture*. London: Routledge, 1999.

Compton, Piers. *The Story of Bisham Abbey*. Reading, Penn.: Thames Valley Press, 1973.

Esdaile, Katherine. *Temple Church Monuments*. London: George Baker, 1933.

Forey, A. *The Templars in the Corona de Aragon*. London: Oxford University Press, 1973.

Gilchrist, R. *Contemplation and Action: The Other Monasticism*. Leicester: Leicester University Press, 1995.

Kennedy, Hugh. *Crusader Castles*. Cambridge, UK: Cambridge University Press, 1994.

Lambert, E. *L'Architecture des Templiers*. Paris: 1955.

Lees, B, Ed, *Records of the Templars in England in the Twelfth Century: the 1185 Inquest. In Records of Economic and Social History of England and Wales (IX)*. London: British Academy, 1935.

Pringle, Denys. *The Churches of the Crusader Kingdom of Jerusalem*. Vol. 1. Cambridge, UK: Cambridge University Press, 1993.

———. *Secular Buildings in the Crusade Kingdom of Jerusalem: An Archaeological Gazateer*. Cambridge, UK: Cambridge University Press, 1997.

Articles

Jacoby, Z. "The Workshop of the Temple Area in Jerusalem in the Twelfth Century: Its Origin, Evolution and Impact." *Zeitschrift fur Kunstgeschichte* 45, (1982): 325–94.

Kedar, B.Z. and D. Pringle. "La Feve: A Crusader Castle in the Jezreel Valley." In *Israel Exploration Journal* 35 (1985): 164–79.

Libor, J. and V. Jesensky. "Hospitaller and Templar Commanderies in Bohemia and Moravia: their Structure and Architectural Forms." Edited by H. Nicholson. *The Military Orders: Welfare and Warfare* 2 (1998): 235.

Perkins, C. "The Knights Templar in the British Isles." *English Historical Review* 25 (1910): 209–30.

Pringle, D. "Templar Castles between Jaffa and Jerusalem." Edited by H. Nicholson. *The Military Orders: Welfare and Warfare* 2 (1998): 89.

Pringle, D. "Templar Castles on the Road to the Jordan." Edited by M. Barber. *The Military Orders: Fighting for the Faith and Caring for the Sick.* (1994): 148–66.

Pringle, D. "Reconstructing the castle of Safed." *Palestine Exploration Quarterly* 117 (1985): 139–48.

Rees, W. "The Templar Manor of Llanmadoc." *Bulletin of the Board of Celtic Studies* 13: III. (1949): 144–5.

Webb, J. "Notes of the Preceptory of the Templars at Garway in the County of Herefordshire." *Archaeologia (XXI)* (1844): 35.

Wood, H. "The Templars in Ireland." *Proceedings of the Royal Irish Academy* 26C, no. 14 (July 1907): 327–77.

Assets, Templar order

Books

Barber, Malcolm. *New Knighthood: A History of the Order of the Temple.* Cambridge, UK: Cambridge University Press, 1994.

Barber, Malcolm and Keith Bate. *The Templars: Selected sources translated and annotated.* Manchester Medieval Sources Series. Manchester and New York: Manchester University Press, 2002.

Bouchard, C. *Holy Entrepreneurs: Cistercians, Knights and Economic Exchange in Twelfth Century Burgundy.* Ithaca and London: Cornell University Press, 1991.

Constable, Giles. *Monastic Tithes, from their Origins to the Twelfth Century.* Cambridge, UK: Cambridge University Press, 1964.

Edbury, P. and D. Metcalf. *Coinage in the Latin Eea.* Oxford: BAR International Series, 1980.

Holt, Richard. *The Mills of Medieval England.* Oxford: Blackwell, 1988.

Little, Lester K. *Religious Poverty and the Profit Economy in Medieval Europe.* London: Longman, 1978.

Lord, Evelyn. *The Knights Templar in Britain.* Harlow: Pearson Education Ltd., 2002.

Nicholson, Helen. *The Knights Templar: A New History.* Stroud: Sutton Publishing, 2001.

Spufford, P. *Handbook of Medieval Exchange.* London: Royal Historical Society, 1986.

_____. *Money and Its Use in Medieval Europe*. Cambridge: Cambridge University Press, 1988.

_____. *Power and Profit: The Merchant in Medieval Europe*. London: Thames & Hudson, 2002.

Usher, Abbott P. *The Early History of Deposit Banking in Mediterranean Europe*. Cambridge, Mass.: Harvard, 1943.

Articles

Abulafia, D. "Marseilles, Acre and the Mediterranean, 1200-1291." Edited by P. Edbury and D. Metcalf. *Coinage in the Latin East: The Fourth Oxford Symposium on Coinage and Monetary History*, British Archaeological reports, International Series 77 (1980): 19–39.

Lloyd, S. "Crusader Knights and the Land Market in the Thirteenth Century." In Cross, P., and S. Lloyd. *Thirteenth Century England*. Woodbridge: Boydell Press, 1986.

Metcalf, D.M. "The Templars as Bankers and Monetary Transfers between East and West in the Twelfth Century." In *Coinage in the Latin East: The Fourth Oxford Symposium on Coinage and Monetary History,* Edited by By P.W. Edbury and Metcalf, D.M., British Archaeological Reports, International Series, 77, (1980): 1-17.

Postan, M. "Credit in Medieval Trade." *Economic History Review*. Series 1, 2, 23. 1928.

Sandys, A. "The Financial and Administrative Importance of the London Temple in the Thirteenth Century." In *Essays in Medieval History presented to Thomas Frederick Tout*. Edited by A.G. Little and F.M. Powicke. 147–62. Manchester: Manchester University Press 1925.

Walker, J. "Alms for the Holy Land: The English Templars and their Patrons." In *The Medieval Military Revolution: State, Society and Military Change In Medieval and Early Modern Europe*. [Ed] A. Ayton and J. Price, London: Taurus Academic Studies, 1995, 63-80.

Bernard of Clairvaux

Books

Bredero, A. H. *Bernard of Clairvaux: Between Cult and History*. Edinburgh: T&T Clark, 1966.

Clanchy, M. *Abelard: A Medieval Life*. Oxford: Oxford University Press, 1997.

Evans, G.R. *Bernard of Clairvaux*. Oxford: Oxford University Press, 2000.

James, B.S., trans. *The Letters of St Bernard of Clairvaux*. Stroud: Sutton Publishing, 1998.

Leclercq, Jean. *A Second Look at Bernard of Clairvaux*. Kalamazoo, Mich.: Cistercians Publications, 1990.

Lekai, L.J. *The Cistercians: Ideal and Reality*. Ohio: Kent State University Press, 1977.

Leyser, H. *Hermits and the New Monasticism: A Study of Religious Communities in Western Europe 1000-1150*. London: Palgrave Macmillan, 1984.

Pranger, M.B. *Bernard of Clairvaux and the Shape of Monastic Thought*. Leiden: Brill Academic Publishers, 1994.

Articles

Bolton, B.M. "The Cistercians and the Aftermath of the Second Crusade." In *The Second Crusade and the Cistericians*, Edited by M. Gervers, 131–140. New York: 1992.

Bredero, A.H. "The Controversy between Peter the Venerable and Saint Bernard of Clairvaux." In *Petrus Venerabilis*, 1956, 53-71.

Gervers, M., editor. "The Influence of Bernard of Clairvaux on the Formation of the Order of the Knights Templar." In *The Second Crusade and the Cistercians*, 57–65. New York: 1992.

Pranger, M.B. "The Virgin Mary and the Love-Language in the Works of Bernard of Clairvaux." In *Citeaux, 40*, 112–137. 1989.

Sommerfeldt, J.R. "The Social Theory of Bernard of Clairvaux." In *Studies in Medieval Cistercian History presented to Jeremiah F. O'Sullivan*, Cistercian Studies Series 13, 35–48. Spencer, Mass.: 1971.

Crusades and the Military Orders

Books

Barber, Malcolm. *The New Knighthood: A History of the Order of the Temple*. Cambridge, UK: Cambridge University Press, 1994.

Barber, Malcolm and Keith Bate, trans. *The Templars: Selected sources translated and annotated.* Manchester Medieval Sources Series. Manchester and New York: Manchester University Press, 2002.

Daftary, F. *The Ismailis: Their History and Doctrines.* Cambridge, UK: Cambridge University Press, 1994.

Daftary, F., editor. *Medieval Ismaili History and Thought, Medieval Ismaili History and Thought.* Cambridge, UK: Cambridge University Press, 1996.

Duby, G. William Marshal: *The Flower of Chivalry.* New York: Pantheon, 1985.

Ehrenkreutz, A.S. *Saladin.* Albany: State University of New York, 1972.

Hamilton, B. *The Leper King and His Heirs: Baldwin IV and the Crusader Kingdom of Jerusalem.* Cambridge, UK: Cambridge University Press, 2000.

Hillenbrand, C. *The Crusades: Islamic Perspectives.* Edinburgh: Edinburgh University Press, 1999.

Maalouf, Amin. *The Crusades through Arab Eyes.* London and New York: Schocken, 1984.

Nicolle, David. *Saladin and the Saracens.* Men at Arms series, no. 171. Oxford: Osprey Publishing, 1986.

———. *Arms and Armor of the Crusading Era 1050-1350,* 2 vols. New York: 1999.

Nicholson, Helen editor. *The Military Orders: Welfare and Warfare,* vol. 2. Aldershot: Ashgate, 1998.

Riley-Smith, Jonathan. *The Knights of St. John in Jerusalem and Cyprus 1050–1310.* London: Macmillan; New York: St. Martin's Press, 1967.

———. *The Crusades: A Short History.* London: Athlone Press, 1987.

———. *The First Crusaders, 1095–1131.* Cambridge, UK: Cambridge University Press, 1997.

———. *Hospitallers: The History of the Order of St. John.* London: Hambledon, 1999.

———. "The Templars and the Teutonic Knights in Cicilian Armenia." In *The Cilician Kingdom of Armenia,* Edited by T.S.R. Boase. Edinburgh: Scottish Academic Press, 1978.

———. *Atlas of the Crusades.* London: Time Books, 1981.

_____. *The Oxford Illustrated History of the Crusades*. Oxford: Oxford University Press, 1995.

Runciman, Steven. *A History of the Crusades*. 3 vols. Harmondsworth: Penguin, 1978.

Schein, Sylvia. *Fideles Crucis: The Papacy, the West, and the Recovery of the Holy Land, 1274-1314*. Oxford: Oxford University Press, 1991.

Southern, R.W. *Western Society and the Church in the Middle Ages*. London: Harmondsworth, 1970.

_____. *Western Views of Islam in the Middle Ages*. Cambridge, Mass.: Harvard University Press, 1962.

Articles

Ayalon, D. "Studies in the Structure of the Mamluk Army." *Bulletin of the School of Oriental and African Studies* XV/2. London, 1953, 203–228.

Barber, M. "Supplying the Crusader States: The role of the Templars." In *The Horns of Hattin*, edited by B.Z. Kedar, 314–326. Jerusalem: Yad Izhak Ben-Zvi and Aldershot: Ashgate Variorum series: 1992.

Bombaci, A. "The Army of the Saljuqs of Rum." In *Instituto orientale di Napoli: Annali* ns XXVIII, 343–369. Naples: 1978.

Favreau-Lillie, M.-L. "The Military Orders and the Escape of the Christian Population from the Holy Land in 1291." *Journal of Medieval History* 19 (1993): 201–27.

Forey, A. "The Military Orders and the ransoming of captives from Islam." 12th to early 14th c. *Studia monastica, XXXIII,* Montserrat, Barcelona: 1991, 259-79.

Forey, A. "The Military Orders and Holy War against Christians in the thirteenth century." *English Historical Review* CIV London: Longman Group Ltd, 1989, 1–24.

Gibb, H.A.R. "The Armies of Saladin." *Cahiers d'Histoire Egyptienne III*. Paris, 1951, 304–320.

Nowell, C.E. "The Old Man of the Mountain." *Speculum* 22 (1947): 497–519.

Pryor, J.H. "The Naval Architecture of Crusader Transport ships." *The Mariner's Mirror 70* (1984).

Riley-Smith, J. "The Templars and the Teutonic Knights in Cicilian Armenia." In *The Cilician Kingdom of Armenia*, edited by T.S.R. Boase, Edinburgh: Scottish Academic Press: 1978. 92–117.

Stiles, Paula R. "Arming the Enemy: Non-Christians' role in the Military Culture of the Crown of Aragon during the Reconquista." In *Noble Ideals and Bloody Realities: Warfare in the Middle Ages*, edited by Christie, N. and M. Yazigi, History of Warfare series 37. Brill: April 2006.

In the New Knighthood

Books

Barber, Malcolm. *The New Knighthood: A History of the Order of the Temple*. Cambridge, UK: Cambridge University Press, 1994.

Bredero, A.H. *Bernard of Clairvaux: Between Cult and History*. Edinburgh: T&T Clark, 1966.

James, B.S., trans. *The Letters of St Bernard of Clairvaux.* trans. Stroud: Sutton Publishing, 1998.

Nicholson, Helen. *The Knights Templar: A New History*. Stroud: Sutton Publishing, 2001.

Prawer, Joshua. *The Crusader's Kingdom*. London: Phoenix Orion, 1972.

Runciman, Steven. *The Eastern Schism: A Study of the Papacy and the Eastern Churches during the 11th and 12th Centuries*. Oxford: Oxford University Press, 1955.

Articles

Arnold, B. "A Transformed Angel (x 3.31.18): The Problem of the Crusading Monk." In *Studies in Medieval Cistercian History presented to Jeremiah F. O'Sullivan*, Cistercian Studies Series 13, 55–62. Spencer, Mass.: 1971.

Greenia, C., trans "In Praise of the New Knighthood." In *The Works of Bernard of Clairvaux, vol. 7, Treatises III*, 126–67. Cistercian Publications: 1977.

Leclercq, Jean. "Saint Bernard's Attitude toward War." In *Studies in Medieval Cistercian History,* vol. II, edited by J.R. Sommerfeldt, Kalamazoo, Mich.: 1976.

Renna, T. "Bernard of Clairvaux and the Temple of Solomon." In *Law, Custom and the Social Fabric in Medieval Europe,* Studies in Medieval Culture 28, Edited by B.S. Bachrach and D. Nicholas. Kalamazoo, Mich.: Medieval Institute Publications, 1990, 73–88.

Werblowsky, R.J. "Introduction." "In Praise of the New Knighthood." In Bernard of Clairvaux: *Treatises III,* Cistercian Fathers 19, Kalamazoo, Mich.: 1977.

de Molay, Jacques

Books

Barber, Malcolm. *The New Knighthood: A History of the Order of the Temple.* Cambridge, UK: Cambridge University Press, 1994.

Demurger, Alain. *The Last Templar: The Tragedy of Jacques de Molay, Last Grand Master of the Temple.* London: Profile Books, 2004. (English translation of 2002 French original)

Forey, Alan. *The Templars in the Corona de Aragon.* London: Oxford University Press, 1973.

Gilmour-Bryson, A. *The Trial of the Templars in Cyprus: A Complete English edition.* Leiden: Brill, 1998.

Articles

Barber, M. "James of Molay, the last Grand Master of the Order of the Temple." *Studia Monastica 14* (1972): 91–124.

Demurger, A. "Jacques de Molay." *Dictionnaire d'histoire et de geographie ecclesiastique.* Paris, Letousey: XXVI.

Forey, A. "Letters of the last Two Templar Masters." *Nottingham Medieval Studies* XLV (2002): 145–71.

Lizerand, Georges, editor. *Le dossier de l'affaire des Templiers.* Librairie Ancienne Honore Champion, Paris: 1923. (See pg 166 for de Molay's evidence given to the papal commissioners on November 28, 1309.)

Organization, Structure, and Rule of the Order

Books

Barber, Malcolm. *The New Knighthood: A History of the Order of the Temple.* Cambridge, UK: Cambridge University Press, 1994.

Barber. M. and Keith Bate. *The Templars: Selected Sources Translated and Annotated.* Manchester Medieval Sources Series, Manchester and New York: Manchester University Press, 2002.

Evergates, Theodore. *Feudal Society in the Bailliage of Troyes under the Counts of Champagne, 1152-1284.* Baltimore: John Hopkins University Press, 1975.

Lord, Evelyn. *The Knights Templar in Britain.* Harlow: Pearson Education Ltd., 2002.

Nicholson, Helen. *The Knights Templar: A New History.* Stroud: Sutton Publishing, 2001.

Partner, Peter. *The Knights Templar and Their Myth.* Rochester. Vt.: Destiny Books, 1990. (Originally published as *The Murdered Magicians*, Oxford: Oxford University Press, 1981.)

Ralls, Karen. *The Templars.* Chicago: Quest Books, 2003.

Seward, Desmond. *The Monks of War.* Harmondsworth: Penguin Books, 1995. (Originally published in 1972.)

Upton-Ward, Judith M., trans. and ed. *The Rule of the Templars: the French Text of the Rule of the Order of the Temple.* Woodbridge, Suffolk: Boydell Press, 1992.

———. trans. and ed. *The Catalan Rule of the Templars: Barcelona, Archivo De La Corona de Aragon, "Cartes Reales" MS 3344: A Critical Edition and English Translation.* Woodbridge, Suffolk: Boydell and Brewer, 2002.

Articles

Barber, M. "The social context of the Templars." *Transactions of the Royal Historical Society 34.* London: Royal Historical Society, 1984, 27–46.

Cerrini, S. "A New Edition of the Latin and French Rule of the Temple." In *The Military Orders.* Vol. 2. *Welfare and Warfare,* edited by H. Nicholson. 207–15. Aldershot: Ashgate, 1998.

Forey, A. "Novitiate and instruction in the Military Orders in the twelfth and thirteenth centuries." *Speculum LXI* (1986): 1–17.

———. "The militarisation of the Hospital of St John." *Studia Monastica XXVI* (1984): 75–89.

Origins of the Order

Books

Barber, Malcolm. *The New Knighthood: A History of the Order of the Temple*. Cambridge, UK: Cambridge University Press, 1994.

Barber, Malcolm and Keith Bate. *The Templars: Selected Sources Translated and Annotated*, Manchester Medieval Sources Series. Manchester and New York: Manchester University Press, 2002.

Hopper, Vincent F. *Medieval Number Symbolism: Its Sources, Meaning, and Influence on Thought and Expression*. New York: Columbia University Press, 1938.

Nicholson, Helen. *The Knights Templar: A New History*. Stroud: Sutton Publishing, 2001.

Nicholson, Helen, editor. *The Military Orders: Welfare and Warfare*. vol. 2. Aldershot: Ashgate, 1998.

Seward, Desmond. *The Monks of War*. Harmondsworth: Penguin Books, [1972] 1995.

Upton-Ward, Judith M., trans. and ed. *The Rule of the Templars: the French Text of the Rule of the Order of the Temple*. Woodbridge, Suffolk: Boydell Press, 1992.

Articles

Barber, Malcolm. "Origins of the Order of the Temple." *Studia Monastica* 12 (1970): 219–240.

Forey, A. "The Emergence of the Military Order in the Twelfth Century." *Journal of Ecclesiastical History 36* (1985): 175–95.

Pilgrimage and Pilgrims

Books

Barber, Richard. *Pilgrimages*. Woodbridge, Suffolk: Boydell & Brewer, 1991.

Chareyron, N. *Pilgrims to Jerusalem in the Middle Ages*. New York: Columbia University Press, 2005.

Couasnon, Charles. *The Church of the Holy Sepulchre in Jerusalem*. Oxford: Oxford University Press, 1974.

Gibson, S. and J. Taylor. *Beneath the Church of the Holy Sepulchre, Jerusalem: The Archaeology and Early History of Traditional Golgotha*. London: n.p., 1994.

Hamilton, B. "Our Lady of Saidnaiya: An Orthodox Shrine Revered by Muslims and Knights Templar at the Time of the Crusades." In *The Holy Land, Holy Lands, and Christian History,* Studies in Church History, 36. Woodbridge, UK: Boydell Press, 2001.

Hopper, Sarah. *To Be a Pilgrim: The Medieval Pilgrimage Experience*. Stroud: Sutton, 2002.

Ohler, Norbert. *The Medieval Traveller*. Translated by C. Hillier. Woodbridge: The Boydell Press, 1989.

Spencer, Brian. *Pilgrim Souvenirs and Secular Badges*. London: Museum of London Press, 1988.

Sumption, Jonathan. *Pilgrimage: An Image of Medieval Religion*. London: Faber & Faber, 1975.

The Pilgrim's Guide to Santiago de Compostela vol II: The Text. Translated by P. Gerson, A. Shaver-Crandell, and A. Stones. London: Harvey Miller Publishers, 1998.

Articles
Birch, D. "Selling the Saints: Competition among Pilgrimage Centres in the Twelfth Century." *Medieval History* 2:2 (1992): 20–34.

Woodruff, C.E. "The Financial Aspect of the Shrine of St Thomas of Canterbury." *Archaeologia Cantiana* 44 (1932).

Relics

Books
Brown, Peter. *The Cult of the Saints: Its Rise and Function in Latin Christianity*. Chicago: University of Chicago Press, 1981.

Geary, P.J. *Furta sacra: Thefts of Relics in the Central Middle Ages*. Princeton, N.J.: Princeton University Press, 1978.

———. *Living with the Dead in the Middle Ages*. Ithaca: Cornell University Press, 1994.

Goldhill, Simon. *The Temple of Jerusalem*. Cambridge, Mass.: Harvard University Press, 2005.

Hamilton, Bernard. *Religion in the Medieval West*. London: Edward Arnold, 1986.

Kingsley, Sean. *God's Gold: The Quest for the Lost Temple Treasure of Jerusalem.* London: John Murray, 2006.

Thiede, C. P. and M. D'Ancona. *The Quest for the True Cross.* London: Weidenfeld & Nicolson, 2000.

Articles

Ackroyd, P.R. "The Temple Vessels—A Continuity Theme." In *Studies in the Religion of Ancient Israel.* Leiden: Brill, 1972.

Birch, D. "Selling the Saints: Competition among Pilgrimage Centres in the Twelfth Century." *Medieval History* 2.2 (1992): 20–34.

Barber, Malcolm. "The Templars and the Turin Shroud." In *Catholic Historical Review 68* (1982): 206–25.

Silberman, Neil A. "In Search of Solomon's Lost Treasures." *Biblical Archaeology Review* 6.4 (1980): 30–41.

Trial of the Templars

Books

Baldwin, John. *The Government of Philip Augustus: Foundations of French Royal Power in the Middle Ages.* Berkeley and London: University of California Press, 1986.

Baldwin, Marshal. *Raymond III and the Fall of Jerusalem (1140-87).* Princeton: Princeton University Press, 1936.

Barber, Malcolm. *The Trial of the Templars.* Cambridge: Cambridge University Press, 1978.

Barber, Malcolm, and Keith Bate, translators. *The Templars: selected sources translated and annotated.* Manchester Medieval Sources Series. Manchester and New York: Manchester University Press, 2002.

Burman, Edward. *Supremely Abominable Crimes: The Trial of the Knights Templar.* London: Allison & Busby, 1994.

Demurger, Alain. *Vie et mort de l'ordre du Temple, 1120-1314.* Paris: Editions du Seuil, 1985, 1989 and 1993.

Gilmour-Bryson, A. *The Trial of the Templars in Cyprus: A Complete English edition.* Leiden: Brill, 1998

———. *The Trial of the Templars in the Papal State and in the Abruzzi.* Biblioteca Apostolica Vaticana, Vatican City: 1982.

Housley, Norman. *The Avignon Papacy and the Crusades 1305-1378*. Oxford: Oxford University Press: 1986.

Lea, H.C. *A History of the Inquisition of the Middle Ages*. 3 vols. 1888; reprint, New York: Russell and Russell, 1955.

Lord, Evelyn. *The Knights Templar in Britain*. Harlow: Pearson Education Ltd., 2002.

Menache, Sophia. *Pope Clement V*. Cambridge: Cambridge University Press, 1998.

Nicholson, Helen. *The Knights Templar: A New History*. Stroud: Sutton Publishing, 2001.

Partner, P. *The Knights Templar and Their Myth*. Rochester, Vt.: Destiny Books, 1990. (Originally published as *The Murdered Magicians*. Oxford: Oxford University Press, 1981.)

Ralls, Karen. *The Templars*. Chicago: Quest Books, 2003.

Seward, Desmond. *The Monks of War*. Harmondsworth: Penguin Books, 1995. (Originally published in 1972.)

Strayer, Jospeh R. *The Reign of Philip the Fair*. Princeton: Princeton University Press, 1980.

Articles
Barber, M. "The Trial of the Templars Revisited." In *The Military Orders: Welfare and Warfare* vol. 2, edited by H. Nicholson, 329 Aldershot: Ashgate, 1998.

———. "The World Picture of Philip the Fair." *Journal of Medieval History 8* (1982): 13–27.

———. "Propaganda in the Middle Ages: the Charges against the Templars," *Nottingham Medieval Studies* 17 (1973): 42–57.

Brown, E.A.R. "The Prince is Father of the King: The Character and Childhood of Philip the Fair of France." *Medieval Studies* 49 (1987): 282–334.

Forey, A. "The Beginnings of the Proceedings against the Aragonese Templars." In *God and Man in Medieval Spain: Essays in Honor of J.R.L. Highfield,* edited by Lomax, D. W. and Mackenzie, D. 81–86. Warminster: 1989.

Ward, J.O. "The Fall of the Templars." *Journal of Religious History* 13 (1984): 92–113.

Tyre, William of

Books

Barber, Malcolm, and Keith Bate, trans. *The Templars: selected sources translated and annotated,* Manchester Medieval Sources Series. Manchester and New York: Manchester University Press, 2002.

Edbury, P. and J. Rowe. *William of Tyre: Historian of the Latin East.* Cambridge: Cambridge University Press, 1988.

Morgan, M.R. *The Chronicle of Ernoul and the Continuations of William of Tyre.* Oxford: Oxford University Press, 1973.

William of Tyre (Guillaume de Tyr). *Chronique.* Edited by R. Huygens, 2 vols, Corpus Christianorum, Continuatio Mediaevalis 63 and 63A. Turnhout: 1986.

William of Tyre (Guillaume de Tyr). *A History of Deeds done beyond the Sea.* Trans. by E.A. Babcock and A.C. Krey, 2 vols, Records of Civilization, Sources and Studies 35. New York, 1943 (reprint 1976).

Articles

Nicholson, H. "Before William of Tyre: European Reports on the Military Orders' Deeds in the East." In *The Military Orders: Welfare and Warfare,* vol. 2. Edited by H. Nicholson, 111. Aldershot: Ashgate, 1998.

Davis, R.H.C. "William of Tyre." In *Relations between East and West in the Middle Ages.* edited by D. Baker, 64–76. Edinburgh: Edinburgh University Press, 1987.

Bibliography

Abulafia, D. "Marseilles, Acre and the Mediterranean, 1200-1291." In *Coinage in the Latin East: The Fourth Oxford Symposium on Coinage and Monetary History.* Edited by Edbury, P, and Metcalf, D., British Archaeological reports, International Series 77. Oxford: Oxford University Press, 1980.

————. *Commerce and Conquest in the Mediterranean 1100–1500.* Aldershot: Ashgate, 1993.

Ambrosini, M.L. *The Secret Archives of the Vatican.* London: Little, Brown & Co., 1970.

Andrews, D., *Cressing Temple.* Chelmsford: Essex County Council, United Kingdom, 1993.

Arnold, B. *German Knighthood: 1050–1300.* Oxford: Clarendon Press, 1985.

————. "A Transformed Angel: The Problem of the Crusading Monk." In *Studies in Medieval Cistercian History* presented in honor of Jeremiah F. O'Sullivan, Cistercian Studies Series 13. Spencer, Mass.: Cistercian Publications, 1971.

Ayalon, D. "Studies in the Structure of the Mamluk Army." *Bulletin of the School of Oriental and African Studies* XV/2, (1953): 203-228.

Aylott, P. "Earthworks at Temple Chelsing and Rennesley," *East Herts Archaeological Society Transactions 1.* (1906): 24–29.

Baldwin, John. *The Government of Philip Augustus: Foundations of French Royal Power in the Middle Ages.* Berkeley and London: University of California Press, 1986.

Baldwin, Marshal. *Raymond III and the Fall of Jerusalem (1140–87).* Princeton, N.J.: Princeton University Press, 1936.

Baldwyne, R.C. and O'Neill, H. "A Medieval Site at Chalk Hill, Temple Guiting." *Bristol and Gloucestershire Archaeological Society Transactions* VLXXXVII (1958).

Barber, Malcolm. "Origins of the Order of the Temple." *Studia Monastica* 12 (1970): 219–240.

———. *The Trial of the Templars*. Cambridge, UK: Cambridge University Press, 1978.

———. "The Templars and the Turin Shroud." *Catholic Historical Review* 68 (1982): 206–225.

———. *The Two Cities: Medieval Europe 1050–1320*. London and New York: Routledge, 1992.

———. *The New Knighthood: A History of the Order of the Temple*. Cambridge, UK: Cambridge University Press, 1994.

———. "The World Picture of Philip the Fair." *Crusaders and Heretics: 12th–14th Centuries*. Variorum Collected Studies Series. Aldershot: Ashgate, 1995. (Originally published in *Journal of Medieval History* 8 [Amsterdam, 1982].)

———. "James of Molay, the Last Grand Master of the Order of the Temple." *Crusaders and Heretics: 12th–14th Centuries*. Variorum Collected Studies Series. Aldershot: Ashgate, 1995. (Originally published in *Studia Monastica* 14 [Barcelona, 1972].)

———. "Supplying the Crusader States: the role of the Templars," *The Horns of Hattin*. Edited by Kedar, Benjamin Z., Jerusalem: Yad Izhak Ben-Zvi Press and Aldershot: Ashgate Variorum series (1992) 314–326.

———. "Lepers, Jews and Moslems: The Plot to Overthrow Christendom in 1321." *History* 66 (1981).

———. "The Trial of the Templars Revisited." *The Military Orders: Welfare and Warfare*. Edited by H. Nicolson. vol. 2. Aldershot: Ashgate, 1998.

———. "The Charitable and Medical Activities of the Hospitallers and Templars, 11th to 15th Centuries." The Whichard Lecture, Greenville, N.C., March 23, 2000.

———. "The social context of the Templars," *Transactions of the Royal Historical Society* 34 (1984): 27–46.

———. "Propaganda in the Middle Ages: the Charges against the Templars," *Nottingham Medieval Studies* 17 (1973): 42–57.

Barber, Malcolm, and Keith Bate, trans. *The Templars: selected sources translated and annotated.* Manchester Medieval Sources Series. Manchester and New York: Manchester University Press, 2002.

Barber, Richard. *The Figure of Arthur.* London: Longman, 1972.

———. *The Knight and Chivalry.* Woodbridge, Suffolk: Boydell & Brewer, 1995. [Originally published in 1970.]

———. *Pilgrimages.* Woodbridge, Suffolk, UK: Boydell & Brewer, 1991.

Barber, R., and J. Barker. *Tournaments.* Woodbridge, Suffolk: Boydell Press, 1989.

Ben-Dov, M. *In the Shadow of the Temple.* Translated by I. Friedman. New York: Harper & Row and Jerusalem: Keter Publishing House, 1985.

Bennett, Prof. M. "Jerusalem's First Crusader King: Godfrey de Bouillon." *BBC History Magazine* (London): May 2001.

Bernard of Clairvaux. "De laude novae militiae ad milites Templi liber." *Sancti Bernardi Opera,* edited by J. Leclercq et.al., vol. 3. Rome, 1963.

———. "In Praise of the New Knighthood." *The Works of Bernard of Clairvaux.* Vol. 7, *Treatise* 3. Translated by C. Greenia. Cistercian Fathers Series, vol. 19. Kalamazoo, Mich.: Cistercian Publications, 1977.

———. *On the Song of Songs.* Translated by Kilian Walsh. Vol. 1. Kalamazoo, Mich.: Cistercian Publications, 1971.

Biddle, Martin. *The Tomb of Christ.* Stroud: Tempus, 1999.

Birch, D. "Selling the Saints: Competition among Pilgrimage Centres in the Twelfth Century," *Medieval History* 2.2 (1992): 20–34.

Boas, A.J. *Crusader Architecture.* London: Routledge, 1999.

Boase, Thomas. *Kingdoms and Strongholds of the Crusaders.* London: Macmillan, 1971.

———. *The Cilician Kingdom of Armenia.* Edinburgh: Scottish Academic Press, 1978.

Bombaci, A. "The Army of the Saljuqs of Rum," *Instituto orientale di Napoli: Annali* XXVIII (1978): 343–369.

Bordonove, G. *La Tragedie des Templiers,* Paris: Pygmalion-Gerard Watelet, 1993.

Bouchard, C. Sword, *Mitre and Cloister: Nobility and the Church in Burgundy, 980–1198*. Ithaca and London: Cornell University Press, 1987.

———. *Holy Entrepreneurs: Cistercians, Knights and Economic Exchange in Twelfth Century Burgundy*. Ithaca and London: Cornell University Press, 1991.

Boulton, D'A.J.D. *The Knights of the Crown: The Monarchical Orders of Knighthood in Later Medieval Europe 1325–1520*. Woodbridge, Suffolk: Boydell Press and New York: St. Martin's Press, 1987.

Boutaric, E. "Clement V, Philippe le Bel et les Templiers," *Revue des questions historiques* X and XI (1871–2).

Bredero, A.H. *Bernard of Clairvaux: Between Cult and History*. Edinburgh: T&T Clark, 1966.

Brown, E.A.R. "The Prince is Father of the King: The Character and Childhood of Philip the Fair of France," *Medieval Studies* 49 (1987): 282–334.

Brown, Peter. *The Cult of the Saints: Its Rise and Function in Latin Christianity*. Chicago: University of Chicago Press, 1981.

———. *Relics and Social Status in the Age of Gregory of Tours*. Reading: Univ. of Reading, 1977.

Brundage, James. *Medieval Canon Law and the Crusader*. Madison: University of Wisconsin Press, 1969.

Bull, M. *Knightly Piety and the Lay Response to the First Crusade*. Oxford: Oxford University Press, 1993.

Bulst-Thiele, Marie L. *Sacrae domus militiae Templi Hierosolymitani magistri: Untersuchungen zur Geschichte des Templeroordens 1118/9–1314*. Göttingen: Vandenhoeck & Ruprecht, 1974.

Burman, Edward. *Supremely Abominable Crimes: The Trial of the Knights Templar*. London: Allison & Busby, 1994.

Butler, Elizabeth M. *The Myth of the Magus*. Cambridge, UK: Cambridge University Press, 1948.

Cerrini, S. "A New Edition of the Latin and French Rule of the Temple." In *The Military Orders*, vol. 2. Welfare and Warfare. Edited by H. Nicholson. Aldershot: Ashgate, 1998.

Chareyron, N. *Pilgrims to Jerusalem in the Middle Ages*. New York: Columbia University Press, 2005.

Chauvin, B., editor. "Citeaux 1098-1099." In *Dossiers d'Archeologie No. 229.* Paris, Dec. 1997–Jan. 1998, and No. 234, June-July 1998.

Christie, N., and M. Yazigi, editors. *Noble Ideals and Bloody Realities: Warfare in the Middle Ages.* History of Warfare 37. Leiden: Brill Academic Press, 2006.

Clanchy, M. *Abelard: A Medieval Life.* Oxford: Oxford University Press, 1997.

Cohn, N. *Pursuit of the Millennium.* Oxford: Oxford University Press, 1970.

———. *Acts of the Lords of Council in Public Affairs 1501–1554.* Selections from the *Acta Domiorum Concili,* introductory to the Privy Council of Scotland. Edited by Robert Kerr Hannay. Edinburgh, 1932. *Europe's Inner Demons: the Demonization of Christians in Medieval Christendom.* London: Chatto and Heinemann, 1975.

Collins, Roger. *Early Medieval Spain: Unity in diversity 400-1000.* 2nd ed., London: Macmillan, 1995.

Compton, Piers. *The Story of Bisham Abbey.* Reading: Thames Valley Press, 1973.

Constable, Giles. *Monastic Tithes, from their Origins to the Twelfth Century.* Cambridge, UK: Cambridge University Press, 1964.

Coppack, G. *The White Monks: The Cistercians in Britain 1128–1540.* Stroud: Tempus, 1998.

Couasnon, Charles. *The Church of the Holy Sepulchre in Jerusalem.* Oxford: Oxford University Press, 1974.

Cowan, I.B., and D. Eason. *Medieval Religious Houses in Scotland.* London: Longman, 1976.

Daftary, F. *The Assassin Legends.* London: I.B. Tauris & Co., 1995.

———. *The Ismailis: Their History and Doctrines.* Cambridge, UK: Cambridge University Press, 1994.

———., editor. *Medieval Ismaili History and Thought.* Cambridge, UK: Cambridge University Press, 1996.

Davis, R.H.C. "William of Tyre." In *Relations between East and West in the Middle Ages.* Edited by D. Baker. Edinburgh: Edinburgh University Press, 1987.

Deansley, Margaret. *A History of the Medieval Church 590–1500.* London: Routledge, 1925.

Dafoe, S. "The Fall of Acre—1291." In *Templar History Magazine 1:2.* Alberta, Canada: 2002.

Davy, M-M. *Bernard de Clairvaux.* Paris: Albin Michel, 2001. [orig. 1990].

Day, J. *The Medieval Market Economy.* Oxford: Oxford University Press, 1987.

Demurger, A. *The Last Templar: The Tragedy of Jacques de Molay, Last Grand Master of the Temple.* London: Profile Books, 2004. (English translation of 2002 French original)

———. *Vie et mort de l'ordre du Temple, 1120-1314.* Paris: Editions du Seuil, 1985, 1989, and 1993.

D'Albon, M. *Cartulaire General de l'Ordre du Templ.* Paris: 1913 and 1922.

Dodds, J. *Architecture and Ideology in Early Medieval Spain.* University Park, Penn.: Pennsylvania State University Press, 1990.

Dove, W. "The Temple Church and its Restoration." In *London and Middlesex Archaeological Society Transactions.* vol 21 no. 3 (1967): 24-37.

Duby, G. *The Three Orders: Feudal Society Imagined.* trans. A Goldhammer, Chicago and London: 1980.

———. *William Marshal: The Flower of Chivalry.* New York: Pantheon, 1985.

———. *The Early Growth of the European Economy,* trans.by Clarke, H., Ithaca, N.Y.: SUNY, 1974.

———. *L'Art cistercien.* Paris: Flammarion, 1991.

Edbury, Peter. *The Kingdom of Cyprus and the Crusades (1191-1374).* Cambridge, UK: Cambridge University Press, 1991.

———. "The Templars in Cyprus." In *The Military Orders I: Fighting for the Faith and Caring for the Sick.* Edited by Barber, M., Aldershot: Ashgate, 1994.

Edbury, P. and D. Metcalf. *Coinage in the Latin East.* Oxford: BAR International Series, 1980.

Edbury, P. and J. Rowe. *William of Tyre: Historian of the Latin East.* Cambridge, UK: Cambridge University Press, 1988.

Edgington, S. and S. Lambert, editors. *Gendering the Crusades.* Cardiff, UK: University of Wales Press, 2001.

Ehrenkreutz, Andrew S. *Saladin.* Albany: State University of New York, 1972.

Elgood, Robert, editor. *Islamic Arms and Armour.* London: Scolar Press, 1979.

Epstein, Steven. *Wage Labor and Guilds in Medieval Europe.* Chapel Hill and London: University of North Carolina Press, 1991.

Erdmann, C. *The Origins of the Idea of Crusading.* Trans. M.W. Baldwin and W. Goffart. Princeton, N.J.: Princeton University Press, 1977

Esdaile, Katherine. *Temple Church Monuments.* London: George Baker, 1933.

Evans, G.R. *Bernard of Clairvaux.* Oxford: Oxford University Press, 2000.

Evergates, Theodore. *Feudal Society in the Bailliage of Troyes under the Counts of Champagne, 1152–1284.* Baltimore: John Hopkins University Press, 1975.

Farmer, D.H. *The Oxford Dictionary of Saints.* Oxford: Oxford University Press, 1978.

Favier, J. *Philippe le Bel.* Paris: Fayard, 1999.

Favreau-Lillie, M.-L. "The Military Orders and the Escape of the Christian Population from the Holy Land In 1291." In *Journal of Medieval History* 19 (1993).

Ferris, E. "The Financial Relations of the Knights Templar to the English Crown." In *American Historical Review* VIII (1902): 139–148.

Fichtenau, H. *Heretics and Scholars in the High Middle Ages 1000-1200.* Trans. by Denise A. Kaiser. University Park, Penn.: Penn State University Press, 2000.

Finke, H. *Papsttum and Untergang des Templeordens.* Vatican document Reg. Aven. no. 305, vol. 564. 2 vols. Munster: Aschendorfsche Bundhandlung, 1907.

Fletcher, Richard. *Moorish Spain.* 2nd ed. Berkeley, Calif.: University of California Press, 2006.

Forey, Alan. "The Emergence of the Military Order in the Twelfth Century." *Journal of Ecclesiastical History* 36 (1985): 175-95.

———. "Women and the Military Orders in the 12th and 13th Centuries." *Studia Monastica* 29, (Barcelona, 1987).

———. *The Military Orders from the Twelfth to the Early Fourteenth Centuries.* Basingstoke: Macmillan, 1992.

———. *The Templars in the Corona de Aragon.* London: Oxford University Press, 1973.

———. "Novitiate and instruction in the Military Orders in the twelfth and thirteenth centuries," *Speculum LXI* (1986): 1-17.

———. "The Military Orders and the ransoming of captives from Islam, 12th to early 14th century." *Studia monastica XXXIII.* Montserrat, Barcelona: 1991.

———. "The Military Orders and Holy War against Christians in the thirteenth century." *English Historical Review CIV.* London: Longman Group Ltd, 1989.

———. "The Failure of the Siege of Damascus," *Journal of Medieval History* 10 (1984).

———. "The Beginnings of the Proceedings against the Aragonese Templars." In *God and Man in Medieval Spain: Essays in Honor of J.R.L. Highfield.* Edited by D.W. D. Mackenzie. Warminster: 1989.

———. "Letters of the last Two Templar Masters." *Nottingham Medieval Studies,* XLV (2002): 145–171.

Fowler, G.H. *Cartulary of Old Warden Abbey,* Bedford: Bedfordshire Record Society, no. 13, 1930.

Frale, B. *L'ultima battaglia dei Templari,* Rome: Viella, 2001.

France, John. *Victory in the East: A Military History of the First Crusade.* Cambridge, UK: Cambridge University Press, 1994.

Garmonsway, G., editor. *The Anglo-Saxon Chronicle.* London: Everyman, 1986.

Geary, P.J. *Furta sacra: Thefts of Relics in the Central Middle Ages.* Princeton, N.J.: Princeton University Press, 1978.

Gerson, P. A. Shaver-Crandell, and A. Stones., translators. *The Pilgrim's Guide to Santiago de Compostela.* Vol II. London: Harvey Miller Publishers, 1998.

———. *Living with the Dead in the Middle Ages*. Ithaca: Cornell University Press, 1994.

Gervers, M. editor. "The Influence of Bernard of Clairvaux on the Formation of the Order of the Knights Templar." In *The Second Crusade and the Cistercians*." New York: Peter Lang, 1992.

———. editor. *The Cartulary of the Knights of St John of Jerusalem in England*. Records of Social and Economic History of England and Wales (NS VI). London: British Academy, 1996.

Gibb, H.A.R. "The Armies of Saladin." *Cahiers d'Histoire Egyptienne III*. Paris: 1951, 304-320.

Gibson, S. and J. Taylor. *Beneath the Church of the Holy Sepulchre, Jerusalem: The Archaeology and Early History of Traditional Golgotha*. London: 1994.

Gies, F. *The Knight in History*. London: Hale, 1986.

Gies. F. and J. Gies. Cathedral, *Forge and Waterwheel: Technology and Invention in the Middle Ages*. New York: Harper Collins, 1994.

Gilchrist, R. *Contemplation and Action: The Other Monasticism*. Leicester: Leicester University Press, 1995.

Gilmour-Bryson, A. *The Trial of the Templars in Cyprus: A Complete English edition*. Leiden: Brill, 1998.

———. *The Trial of the Templars in the Papal State and in the Abruzzi*. Biblioteca Apostolica Vaticana, Vatican City: 1982.

Glick, T.F. *Islamic and Christian Spain in the Early Middle Ages: Comparative perspectives on social and cultural formation*, Princeton, N.J.: Princeton University Press, 1979.

Goetinck, G. *Peredur: A Study of Welsh Tradition in the Grail Legends*. Cardiff: University of Wales Press, 1975.

Goldhill, S. *The Temple of Jerusalem*. Cambridge, Mass.: Harvard University Press, 2005.

Gooder, E. *Temple Balsall*. Chichester: Phillimore, 1995.

Green, M., and R. Howell. *A Pocket Guide to Celtic Wales*. Cardiff: University of Wales Press, 2000.

Greenia, C., translator. "In Praise of the New Knighthood." In *The Works of Bernard of Clairvaux*, vol. 7, *Treatises III*. Kalamazoo, Mich.: Cistercian Publications, 1977, 126–67.

Hamilton, B. *The Leper King and his Heirs: Baldwin IV and the Crusader Kingdom of Jerusalem*, Cambridge, UK: Cambridge University Press, 2000.

———. *The Latin Church in the Crusader States: The Secular Church.* London: Variorum, 1980.

———. *The Christian World of the Middle Ages.* UK: Sutton Publishing, 2003.

———. "Our Lady of Saidnaiya: an Orthodox Shrine Revered by Muslims and Knights Templar at the Time of the Crusades." *The Holy Land, Holy Lands, and Christian History: Studies in Church History* 36 (2001).

———. *The Medieval Inquisition.* London: Holmes and Meirer, 1981.

———. *Religion in the Medieval West.* London: Edward Arnold, 1986.

Hannay, Robert Kerr, editor. *Acts of the Lords of Council in Public Affairs 1501–1554.* Selections from the *Acta Domiorum Concili,* introductory to the Privy Council of Scotland. Edinburgh, 1932.

Harris, J. *Byzantium and the Crusades.* London and New York: Hambledon and London, 2003.

Henderson, J. *The Construction of Orthodoxy and Heresy.* Albany: State University of New York Press, 1998.

Hillgarth, J.N. *Ramon Lull and Lullism in Fourteenth Century France.* Oxford: Clarendon Press, 1971.

Hillenbrand, C. *The Crusades: Islamic Perspectives.* Edinburgh: Edinburgh University Press, 1999.

Holt, James C. *Magna Carta,* Cambridge, UK: Cambridge University Press, 1992.

Holt, P.M. *Early Mamluk Diplomacy (1260-1290): Treaties of Baybars and Kalawun with Christian Rulers.* Leiden: Brill, 1995.

Holt, Richard. *The Mills of Medieval England.* Oxford: Blackwell, 1988.

Holt, R. and G. Rosser. *The Medieval Town 1200-1540.* London: Longman, 1990.

Hopper, Sarah. *To Be a Pilgrim: The Medieval Pilgrimage Experience.* Stroud: Sutton, 2002.

Hopper, Vincent F. *Medieval Number Symbolism: Its Sources, Meaning, and Influence on Thought and Expression.* New York: Columbia University Press, 1938.

Housley, Norman. *The Italian Crusades: The Papal-Angevin Alliance and the Crusades against Christian Lay Powers 1254–1343*. Oxford: Clarendon Press, 1982.

———. *Documents on the Later Crusades, 1274-1580*. Basingstoke: Macmillan, 1996.

———. *The Avignon Papacy and the Crusades 1305-1378*. Oxford: Oxford University Press: 1986.

Howarth, Stephen. *The Knights Templar*. London: Continuum, 1985.

Jacoby, Z. "The Workshop of the Temple Area in Jerusalem in the Twelfth Century: Its Origin, Evolution and Impac," in *Zeitschrift fur Kunstgeschichte 45* (1982).

Jung, Emma, and Marie-Louise von Franz. *The Grail Legend*. Translated by C.G. Jung Foundation. 2d ed. Princeton: Princeton University Press, 1970.

Kaeuper, R.W. *Chivalry and Violence in Medieval Europe*. Oxford: Oxford University Press, 1999.

Kaeuper, Richard and E. Kennedy. *The Book of Chivalry of Geoffroi de Charny: Text, Context, and Translation*. Philadelphia: University of Pennsylvania Press, 1996.

Kedar, Benjamin Z. "A Twelfth Century description of the Jerusalem Hospital." In *The Military Orders: Welfare and Warfare*. Edited by H. Nicholson. Aldershot: Ashgate, 1998.

———. *Crusade and Mission: European Approaches Toward the Muslims*. Princeton, N.J.: Princeton University Press, 1984.

Kedar, Benjamin, and Denys Pringle. "La Feve: A Crusader Castle in the Jezreel Valley." In *Israel Exploration Journal*. 35 (1985).

Keen, Maurice. *Chivalry*. New Haven and London: Yale University Press, 1984.

Kennedy, Hugh. *Crusader Castles*. Cambridge: Cambridge University Press, 1994.

———. *Muslim Spain and Portugal: A political history of al-Andalus*. London: Longman, 1996.

Kenyon, Kathleen. *Digging up Jerusalem*. London: Ernest Benn Ltd., 1974.

Kieckhefer, Richard. *European Witch Trials: Their Foundation in Learned and Popular Culture 1300–1500*. London: Routledge, 1976.

———. *Magic in the Middle Ages.* Cambridge, UK: Cambridge University Press, 2000.

Kienzle, Beverley M. *Cistercians, Heresy and Crusade in Occitania, 1145-1229.* Woodbridge and Rochester, N.Y.: York Medieval Press Publication, 2001.

Kinder, T.N. *L'europe cistercienne.* La Pierre-qui-Vire: Zodiaque, 1998.

Kingsley, Sean. *God's Gold: The Quest for the Lost Temple Treasure of Jerusalem.* London: John Murray, 2006.

Kirshner, J., editor. *Business, Banking and Economic Thought in Late Medieval and Early Modern Europe.* Chicago: University of Chicago Press, 1974.

Knowles, D. *The Evolution of Medieval Thought.* London: 1962.

Krey, A.C. *The First Crusade: The Accounts of Eyewitnesses and Participants.* Princeton: Princeton University Press, 1921.

Lambert, E. *L'Architecture des Templiers.* Paris: 1955.

Lambert, Malcolm. *Medieval Heresy.* Oxford: Blackwell, 1992.

———. *The Cathars.* Oxford: Blackwell, 1998.

Lawrence, Hugh. *Medieval Monasticism.* London: Longman, 1984.

———. *The Friars.* London: Longman, 1994.

Lea, H.C. *A History of the Inquisition of the Middle Ages.* 3 vols. 1888; reprint, New York: Russell and Russell, 1955.

Leclercq, Jean. "Saint Bernard's Atttitude toward War." *Studies in Medieval Cistercian History* vol. 2. Edited by J.R. Sommerfeldt, Kalamazoo, MI: Cistercian Publications, 1976.

———. *A Second Look at Bernard of Clairvaux.* Kalamazoo, Mich.: Cistercians Publications, 1990.

———. *The Love of Learning and the Desire for God.* Translated by C. Misrahi. New York: Fordham University Press, 1982.

Leff, Gordon. *Heresy in the Later Middle Ages.* Manchester: Manchester University Press, 1967.

Lees, B., editor. *Records of the Templars in England in the Twelfth Century: the 1185 Inques.* Records of Economic and Social History of England and Wales (IX), London: British Academy, 1935.

Lekai, L.J. *The Cistercians: Ideal and Reality.* Ohio: Kent State University Press, 1977.

Lerner, R. *The Heresy of the Free Spirit in the Later Middle Age.* Notre Dame and London: Notre Dame University Press, 1972.

Leroux-Dhuys, J-F and H. Gaud. *Les Abbayes cisterciennes en France et en Europe.* Paris: Editions Place des Victoires, 1998.

Lewis, Bernard. *The Assassins.* New York: Basic Books, 1968.

_____. *The Arabs in History.* Oxford: Oxford University Press, 1993. (Sixth and fully rev. ed of 1950 orig.)

Leys, A. *The Sandford Cartulary.* Vols 19 and 22. Oxford: Oxfordshire Record Society, 1938.

Leyser, H. *Hermits and the New Monasticism: A Study of Religious Communities in Western Europe 1000-1150.* London: 1984.

Libor, J. and V. Jesensky. "Hospitaller and Templar Commanderies in Bohemia and Moravia: their Structure and Architectural Forms." *The Military Orders: Welfare and Warfare.* Vol. 2. Edited by H. Nicholson. Aldershot: Ashgate, 1998.

Little, Lester K. *Religious Poverty and the Profit Economy in Medieval Europe.* London: Longman, 1978.

_____. "Pride goes before Avarice: Social Change and the Vices in Latin Christendom." *American Historical Review* 76 (1971): 16–49.

_____. *Benedictine Maledictions: Liturgical Cursing in Romanesque France.* Ithaca, N.Y.: Cornell University Press, 1996.

Lizerand, Georges, editor. *Le dossier de l'affaire des Templiers.* Librairie Ancienne Honore Champion, Paris: 1923. See page 166 for de Molay's evidence given November 28, 1309.

Lloyd, S. *English Society and the Crusades 1216-1307.* Oxford: Clarendon Press, 1988.

_____. "Crusader Knights and the Land Market in the Thirteenth Century." In *Thirteenth Century England.* Woodbridge: Boydell Press, 1986.

Loomis, Roger S. *The Grail: From Celtic Myth to Christian Symbol.* Princeton: Princeton University Press, 1991. (Originally published in 1963.)

Lord, Evelyn. *The Knights Templar in Britain.* Harlow: Pearson Education Ltd., 2002.

Luttrell, A. *Two Templar-Hospitaller Preceptories North of Tuscania.* Rome: 1971.

_____. "The Hospitallers and the Papacy, 1305-1314." In *Forschungen zur Reichs-, Papst-und Landesgeschichte (Melanges Peter Herde)*. Edited by K. Borchardt and E Bunz, Stuttgart: A Hiersemann, 1998.

Maalouf, Amin. *The Crusades through Arab Eyes*. London and New York: Schocken, 1984.

MacNiociall, G. "Documents relating to the suppression of the Templars in Ireland." *Analecta Hibernica*, vol. 24. Dublin: 1967.

Macquarrie, Alan. *Scotland and the Crusades 1095-1560*. Edinburgh: John Donald, 1985.

Map, Walter. *De nugis curialium*. Edited and translated by M. R. James, C.N.L. Brooke, and R. B. Mynors. Oxford: Oxford University Press, 1983.

Marshall, C. *Warfare in the Latin East, 1192–1291*. Cambridge, UK: Cambridge University Press, 1992.

Martin, E.J. *The Templars in Yorkshire*. York: 1929–30.

Mazar, Eilat. *The Complete Guide to the Temple Mount Excavations*. Jerusalem: Shahom Academic Research and Publication, 2002.

Menache, Sophia. *Pope Clement V*. Cambridge: Cambridge University Press, 1998.

Metcalf, D.M. "The Templars as Bankers and Monetary Transfers between East And West in the Twelfth Century." *Coinage in the Latin East: The Fourth Oxford Symposium on Coinage and Monetary History*. Edited by P.W. Edbury and Metcalf, D.M., British Archaeological Reports, International Series, 77 (1980).

Molin, Kristian. *Unknown Crusader Castles*. London: Hambledon and London, 2001.

Moore, R.I. *The Origins of European Dissent*. 2nd ed., Oxford: OUP, 1985.

Morgan, M.R. *The Chronicle of Ernoul and the Continuations of William of Tyre*. Oxford: Oxford University Press, 1973.

Muldoon, James. *Popes, Lawyers and Infidels: The Church and the non-Christian world 1250-1550*. Philadelphia: University of Pennsylvania Press, 1979.

Munroe, D.C. "Urban and the Crusaders." In *Translations and Reprints from the Original Sources of European History*. Vol. 1:2. Philadelphia: University of Pennsylvania, 1895.

Mutafian, C. *La Cilicie au carrefous des empires.* 2 vols., Paris: Les Belles Lettres, 1988.

Nasr, S.H. ed. *Ismaili Contributions to Islamic Culture.* Tehran: Imperial Iranian Academy of Philosophy, 1977.

Newby, P. H. *Saladin in His Time.* London: Faber & Faber, 1983. New York: Dorset Press, 1992.

Nicholson, Helen. *The Knights Templar: A New History.* Stroud: Sutton Publishing, 2001.

———. *Love, War, and the Grail: Templars, Hospitallers and Teutonic Knights in Medieval Epic and Romance 1150–1500.* History of Warfare Series, vol. 4. Leiden: Brill, 2001.

———. "Before William of Tyre: European Reports on the Military Orders' Deeds in the East," in *The Military Orders: Welfare and Warfare,* vol. 2. Edited by H. Nicholson. Aldershot: Ashgate, 1998.

———. *Templars, Hospitallers, and Teutonic Knights: Images of the Military Orders, 1128-1291.* Leicester: Leicester University Press, 1993.

Nicolle, David. *Arms and Armor of the Crusading Era 1050-1350,* 2 vols. New York: 1999.

———. *Medieval Warfare Source Book: Vol II, Christian Europe and its Neighbours.* UK: 1996.

———. *Saladin and the Saracens.* Men at Arms series, no. 171, Oxford: Osprey Publishing, 1986.

Ohler, Norbert. *The Medieval Traveller.* Translated by C. Hillier. Woodbridge: The Boydell Press, 1989.

O'Sullivan, J.F. *Studies in Medieval Cistercian History.* Spencer, Mass.: Cistercian Publications, 1971.

Parker, Thomas M. *The Knights Templar in England.* Tucson: University of Arizona Press, 1965.

Partner, P. *The Knights Templar and Their Myth.* Rochester. Vt.: Destiny Books, 1990.

Patrich, J. "Monasteries." Translated by E. Stern. In *The New Encyclopedia of Archaeological Excavations in the Holy Land.* Vol. 3. Jerusalem: 1993.

Pelikan, J. editor. *Sacred Writings, Christianity: The Apocrypha and the New Testament.* New York: Quality Paperback Book Club, 1992.

Perkins, C. "The Knights Templar in the British Isles." *English Historical Review* 25 (1910): 209-30.

Pernaud, R. *Les Templiers*. Paris: 1974.

Phillips, J.R.S. *The Medieval Expansion of Europe*. Oxford: Oxford University Press, 1998. 2nd edition.

Philips, W.E. "The Plight of the Song of Songs." In the *Journal of the Academy of Religion* 42 (1974).

Postan, M. "Credit in Medieval Trade." *Economic History Review*. series 1, 2, 1928.

———. *Essays on Medieval Agriculture and General Problems of the Medieval Economy*, Cambridge: Cambridge University Press, 1973.

———. *The Medieval Economy and Society: An Economic History of Britain, 1000-1500*. London, 1972.

Pranger, M.B. *Bernard of Clairvaux and the Shape of Monastic Thought*. Leiden: Brill Academic Publishers, 1994.

———. "The Virgin Mary and the Love-Language in the Works of Bernard of Clairvaux." *Citeaux* 40 (1989): 112-137.

Prawer, Joshua. *The Crusader's Kingdom*. London: Phoenix Orion, 1972.

———. *Crusader Institutions*. Oxford: Clarendon Press, 1980.

Pressouyre, L., and Kinder, T.H., editors. *Saint Bernard et le monde cistercien*, Paris: CNMHS/SAND, 1990.

Pringle, Denys, "Templar Castles between Jaffa and Jerusalem." In *The Military Orders: Welfare and Warfare*, vol. 2. Edited by H. Nicholson, Aldershot: Ashgate, 1998.

———. "Templar Castles on the Road to the Jordan." *The Military Orders: Fighting for the Faith and Caring for the Sick*. Edited by M. Barber. Aldershot: Ashgate Variorum (1994): 148–66.

———. *The Churches of the Crusader Kingdom of Jerusalem*. vol. 1, Cambridge: Cambridge University Press, 1993.

———. "Reconstructing the Castle of Safed", *Palestine Exploration Quarterly* 117 (1985): 139–48.

———. *Secular Buildings in the Crusade Kingdom of Jerusalem: An Archaeological Gazateer*. Cambridge: Cambridge University Press, 1997.

Proceedings of the Society of Antiquaries of Scotland. vol 12, Edinburgh, 1877–78.

Pryor, J.H. "The Naval Architecture of Crusader Transport ships." *The Mariner's Mirror* 70 (1984).

Pugh, Ralph. *Imprisonment in Medieval England,* Cambridge: Cambridge University Press, 1968.

Ralls, Karen. *The Templars.* Chicago: Quest Books, 2003.

Rashdall, Hastings. *The Universities of Europe in the Middle Ages,* rev. ed. Translated by F.M. Powicke and A.B. Emden. 3 vols. Oxford: Oxford University Press, 1936.

Rees, W. "The Templar Manor of Llanmadoc." *Bulletin of the Board of Celtic Studies* 13. (1949): 144–5.

Renna, T. "Bernard of Clairvaux and the Temple of Solomon." In *Law, Custom and the Social Fabric in Medieval Europe.* Studies in Medieval Culture, 28. Edited by B.S. Bachrach and D. Nicholas. Kalamazoo, Mich.: Medieval Institute Publications, 1990.

Richard, J. "Hospitals and Hospital Congregations in the Latin Kingdom during the First Period of the Frankish Conquest." *Outremer Studies in the History of the Crusading Kingdom of Jerusalem presented to Joshua Prawer.* Edited by B. Kedar, H. Mayer, and R. Smail. Jerusalem: Yad Izhak Ben-Zvi Institutem, 1982.

Riley-Smith, Jonathan. *The Knights of St. John in Jerusalem and Cyprus 1050–1310.* London: Macmillan; New York: St. Martin's Press, 1967.

———. *The Crusades: A Short History.* London: Athlone Press, 1987.

———. *The First Crusaders, 1095–1131.* Cambridge: Cambridge University Press, 1997.

———. *Hospitallers: The History of the Order of St. John.* London: Hambledon, 1999.

———. "The Templars and the Teutonic Knights in Cicilian Armenia," in *The Cilician Kingdom of Armenia.* Edited by T.S.R. Boase. Edinburgh: Scottish Academic Press, 1978.

———. *Atlas of the Crusades.* London: Time Books, 1981.

———. *The Oxford Illustrated History of the Crusades.* Oxford: Oxford University Press, 1995.

Roach, A.P. *The Devil's World: Heresy and Society 1100-1300*, Harlow: Pearson Longman, 2005.

Rohricht, R. *Regesta Regni Hierosolymitani*. Innsbruck, Austria, 1893, 19, no. 83.

Roux, J-P. *Histoire de l'empire mongol*, Paris: 1994.

Rudolph, Kurt. *Gnosis: The Nature and History of Gnosticism*. Translated by R. M. Wilson. Edinburgh: Edinburgh University Press, 1984.

Runciman, Steven. *The Eastern Schism: A Study of the Papacy and the Eastern Churches during the 11th and 12th Centuries*. Oxford: Oxford University Press, 1955.

———. *A History of the Crusades*. 3 vols. Harmondsworth: Penguin, 1978.

Sandys, A. "The Financial and Administrative Importance of the London Temple inthe Thirteenth Century." In *Essays in Medieval History presented to Thomas Frederick Tout*. Edited by A.G. Little and F.M. Powicke. Manchester: Manchester University Press, 1925.

Sayers, J. *Original Papal Documents in England and Wales from the Accession of Innocent III to the Death of Pope Benedict XI (1198-1304)*. Oxford: Oxford University Press, 1999.

Schein, Sylvia. *Fideles Crucis: The Papacy, the West, and the Recovery of the Holy Land, 1274-1314*. Oxford: Oxford University Press, 1991.

Selwood, Dominic. *Knights of the Cloister: Templars and Hospitallers in Central-Southern Occitania c.1100/c.1300*. Woodbridge, Suffolk: Boydell Press, 1999.

Seward, Desmond. *The Monks of War*. Harmondsworth: Penguin Books, [1972 orig.] 1995 edition.

Silberman, Neil A. *Digging for God and Country: Archaeology and the Secret Struggle for the Holy Land, 1799–1917*. New York: Knopf, 1982.

Simon, Edith. *The Piebald Standard*. London: Cassell, 1959.

Sire, H.J.A. *The Knights of Malta*. New Haven and London: Yale University Press, 1994.

Slezer, J. *Theatrum Scotiae*. London, 1693.

Smail, R.C. *Crusading Warfare 1097-1193*. Cambridge: Cambridge University Press, 1956.

Smalley, B. *The Study of the Bible in the Middle Ages,* 3rd ed. Oxford: Oxford University Press, 1983.

Stevenson, David. *The Origins of Freemasonry.* Cambridge: Cambridge University Press, 1990.

Southern, R.W. *Western Society and the Church in the Middle Ages.* London: Harmondsworth, 1970.

———. *Western Views of Islam in the Middle Ages.* Cambridge, Mass.: Harvard University Press, 1962.

Spencer, Brian. *Pilgrim Souvenirs and Secular Badges.* London: Museum of London Press, 1988.

Spufford, Peter. *Handbook of Medieval Exchange.* London: Royal Historical Society, 1986.

———. *Money and Its Use in Medieval Europe.* Cambridge: Cambridge University Press, 1988.

———. *Power and Profit: The Merchant in Medieval Europe.* London: Thames & Hudson, 2002.

Stiles, Paula R. "Arming the Enemy: Non-Christians' role in the Military Culture of the Crown of Aragon during the Reconquista." In *Noble Ideals and Bloody Realities: Warfare in the Middle Ages,* History of Warfare 37. Edited by M. Christie and M. Yazigi. Leiden: Brill, 2006.

Strayer, Jospeh R. *The Reign of Philip the Fair.* Princeton: Princeton University Press, 1980.

———. *Dictionary of the Middle Ages.* 13 vols. New York: 1982–9.

Stoyanov, Yuri. *The Other God: Dualist Religion from Antiquity to the Cathar Heresy.* New Haven and London: Yale University Press, 2000.

Sumption, Jonathan. *Pilgrimage: An Image of Medieval Religion.* London: Faber & Faber, 1975.

The Letters of St Bernard of Clairvaux, trans. By B.S. James, Stroud: Sutton Publishing, 1998.

Thiede, C.P. and M. D'Ancona. *The Quest for the True Cross.* London: Weidenfeld & Nicolson, 2000.

Thompson, J.A.F. *The Western Church in the Middle Ages.* London: 1998.

Turner, R.V. and R. Heiser. *The Reign of Richard the Lionheart.* Harlow; Pearson Education, 2000.

Tyre, W. *A History of Deeds Done Beyond the Sea,* trans. Babcock, E.A. and Krey A.C., New York: Columbia University Press, 1943.

Tyerman, C. *England and the Crusades.* Chicago: University of Chicago Press, 1988.

Ullendorff, E. and C.F. Beckingham. *The Hebrew Letters of Prester John.* Oxford: Oxford University Press, 1982.

Upton-Ward, Judith M. trans. and ed. *The Rule of the Templars: the French Text of the Rule of the Order of the Temple.* Woodbridge, Suffolk: Boydell Press, 1992.

————. trans and ed. *The Catalan Rule of the Templars: Barcelona, Archivo De La Corona de Aragon, "Cartes Reales." MS 3344: A Critical Edition and English Translation.* Woodbridge, Suffolk: Boydell and Brewer, 2002.

Usher, Abbott P. *The Early History of Deposit Banking in Mediterranean Europe.* Cambridge, Mass.: Harvard, 1943.

van der Broek, R. and W. Hanegraaff. *Gnosis and Hermeticism: From Antiquity to Modern Times.* Albany: State University of New York Press, 1998.

Waddell, C. *Narrative and Legislative Texts from early Citeaux.* An Edition, Translation and Commentary. Citeaux: Commentarii Cistercienses, Textes et Documents, Vol. 9, 1999.

————. *Cistercian Lay Brothers Twelfth-century uses with related texts.* Citeaux: Commentarii Cistercienses, Textes det Documents, Vol. 10, 2000.

————. *Statutes from Twelfth-century Cistercian General Chapters.* Citeaux: Commentarii Cistercienses, Textes et Documents. vol. 11, 2002.

Wakefield, Walter L. *Heresy, Crusade and Inquisition in Southern France, 1100-1250.* Berkeley: University of California Press, 1974.

Wakefield, Walter L. and A. Evans. *Heresies of the High Middle Ages.* New York: Columbia University Press, 1969.

Walford, C. Fairs: *Past and Present: A Chapter in the History of Commerce.* London: Elliot Stock, 1883.

Walker, A. *The Knights Templar in and around Aberdeen*. Aberdeen: Aberdeen University Press, 1887.

Walker, J. "Alms for the Holy Land: The English Templars and their Patrons." In *The Medieval Military Revolution: State, Society and Military Change in Medieval and Early Modern Europe*. Edited by A. Ayton and J. Price. London: Taurus Academic Studies, 1995.

Ward, J.O. "The Fall of the Templars," *Journal of Religious History* 13 (1984): 92–113.

Warren, W.L. *King John*. New Haven: Yale University Press, 1997.

Wasserman, James. *The Templars and the Assassins: The Militia of Heaven*. Rochester, Vt.: Inner Traditions, 2001.

Werblowsky, R.J. "Introduction, *In Praise of the New Knighthood*." Bernard of Clairvaux: *Treatises III*, Cistercian Fathers 19, Kalamazoo, MI: Cistercian Publications, 1977.

Wilkinson, J., J. Hill, and W.F. Ryan, editors. *Jerusalem Pilgrimage 1099–1185*. London: Hakluyt Society, 1988.

William of Tyre, (Guillaume de Tyr). *Chronique*. Edited by R. Huygens. 2 vols. Corpus Christianorum, Continuatio Mediaevalis 63 and 63A, Turnhout: 1986.

———. *A History of Deeds done beyond the Sea*. Translated by E.A. Babcock and A.C. Krey. 2 vols. Records of Civilization, Sources and Studies 35, New York, 1943 (reprint 1976)

Wilson, C.W., translator. *The Pilgrimage of the Russian Abbot Daniel in the Holy Land, 1106-7 A.D.* London: Eastern Orthodox Books, 1888.

Wise, Terence. *Wars of the Crusades 1096-1291*. Oxford: Osprey Publishing. 1978.

Wood, H. "The Templars in Ireland." *Proceedings of the Royal Irish Academy*, 26C. no. 12, Dublin: July 1907.

Wood, Ian. *The Merovingian Kingdoms 450–751*. Harlow: Pearson Education Ltd., 1994.

Ziegler, Philip. *The Black Death*. New York: HarperPerennial, 1969.

Index

About the Author

KAREN RALLS, M.A., PH.D., medieval historian, religious studies scholar, and international lecturer, obtained her doctorate from the University of Edinburgh. She was Postdoctoral Fellow at Edinburgh for six years prior to relocating to Oxford, England, where she now conducts further specialist medieval period research. A member of the American Academy of Religion (AAR), the Oxford University Religious Studies Society, and the British Association for the Study of Religion (BASR), Dr. Ralls lectures worldwide, speaks at international conferences, and has appeared on numerous American, British, and European TV documentaries for The History Channel, Discovery, and National Geographic. She is also the medieval editor and writer of a regular column for *Sacred History,* an American magazine for general readers, which was selected in 2006 by *Library Journal* as one of the "Top 30 new periodical releases" in the United States. Originally from the United States, Dr. Ralls's recent books include *The Templars and the Grail* (Quest, 2003), and the academic titles *Music and the Celtic Otherworld* (St. Martin's Press/Edinburgh University Press, 2000) and *Indigenous Religious Music* (Ashgate Academic, 2002). Her interests include music and art history; in 2005, she completed a specialist Medieval and Renaissance Art History course at the highly regarded Victoria and Albert Museum in London. For more information, please see her award-winning Website *www.ancientquest.com.*